Communication Among Grandmothers, Mothers, and Adult Daughters

A Qualitative Study of Maternal Relationships

LEA's Series on Personal Relationships
Steve Duck, Series Editor

www.erlbaum.com

Communication Among Grandmothers, Mothers, and Adult Daughters

A Qualitative Study of Maternal Relationships

Michelle A. Miller-Day
The Pennsylvania State University

LAWRENCE ERLBAUM ASSOCIATES, PUBLISHERS
2004   Mahwah, New Jersey   London

Lawrence Erlbaum Associates, Inc., Publishers
10 Industrial Avenue
Mahwah, New Jersey 07430

Cover design by Kathryn Houghtaling Lacey

Library of Congress Cataloging-in-Publication Data

Miller-Day, Michelle A.
Communication among grandmothers, mothers, and adult daughters :
    a qualitative study of maternal relationships / Michelle A. Miller-Day.
        p.   cm. — (LEA's series on personal relationships)
    Includes bibliographical references and index.
ISBN 0-8058-3979-8 (cloth : alk. paper)
1. Parent and adult child. 2. Mothers and daughters. 3. Intergenerational
    relations. I. Title. II. Series.
HQ755.86.M55   2004
306.874—dc22   2003064201
                                                            CIP

Books published by Lawrence Erlbaum Associates are printed on acid-free paper,
and their bindings are chosen for strength and durability.

Printed in the United States of America
10   9   8   7   6   5   4   3   2   1

Contents

Series Foreword

Steve Duck
University of Iowa

This series from Lawrence Erlbaum Associates reviews the progress in the academic work on relationships in respect of a broad array of issues, and does so in an accessible manner that also illustrates its practical value. The LEA series also includes books intended to pass on the accumulated scholarship to both the next generation of students and those who deal with relationship issues in the broader world beyond the academy. The series thus comprises not only monographs and other academic resources that exemplify the multidisciplinary nature of this area, but also textbooks suitable for use in the growing numbers of courses on relationships.

The series provides a comprehensive and current survey of theory and research in personal relationships through the careful analysis of the problems encountered, and solved, in research, yet it additionally considers the systematic application of that work in a practical context. These resources are intended to be not only comprehensive assessments of progress on particular topics, but also significant influences on the future directions and development of the study of personal relationships. Although each volume is focused and centered, authors attempt to place their respective topics in the broader context of other research on relationships and within a range of wider disciplinary traditions. Thus, the series not only offers incisive and forward-looking reviews but also demonstrates the broader theoretical implications of relationships for the range of disciplines from which the research originates. Series volumes include original studies, reviews of relevant theories and research, and new theories oriented toward understanding personal relationships both in themselves and within the context of broader theories of family process, social psychology, and communication. Reflecting the diverse composition of personal relationship study, readers in numerous disciplines—social psychology, communication, sociology, family studies, developmental psychology, clinical psychology, personality, counseling, women's studies, gerontology, and others—will find valuable and insightful perspectives in the series.

Apart from the academic scholars who research the dynamics and processes of relationships, there are many other people whose work involves them in the operation of relationships in the real world. For such people as nurses, police officers, teachers, therapists, lawyers, drug and alcohol counselors, marital counselors, and those who take care of the elderly, a number of issues routinely arise concerning the ways in which relationships affect the people whom they serve. Examples include the role of loneliness in illness and the ways to circumvent it, the complex impact of family and peer relationships on a drug-dependent person's attempts to give up the drug, the role of playground unpopularity on a child's learning, the issues involved in dealing with the relational side of chronic illness, the management of conflict in marriage, the establishment of good rapport between physicians and seriously ill patients, the support of the bereaved, and the correction of violent styles of behavior in dating or marriage. Each of these is a problem that may confront some of the previously mentioned professionals as part of their daily concerns, and each demonstrates the far-reaching influences of relationship processes on much else in life that is presently theorized independently of relationship considerations.

The present volume is devoted to exploring women's experiences of their maternal relationships across the life span and analyzing communication among these women. The book explores the multiple roles, contexts, and dimensions of these relationships simultaneously in natural environments, and employs a qualitative approach based on the personal lives of the participants. We are all used to understanding the mother–daughter relationship as a unique bond in which daughters are seen as extensions of their mothers, and there are many developmental theories that take such an approach. Michelle Miller-Day fills out—and in many cases questions—this set of assumptions and takes a life-span approach to studying families, emphasizing the need for more information about how multiple generations (grandparents, parents) impact family members. Communication within the grandmother–mother–daughter relationship is explored from a layered, intergenerational perspective that integrates and juxtaposes alternative experiences of the social world; from this emerges a rich and complex understanding of the importance of intergenerational relationships.

The present volume is a good example of the series' concerns, because it attends to a particular approach to relationships that has been systematically outlined and developed over a number of years in a comprehensive study. The approach is well developed, and the styles that support it are clearly depicted, some dedicated to the overall approach and some depicting its specific application to particular issues.

The strength of the systematic research in approaching this important relationship is one of the ways in which this book can contribute substantially to an understanding of broad relationship processes. For theorists, therapists, and the rest of us, this theme is of immense significance and the present book represents one of the best discussions to date.

Preface

I am both a mother and a daughter; I have been a stepmother to a stepdaughter; and I am currently the mother of two biological sons. These multiple roles have colored how I view the world and have influenced the way that I have written this book.

Although I do not have a biological daughter, and legally no longer have a stepdaughter, I have devoted much of my professional life to understanding relational communication between mothers and daughters. I became interested in the mother–daughter relationship even before I had step- or biological children of my own, and my relationship with my mother was not particularly problematic. In fact, I would say that my relationship with my mother has always been very satisfying and fraught with little conflict. Thus, my interest in the mother–daughter relationship did not originate from a deep-seated desire to resolve conflicts in my own relationship with my mother.

In truth, my interest in the mother–daughter relationship emerged from a scholarly exploration of the family relationships among women and their problem behaviors—behaviors that placed their health at risk, such as eating disorders and drug abuse. I knew intellectually that women's self-destructive "problem" behaviors could often be understood by closely examining the relationships within their family of origin (Bennett & Wolin, 1990; Laliberte, Boland, & Leichner, 1999; Levitt, 2001; Turner, 1995). I also "knew" intuitively that mothers were important in daughters' lives (after all, my mother was important to me), but other than my own experience, I didn't know much about how other women experienced the mother–daughter relationship and if that experience affected, in any way, daughters' attitudes regarding their problem behaviors. Therefore, as a scholar, my initial inquiry focused on how mothers and daughters experienced their relationship with each other, how that relationship defined a woman's sense of self, and how communication between mothers and daughters affected daughters' attitudes regarding their problem behaviors.

Much of the mother–daughter research that I subsequently conducted over the years has been situated in a *transactive* view of communication (Mortensen, 1972), which "conceptualizes communication between dyad members as a constant, changing process in which the participants are mutually and simultaneously adapting their communication to that of the other member" (Whitchurch & Dickson, 1999, p. 689). In the mid-1990s, I embarked on an ongoing investigation of how mothers and daughters symbolically negotiated their relationship (Miller, 1995, 1997; Miller-Rassulo, 1992). Daughters in these studies reported feeling overshadowed by their mothers; this shadow casting, as perceived by daughters, contributed to the daughters' problem behavior, such as attempted suicide (Miller, 1995), and deeply affected daughters' negotiations of their identities independent from their mothers (Miller, 1997). The mother–daughter connection is a loving one that seems to bind women together across generations, even while they pursue separate identities. This latter point is particularly important, because this connection is often maintained across several decades, and mothers and their daughters continue to negotiate their relationship throughout the life span.

In this book, I build on and extend earlier qualitative research to include the experiences of multiple families as well as maternal grandmothers. The desire to broaden my examination of the mother–daughter relationship to the bonds across three generations was provoked by a growing interest among scholars from several disciplines in studying families from a life-span approach (Fingerman, 1995, 1996, 1998a, 1998b, 2001; Nussbaum, Pecchioni, Robinson, & Thompson, 2000). By including aged mothers and their adult daughters and younger mid-life mothers with their young adult daughters, I sought to catch a glimpse of how this relationship is experienced at different points in a woman's life. Moreover, by including three generations of women, I sought to gather multigenerational perspectives on family and examine these for patterns of maternal interaction transmitted across generational boundaries. In essence, the grandmother–mother–adult daughter triad is the conjunction of two mother–daughter bonds. A review of the research literature demonstrates a lack of information about adult mother–daughter relationships across generational boundaries. Consequently, to build on the scholarly literature on maternal relationships as well as on my previous line of research, I elected to include grandmothers in my subsequent investigation of mother–daughter communication. Drawing on 8 months of qualitative research, using observations of and extensive interviews with six sets of middle-income, Caucasian grandmothers, mothers, and daughters, this book provides a heuristic account of intergenerational mother–daughter relational communication, building toward a grounded theory of mother–daughter communication that I have called *necessary convergence of meaning.*

Watching theory evolve is something akin to descriptions of an out-of-body experience. Although I participated in the development of the theory, the process created a unique energy of its own that has propelled me from data collection, analysis, interpretation, and back again through these elements until the theory took form and the function of it became visible. In this book, I tell the "story" of this research process. I narrate and recount the steps, share my insights, and document my decisions along the way. As Maines (1993) suggested, social scientists are narrators who must use words and discursive representations to convey their work. Indeed, both Maines (1993) and Davis (1974) conceptualized social scientists as "spinners of professional tales" who are called on to "textualize" research reports. As a social scientist (and as a mother and a daughter), my voice is firmly situated in the pages of this book, sharing my account of what I saw, heard, and learned while studying 18 women and their families. The book is written to represent not only the experiences and perceptions of the women who participated in this research, but also my own experiences along the way that were salient to the interpretation of data. This perspective allows the reader to be situated in the world of grandmothers, mothers, and daughters as they experience, describe, and analyze their family communication.

The first chapter provides a brief overview of differing theoretical perspectives on the mother–daughter relationship. I also offer a rationale for examining intergenerational communication among grandmothers, mothers, and adult daughters, and provide a brief summary of my own line of research in order to provide a context for understanding this study. This chapter articulates the purpose of the research and reinforces the goal of this book: to provide a descriptive, heuristic account of grandmother–mother–adult daughter relational communication as it occurred in the natural setting of Elkwood, USA.

Chapter 2 outlines the methodological approach and procedures used in this research. I argue for the creation of a new knowledge about family relationships gained through the use of naturalistic, interpretive approaches to family research, and also introduce the reader to various types of qualitative approaches. This chapter focuses on documenting the steps taken on my research journey, from conceptualization through interpretation of the data. Before discussing the results of this interpretation, chapter 3 introduces the reader to the research setting and to the participants whose lives are represented in these pages. Following a description of the town of Elkwood are composites of the participants and their maternal relationships. These composites are intended to be introductory, and are presented as thumbnail sketches of the women, their relationships, and their interconnectedness across generations.

Chapter 4 provides a description and interpretation of the dialectical tensions that emerged as central to understanding maternal relationships in

Elkwood. This chapter focuses on sharing the stories of the participating 18 women, painting a picture of two distinct kinds of cohesive maternal relationships—connected and enmeshed—and finally interpreting and discussing these patterns. Chapter 5 aims to identify, interpret, and discuss different patterns of interaction and discursive practices that characterized the different Elkwood relationships. Chapter 6 presents a grounded theory of mother–daughter interaction that I have termed *necessary convergence*. Although it is in its initial stages of development, I argue this theoretical framework of appropriation of meaning may be transferable to other Caucasian mother–daughter relationships and may be useful in understanding how mother–daughter communication may potentially increase a daughter's risk for developing problem behaviors. Finally, chapter 7 discusses some implications of the findings and offers directions for future study.

de Kanter (1993) indicated that there are two births—the birth of the body that does violence to many mothers' bodies, and the birth of the self that does violence to mothers' expectations and hopes. It is this second birth that I have learned about from the women whose voices are represented in these pages.

In sum, this book provides a portrait of 18 women from Elkwood, USA, and offers a descriptive, heuristic account of these maternal relationships. Viewing maternal relationships through the multiple lenses of social scientist, mother, and daughter has afforded me an opportunity to engage in my fieldwork, empathize with the women, and yet pull back the lens to interpret the intersubjective meanings unfolding before me. Of course, these meanings were ultimately interpreted through my viewpoint and guided by the rich theoretical foundations available to me as a scholar. It is my hope that by reading this book the reader may gain insight into his or her self, sister, mother, grandmother, or other woman, and understand more completely the richly textured nature of maternal relationships.

ACKNOWLEDGMENTS

Many people contributed to the development of this book, first and foremost the women of Elkwood, USA, and the many other women with whom I have worked over the years, learning about their lives and their intimate connections. I've discovered so much from the wisdom of other women, and many have been very willing to disclose their wisdom to a stranger newly introduced into their acquaintance.

This project could not have begun without the cooperation and inspiration of my own family, others in my hometown, and the family who was the subject of an earlier study. These women allowed me to pilot the study procedures within their homes and in their community. I learned an incredible amount by just talking with these women and watching them "in action." These maternal relationships taught me what questions to ask and where to focus my observations.

I am also grateful to the graduate students who studied with me and assisted me at the Pennsylvania State University, especially Maggie J. Pitts and Jen Davis. My students have not only made editorial contributions to this book, but they have also furthered my conceptualizations about grandmother, mother, and adult daughter relationships in ways that I did not anticipate before I began writing. My students have inspired me by their questions and heartened me by their own stories.

My husband, Ed Day, my children, and my colleague Michael Hecht have all encouraged this project and provided much-needed support. Likewise, my own mother, Donna Miller, was an inspiration to me, along with my sisters and the next generation in my family, including nieces and grandnieces. I am grateful for their support.

Finally, I express my gratitude to Linda Bathgate at Lawrence Erlbaum Associates, Publishers Inc. She supported me with patience and conducted her job efficiently in order to make this book a reality. Along with Linda, Kristin Valentine, Lee Carpenter and the editorial staff members at LEA were instrumental in making sure that this volume is in now in your hands.

To all of these individuals, I express my appreciation. To women in general, I hope that by reading this book you begin to comprehend how understanding more about your maternal relationships can surely provide a key to an increased understanding of self.

—*Michelle A. Miller-Day*

I

Setting the Scene

1

Velvet Chains: Understanding Maternal Relationships

Clever men create themselves, but clever women are created by their mothers. Women can never quite escape their mothers' cosmic pull, not their lip-biting expectations or their faulty love. We want to please our mothers, emulate them, disgrace them, outrage them, and bury ourselves in the mysteries and consolations of their presence. When my mother and I are in the same room we work magic on each other .... It's my belief that between mothers and daughters there is a kind of blood-hyphen that is, finally, indissoluble.

—(Shields, 1987, p. 127)

Reminiscing about the birth of her first daughter, a young woman I spoke with said, "I held her in my arms, looked into her face and I saw ... well, I saw me. Another chance. I hoped that she might do all the things in the world I couldn't ... or didn't." (Amanda Rhines, personal communication, April, 2003). Another mother looked more apprehensive when sharing her recollection, "[When my daughter was born] I feared for her, for all the things that can happen to young girls!" (W. Spritzer, personal communication, April, 2003). Mothers, daughters, daughters who become mothers, and mothers who become grandmothers—women co-authoring lives across the life course. This is what I am learning about mothers and daughters across generations. The agency is in the authorship.

Each maternal relationship has a *story*. The cast of characters changes, the settings are altered, and the stories evoke a range of unresolved contradictions, joys, hopes, and tensions. The "story" of mothers and daughters and the awk-ward co-existence of both the positive and negative qualities inherent in these relationships has been the subject of many theories over the years, and promises to continue to provoke personal introspection and scholarly examination. As many women reading this book may attest, adolescents tend to feel engulfed by their mothers, the "blood-hyphen" chaining them together throughout a life-time. These chains, however, seem to be *velvet* chains—chains of security, love, and devotion that may keep a daughter anchored to maternal protection, but may well hold her back from experiencing the world as an individual.

Just last week as I sat in a conference room with other faculty from my college, a woman next to me asked, "What is your area of research?" I said, "Right now I'm writing a book about mothers and daughters across generations." Upon hearing this statement she and two other female faculty members within earshot issued a collective sigh, "Ahhhhh." The reactions I get from other women when talking about maternal relationships are layered with interest, exasperation, and power-ful emotion. In some ways, the mother–daughter relationship holds a curious fas-cination for women because it promises a key to the understanding of self (Walters, 1992). To understand themselves, whether they like it or not, many women feel they have to look first to their relationship with their mother, achiev-ing selfhood in a relational context. Therapists and researchers over the past de-cade have reported that women often have difficulty with defining self unless they first contextualize that self in the mother–daughter relational experience (Adelson, 1998; Kabat, 1998; Pipher, 1994; van Mens-Verhulst, Schreurs, & Woertman, 1993).

Rich (1986) once wrote that the mother–daughter relationship "is the great unwritten story." Perhaps she was trying to convey that although authored on an ongoing basis by the women in these relationships, the story has yet to be adequately documented. However, scholars and authors have ex-pended a great deal of effort in writing that story over the years. Recent re-search efforts have examined the complex relationship between adult mothers and daughters, focusing on several elements of that relationship, such as aging mothers and daughters (Fingerman, 1996, 1998a, 1998b, 2000, 2001; Soerensen, 1998; Walker & Thompson, 1983), depression (Powers & Welsh, 1999), disclosure (Koerner, Jacobs, & Raymond, 2000), eating (Benedikt, Wertheim, & Love, 1998; Herzog, Kronmueller, Hartmann, Bergmann, & Kroeger, 2000; Hill & Franklin, 1998; Stolley & Fitzgibbon, 1997), personal identity development (Chodorow, 1978; Dahl, 1995; Graber & Brooks-Gunn, 1999; Pipher, 1994; Smith, Hill, & Mullis, 1998), sexual be-havior (Fingerman, 1989; Lefkowitz, Kahlbaugh, & Sigman, 1998), and story-telling (Schely-Newman, 1999). Yet, a search of the extant literature in the field of relational communication revealed no studies concerned with the adult mother–daughter relationships across different points in the life span, across generations, and focusing on the communicative aspects of negotiating maternal relationships.

Although variable analytic research is illuminating, some scholars contend that a weakness in much of the general parent–child literature is that parental relationships are studied one dimension at a time, rather than examining the multiple roles, contexts, and dimensions of these relationships simultaneously and in natural environments (Holstein & Gubrium, 1994).

However, ethnographic and descriptive accounts by Adelson (1998), Bonner (1993), de Waal (1993), McMahon (1995), Miller-Rassulo (1992), Miller (1995), and Warloe (1998) do begin to paint a picture of the multiple dimensions of the contextualized mother–daughter relationship. Adelson (1998) reported a case study of the psychotherapeutic treatment of a woman who, at the age of 60, was emotionally disabled due to her unresolved relational identity with her mother. Whereas de Waal (1993) explored the changing power balance in families focusing on daughters' perceptions of their mothers' mothering strategies, McMahon (1995) analyzed the meaning of motherhood for 59 mothers in terms of the costs and rewards of having children. Miller-Rassulo (1992) investigated the personal accounts of both daughters and mothers, describing their experiences in the mother–daughter relationship and then examining one particular family—four generations of women—and their intergenerational family communication patterns (Miller, 1995). Bonner (1993) focused on the multigenerational maternal relationships in her autoethnographic account, which was prompted by her own volatile and consuming relationship between her grandmother and mother in the Soviet Union. Finally, Warloe (1998) edited an anthology of letters from daughters to their mothers who were both living and dead, rendering an image of the centrality of mothers in women's lives.

A common thread in contemporary scholarship, whether it is descriptive or predictive, is the recurrence of blaming mothers for everything from a daughter's fear of success to her latest bad haircut.[1] Mother blaming is certainly not a new phenomenon. In fact, it has been a pervasive theme in the psychological literature (Caplan, 2000; Chodorow, 1978; Debold, Wilson, & Malave, 1993; Friday, 1977). Mothers have been depicted as almost totally responsible for their offspring's attitudes, self-esteem, and identity formation, and are often blamed when anything goes awry (McFarland & Watson-Rouslin, 1997). Gerstel and Zussman (1999) argued that "In some ways, middle-class mothers today resemble those nineteenth-century middle-class mothers who found themselves anxious all the time after their exposure to elite reformers and experts who kept telling them how to manage all the details of child rearing from toilet training to the expression of emotions" (p. 63).

---

[1] I know that in my household, Mom (i.e., me) is usually the first one to bear the brunt of my children's disappointments and wrath. It is very easy to blame moms because ... well ... we will usually take it.

Over the past few decades, scholars from multiple disciplines have sought to understand the complexities of mother–offspring relationships. Consequently, there is a wealth of information from different theoretical perspectives that are useful in explaining this relationship. This multidisciplinary background necessitates a quick review of contemporary theories that have helped provide insight into this unique relationship.

PERSPECTIVES ON UNDERSTANDING MOTHERS AND DAUGHTERS

In their study of 160 women's relationships with their mothers, McFarland and Watson-Rouslin (1997) pointed out that there is a mythology of motherhood. They suggested that mothers have always been held to incredibly high expectations, "responsible for everything from their children's self esteem to their attitudes about sex. If a mother cares too much, she is overprotective or, in the jargon of the 1990's, 'codependent'; if she does not care enough, she is cold and withholding. A mother is rarely, if ever, good enough" (p. 4).

The literature surrounding the mother–daughter relationship promotes the image of this relationship as a unique bond in which daughters are seen as extensions of their mothers. According to Jung and Kerenyi (1969), "every mother contains her daughter within herself, and every daughter her mother" (p. 162). This bond was pivotal to Freud's (1905, 1917, 1923, 1932) classic theories that have dominated psychoanalytic perceptions of the mother–daughter relationship.

The traditional Freudian psychoanalytic perspective casts the mother–daughter relationship at the center of the drama of a girl's struggle to become a female human being with a heterosexual, individual identity. Within this orientation, which is still influential today, sexual identity and separation from the loving, caring, nurturing, and powerful relationship with the mother are seen as necessary steps in any daughter's developmental process (Surrey, 1993). According to the traditional Freudian perspective, in the pre-Oedipal phase the infant daughter's bond with the mother figure is central to the infant's world, with this bond characterized as symbiotic, whereas her bond with the father is delayed until the Oedipal phase (Lykke, 1993; Woertman, 1993). Thus, because of early attachment and identification, daughters unconsciously internalize maternal values, behaviors, and identity. According to this early Freudian premise, daughters eventually begin to resent their feminine identity and blame mothers for their lack of a penis, either literally or as symbolic of a lack of power in a patriarchal society (Phillips, 1991). A central claim of this early psychoanalytic perspective is that struggles between mothers and daughters are rooted in this symbiotic attachment and the daughter's desire for separation of *self* from mother.

Self, in early to mid-20th-century writings, is typically portrayed as existing in space, possessing attributes (physical, cognitive, spiritual), demarcated or bounded in some way, and acting from a place of separation or containment with the world "out there" (Mahler, 1963, 1972). This emphasis on defining and establishing boundaries has reinforced the self as a separate controlled entity, with others in competition rather than connection. Within this theoretical position connectedness is subjugated to the need to protect the separate self, and thus separating and individuating from the mother is key to the development of any healthy mother–daughter relationship (Surrey, 1993).

In the early part of the 20th century, Freudian psychological perspectives dominated scholarly thought regarding the mother–daughter relationship, but have come under attack by feminist scholars in the latter part of the century.[2] In the 1960s and 1970s, feminist scholars began to claim that a predominantly male and sexist point of view characterized the classic psychoanalytical orientation. Therefore, a chorus of feminist voices rang out for the amendment of traditional Freudian psychoanalytic thought regarding mothers and daughters, and called for a new psychology of women (see, e.g., Jean Baker Miller's 1976 work). These voices sought to replace the male-biased theory of separation (Oedipal) with an emphasis on female connectedness (Bjerrum-Nielson & Rudberg, 1994).

The object-relations perspective emerged in the 1970s as central to the discussion of connectedness between mothers and daughters. The object-relations theoretical perspective (Chodorow, 1978) was grounded in traditional psychoanalytic thought, yet challenged it as well, and concentrated on the psychosocial development of girls. Chodorow (1974, 1978) cited evidence that women both reproduce caring and mothering and transmit these intergenerationally. According to Chodorow (1974) and Chodorow and Contratto (1992), a tension exists in the mother–daughter relationship wherein girls need to differentiate from their mothers and transfer their libidinous feelings to the opposite gender in order to develop as heterosexual human beings. Yet, girls also have to identify with their mothers to accept the adult female role. The object-relations perspective emphasizes the duality of the daughter's individuation process, in which she must *both* identify and separate from her mother. The separation to create a unique sexual identity pulls a daughter away from her mother, whereas her development of gender identity pulls her closer to her mother (Wodak & Schultz, 1986). According to the object-relations theory, the first connection we have as infants is with mother (or the caretaker, who is typically female), and inasmuch as gender is so meaningful in our culture, difference from mother becomes important to boys and sameness with mother becomes important to girls.

---

[2]The works of Janneke van Mens-Verhulst, Karlein Schreurs, and Liesbeth Woertman, along with the writings of Janet Surrey, are pivotal to the arguments and history provided in this chapter. Their work and the writings of the authors cited here have stimulated a decade of new scholarly debate about women's developmental processes, mother–daughter connections, and identity.

Joining in the conversation about mothers and daughters in the 1960s and
1970s, authors such as de Beauvoir (1965), Friedan (1964), French (1987),
Hammer (1976), and Rich (1986) explored maternal relationships, expressing the ambivalence felt by many women of this era regarding explanations
and experiences of the mother–daughter relationship. "My mother/my self"
was the theme of Nancy Friday's (1977) best-selling book of the same name,
which illuminated the symbiotic nature of the mother–daughter relationship
yet continued the psychoanalytic thesis that mothers were responsible for
constructing daughters' gender identity. Still, in the late 1970s and early
1980s many feminist authors remained entrenched in the earlier traditional
Freudian perspectives, focusing on mother as nurturer and responsible for
nurturing, while at the same time identifying mother as the major obstacle to
female autonomy and equality with men.[3]

Indeed, popular and scholarly debates of the past 30 years have focused on
the role and function of mothers in oppressing their daughters. Some feminist
and social learning theorists in the past several decades have argued that girls
learn their gender identity from their mothers, and that behaviors such as sup-
pressing desire, deference, and submission are gendered, learned behaviors.
Moreover, these theorists suggest that when a strong mother–daughter connection is accompanied by a daughter's strong gender identification, girls are
at greater risk for developing into passive and dependent women (Chodorow
& Contratto, 1992; Friday, 1977). Furthermore, some psychologists argue
that mothers become unwitting accomplices in perpetuating the oppression of
women by socializing their daughters into traditional female roles (Debold et
al., 1993; Eichenbaum & Orbach, 1982).

Instead of focusing on daughter's identification with mother as an obstacle
to development, other scholars over the past few decades have highlighted
mothers' identification with their daughters (Boyd, 1989; Eichenbaum &
Orbach, 1989). This shift in the 1980s redirected the locus of inquiry, yet maintained an implicit condemnation of mothers for daughters' oppression.
Eichenbaum and Orbach's (1982, 1984, 1989) writings emphasized the mother
(unconsciously) sabotaging her daughter's process of differentiation. According to this NeoFreudian perspective,[4] mother sees herself in her daughter and
acts toward her daughter as she does herself, becoming like her own mother and
her own child (Boyd, 1989; Hammer, 1976). The scholarly discussion about this
ongoing struggle between identity and differentiation, separation and autonomy in the mother–daughter relationship continues to play out today in academic discourse (e.g., see Adelson, 1998; Bonner, 1993; Cowen & Wexler,
1997; Fingerman, 1998b; Kabat, 1998; Kenemore & Spira, 1996; Kerpelman &
Smith, 1999; Smith et al., 1998; van Mens-Verhulst et al., 1993).

---

[3]For more comprehensive reviews of the feminist work during this time in history, see
Everingham (1994) and Walters (1992).
[4]NeoFreudian refers to any psychoanalytic system based on but modifying Freudian doctrine.

In much of the Freudian and NeoFreudian psychoanalytic theories that dominated the majority of this past century, motherhood was vilified and successful mothering was often measured by how "independent" children were of their mothers as they moved into adulthood. However, in the 1980s, scholars such as Gilligan (1982) and Miller (1986) claimed that although separation and differentiation are important in the mother–daughter relationship, they function differently for girls than for boys. These scholars, among others (especially in the early 1990s, such as Gilligan, Rogers, & Dolman, 1991; Jordan 1993; van Mens-Verhulst et al., 1993), challenged the notion that a daughter's independence from mother is essential for female development. According to this perspective, men and women experience interpersonal relationships and issues of dependency differently. Within this orientation, boys' separation from mother is considered essential for the development of masculinity. However, for girls and women, femininity is defined through attachment; therefore, separation is a *threatening* rather than a *necessary* development in the mother–daughter relationship. Within this perspective, relationship is central to women's lives, and not merely an obstacle. This discernable shift in the outlook on mother–daughter relationships is interesting, considering that most theoretical approaches prior to the late 1980s typically viewed relationship and attachment as secondary to intrapsychic development.

In the early 1990s, women began to realize that they did not need to denigrate or reject their mothers in order to form unique identities. In fact, the most recent literature on the mother–daughter relationship claims that identity is formed within, and not to the exclusion of, relationship (Coll, Surrey, & Weingarten, 1998; McFarland & Watson-Rouslin, 1997; Surrey, 1993; van Mens-Verhulst et al., 1993). Current research also suggests that many mothers and daughters express greater identification and experience more satisfaction in their relationship than do other parent–child dyads (Bergman & Fahey, 1997; Kerpelman & Smith, 1999). This orientation toward the mother–daughter relationship is grounded in the strength of maternal connection and identification—in *relationship*—not in separation.

WOMEN IN RELATIONSHIP

Gilligan and Price (1993) claimed that a paradigm shift has occurred in psychology—a shift from looking at self as autonomous to viewing self as lived essentially in relationship. Adams and Marshall (1996) presented a social-psychological theory of identity that situated the development of personal identity in the context of negotiating relational identities, and both Jordan (1993) and van Mens-Verhulst et al. (1993) advocated a movement toward a communicatively developed relational self, emphasizing the self as inseparable from dynamic interactions. These theorists suggested that this conceptual movement was particularly salient for understanding the mother–daughter relationship (Jordan, 1993; van Mens-Verhulst et al., 1993).

The contemporary relational approach to understanding mothers and daughters stresses connection and mutuality, emerging from the work of Surrey (1993) and Gilligan (1982). Theoretically, this shift embraces a "move from static to dynamic modeling, a movement from steady states to processes; a move from theorizing about separate and contained self to theorizing about an intersubjective self; from uni-perspectival to multiple perspective integration" (van Mens-Verhulst et al., 1993, p. 110). Therefore, intersubjective meanings, the multiple perspectives of the participants, and connections are necessary to truly understand the mother–daughter relationship. As van Mens-Verhulst et al. (1993) stated, this is central because connections and disconnections characterize most meaningful relationships.

A relational framework suggests that the relational connection between mothers and daughters is characterized, above all, by communication (Jordan, 1993). Women describe communication as the prime source of establishing their relational identity with their mother or daughter (Mann, 1998). It is through mutually responsive communication that mothers and daughters establish patterns of relational communication that link them to one another, shaping each woman's sense of self.

Surprisingly, few scholars have examined the patterns of relational communication that occur between mothers and adult daughters as they negotiate their relationship. Socialization literature is teeming with investigations of maternal influence on young children's development, yet few focus on the role of communication in establishing and constituting the mother–daughter relationship. Moreover, much of the research stops at adolescence, failing to explore the ongoing negotiations and renegotiations of mothers and daughters over the life cycle. As a daughter becomes a mother of her own daughters, she must participate in a process of (re)negotiating her identity and her relationships across time with both her mother and her daughters (Kroger, 2000).

MOTHER–DAUGHTER COMMUNICATION

In terms of general mothering relationships, sociolinguistic research has provided a body of research on mother–infant communication and caregiver talk. The position that underpins much of this linguistic research is tied to social learning theories that focus on parent effects (Peterson & Rollins, 1987). This perspective explores the extent to which parental "styles, behaviors, and characteristics contribute to various social and psychological qualities in children" (Peterson & Hann, 1999, p. 327). Although interaction is at the center of these theories, the general emphasis is on parents' conveyance of a social reality through their interactions with the children, shaping children's behaviors. Along those lines, much of the research on mother–infant interaction suggests that mothers are primarily responsible for infants' language learning (Wodak & Schultz, 1986). Linguistic analyses suggest that mothers mirror their infants' nonverbal behaviors, and that this empathy is often translated into linguistic expression (Ryan, 1974). Linguistic research has also identified three characteristics of mother–infant speech: symbiotic, authoritative, and pedagogic (Wodak & Schultz, 1986).

Other linguistic studies suggest that mothers, more than fathers, strive to manipulate children's behavior in more subtle, indirect ways (Borker, 1980). This research finds that mothers learn to use communication techniques that combine high dominance with high affiliation, which permits them to be dominating without appearing domineering (Rogers-Millar & Millar, 1979). Wodak and Schultz (1986) claimed this indirect control is a model of feminine discourse and that daughters begin to repeat their mothers' communication patterns—both their mother's styles of communication and their repetition of words. Indeed, the mother–daughter literature is filled with references to the phenomenon of hearing us speak in our mother's voice (Eichenbaum & Orbach, 1982, 1984, 1992; McFarland & Watson-Rouslin, 1999; Miller, 1995; Miller-Rassulo, 1992).

Although this linguistic research is illuminating and helpful, a closer review of scholarship conducted by relational scholars, devoted to a full view of the relationship, is necessary to understand the centrality of communication in the mother–daughter relationship. Montgomery and Baxter (1998) noted, "Communication is an interactive, involving, and situated process that produces multiple meanings that simultaneously both differentiate and connect participants. Communication is the vehicle of social definition; participants develop their senses of self, [and] partners develop their senses of relationship … through the process of communication" (p. 161).

Unfortunately, little research has been devoted to understanding how mother–daughter relationships are communicatively constituted at any given point across the life span. Especially lacking is research on mothers and their adult daughters outside the context of mothers' frailty. Studies conducted by Schely-Newman (1999), Langellier and Hall (1990), and Langellier and Peterson (1992) did examine the nature and function of storytelling among women and their adult daughters, shedding light on the significance of narrative and patterned communication in establishing family themes and feminine identity. Guerro and Afifi (1995) looked at the issue of topic avoidance between mothers and their young adult children, whereas Randall (1995) demonstrated the use of conversational analysis as a tool in understanding mothers and their relationship with their young adult daughters.

Fingerman's (2001) research is very insightful and sheds light on sources of tension in the aging mother–adult daughter relationship. Her work focuses on the relationships of healthy elderly mothers and their adult daughters and extends the knowledge of mother and daughter relationships beyond the typical scenario of the adult daughter mainly as caregiver. Rastogi and Wampler (1999), whose work is equally helpful and promising, introduced the Mother and Adult Daughter (MAD) questionnaire, which measures mother–adult daughter closeness within the frameworks of intergenerational, feminist object relations and attachment theories. These social scientific studies have made enormous contributions to increasing our knowledge about the function of communicative interaction in mother–adult daughter relationships.

Many of these studies, along with the relational approach to understanding women's development (Jordan, 1993; van Mens-Verhulst et al., 1993), inform my inquiry into the mother–daughter relationship. As in most interpretivist/qualitative research, my questions are guided by my current knowledge of the mother–daughter relationship, yet are not restricted to that understanding. This overview of the different theoretical approaches situates my current study by providing a necessary foundation for an interpretivist construction of maternal relational communication.

BUILDING ON A FOUNDATION: ABDUCTIVE RESEARCH

The nature of grounded theoretical research is that of *discovery*. The researcher works back and forth between both the data and existing theoretical knowledge toward building a substantive theory—a theory developed from the study of one small area of investigation using a specific, purposeful sample from a particular population (Strauss & Corbin, 1998). A substantive theory has limited but useful explanatory power for the specific populations from which it was derived; it applies back to them and may be transferred to populations with similar characteristics. This process mixes both inductive and deductive processes and thus is characterized as an abductive process of building from the data toward an emergent whole and fluidly working between the parts and the whole, integrating raw data, existing theory, and interpretations of the researcher throughout this ongoing process. Negative cases are often important and researchers seek to account for all they can with existing knowledge, and then to discuss the results for which they cannot account. This approach assumes that as researchers gather new data they will work back and forth between data and theory, building a foundation of description toward a theoretical explanation. This is important to the research reported in this book because, as indicated in the preface, for the past few years I have attempted to increase my own and others' understanding of the role of communication in the mother–daughter relationship. This current study is built on this existing research foundation.

In Miller-Rassulo (1992), I reported a phenomenological study that addressed the question: How do mothers and daughters experience their relationship? Female participants were asked, "How do you experience your relationship (right now) with your daughter/mother?" and "How did you experience your relationship with your daughter (when she was growing up) or your mother (in your childhood and adolescence)?" Based on in-depth interviews with middle-class, Caucasian mothers and daughters, this study provides a framework of experience from which to develop an inductive understanding of these women, their communication, and their relationships with their mothers and daughters.

In Miller (1995), I conducted a detailed ethnographic case study of one particular family and four generations of its women who had made serious suicide attempts. Building on what was learned in earlier interviews with a variety of women, in this study I elected to focus less on the phenomenological experience—or the *essence*—of the mother–daughter relationship and more on the intergenerational transmission of messages that contributed to the women's suicidal behavior. Working from my tacit knowledge as a daughter and my scholarly knowledge, my examination of this family led to a tentative model of intergenerational transmission of suicide risk. This model was based on a case study, so the next step in the research process was to apply this model to additional families. By adding families I sought to build on my previous findings, describe and explain maternal relationships further, transfer my preliminary findings across contexts, and then build a greater theoretical understanding of the communication that occurs among middle-class, Caucasian mothers and daughters.

Furthermore, based on the grounded data obtained to date in the research (Miller, 1995; Miller-Rassulo, 1992), an important part of the mother–daughter relationship puzzle was grandmothers and their relationships with their daughters and granddaughters. In this previous research, not only was grandmothers' communication with daughters and granddaughters central to the identity of women, but the grandmothers appeared to provide a mediating influence on the mother–daughter relationship itself (Miller, 1995). Therefore, based on both the literature's claims that patterns of communication are often passed down from one generation to the next (Bartle-Haring & Sabatelli, 1998), and on the findings from my own ongoing research, I decided to expand my research focus to include grandmothers.

Multigenerational approaches include the basic assumptions that family patterns are shared, transformed, and manifested through transgenerational transmission; have boundaries that are hierarchical in nature; and develop functional and dysfunctional patterns based on the legacy of previous generations and here-and-now happenings (Hoopes, 1987). My early investigations explored mother–daughter transmission of family cultural values and expectations (Miller, 1995, 1997; Miller-Rassulo, 1992). The picture that emerged from this research was that of mothers who struggled toward achievement in their lives, only to be overshadowed by their mothers and consequently casting a shadow on their daughters. These studies did not include a focus on grandmothers, so the addition of grandmothers allowed me to broaden the scope of this area of inquiry beyond one generation of mothers and daughters. The desire to expand my examination to three generations was further provoked by a growing interest among a multidisciplinary group of scholars in studying families from a life-span approach (Fingerman, 1996, 1998a, 1998b; Nussbaum, 1989; Nussbaum & Bettini, 1994; Williams & Nussbaum, 1999).

The life-span approach to studying families emphasizes the need for more information about how multiple generations (grandparents, parents) impact family members (Bartle-Haring & Sabatelli, 1998; Harvey & Bray, 1991; Kaufman & Uhlenberg, 1998, Tinsley & Parke, 1984) and how relationships are negotiated at different points across the life span (Fingerman, 1996, 2001). Moreover, Bowen (1978) asserted that rules and styles of communicating are often transmitted intergenerationally; thus, it is imperative that research on family communication explores the relational and symbolic links to previous generations. van Mens-Verhulst et al. (1993) suggested that most mother–daughter theories do not pay attention to generational shifts, presuming that each generation can be considered a rerun of preceding mother–daughter relationships, obscuring some real differences between generations. Using the relational framework of both van Mens-Verhulst et al. (1993) and Jordan (1993), I seek to examine maternal relationships within a context of multiple and overlapping relationships.

I describe communication within the grandmother–mother–daughter relationship from a layered, intergenerational perspective. Layering is a device for integrating and juxtaposing alternative experiences of the social world. This perspective allows you to be situated in the world of grandmothers, mothers, and adult daughters and granddaughters as they experience, describe, and analyze their family communication. Additionally, this device allows my authorial voice to enter into the emergent story. Hence, this book was meant to represent both my experiences conducting this study and the experiences of the participants.

The purpose of this book, then, is to examine women's experiences of their maternal relationships across the life span and analyze communication among these women. In the end, this qualitative report provides discovery, description, and interpretation of data, leading toward both a heuristic model for understanding issues central to negotiating women's maternal relationships and a grounded theory for the specific dimensions of mother–daughter communication.

2

The Qualitative Research Journey: "How Did I Get Here and Where Am I Going?"

Research is formalized curiosity.

It is poking and prying with purpose. It is a seeking that he who wishes may know the secrets of the world and they that dwell therein.

—(Zora Neale Hurston, 1942, p. 174)

When I was in graduate school, I experienced a transforming moment in my education and career. Donna, one of the subjects in a study I conducted, was reading a manuscript I had written for a graduate communication course when she uttered the words, "Where is the depth? Where is the feeling? Where am *I* in all of these words?"

"Well," I responded, "right there on page 17!"

"I know that I'm the *subject*," Donna went on, "and I know that you are *the researcher*. But … uhmmm … I really don't get a sense of either one of us in the paper."[5]

---

[5]For a more extensive discussion of this transforming event and my subsequent foray into alternative (re)presentations of social research, see Banks and Banks (1998).

She was absolutely right! The people who participated in the study were not subject to my manipulation; they actively and voluntarily *participated* in this interview- and survey-based investigation. Donna, along with the others, provided a unique voice during the collection of the data, yet that voice was ultimately muted by the deadening thud of an aggregate statistic. As I noted in (Miller, 1986), 72% of the women in this study believed that their fathers underestimated their achievements. *Thud*

In response to her admonition I challenged myself, "Okay, it's important to know that there were so many of the women in this study who experienced the same thing ... but ...," I thought, "did they really experience the same thing? What was that feeling?" I turned to Donna. "You *thought* your father underestimated your achievements, but that is not a feeling, is it? All of the feelings that you shared with me in our interview have been washed out and diluted in this report." Ultimately, the power of her personal experience had been rendered impotent in the final reporting of the research findings.

Since that time, I have never underestimated the power of collecting, analyzing, and reporting the experiences of others in human interaction. In my work with families I am often reminded that aggregate data are helpful, but the in-depth specificity of interpretive data brings our understanding of certain social phenomenon into clear focus.

I am awed by the methodological pluralism that is the hallmark of contemporary research on families. We have learned so much about families over the years through the use of multiple methods of inquiry. Yet, along the way, somewhere in the 1940s and early 1950s, choices of research methodologies in studying family relationships became restricted (Gilgun, 1999). More recent reviews such as Gilgun (1999), in her exemplary review of methodological choices in family research, as well as Allen (2000), among others (Biglan, 1995; Deatrick, Faux, & Moore, 1993; Gilgun, Daly, & Handel, 1992; Miller, 1995; Socha & Stamp, 1995), challenge the contemporary reliance on statistically generalizable, aggregate data in family research, and strongly advocate for a more conscious and inclusive approach to family studies. This inclusive approach is based on the notion of honoring lived experience and *verstehen*, or understanding, of family life and familial relationships situated in cultural and social contexts. It is this in-depth understanding of others in our research that is at the center of interpretive research as well as at the heart of this book.

Investigating family relationships within an interpretivist paradigm, a researcher: (a) is the primary instrument for data collection and analysis, (b) seeks to understand family relationships in their natural contexts, (c) acknowledges the intersubjective nature of human meaning, (d) acknowledges researcher bias with an effort to see things from the others' perspective while bracketing one's own biases, and (e) seeks to understand and describe patterns of human meaning making with a focus on language as a demonstration of meaning (Bishop, 1999; Gioia & Pitre, 1990; Rossman & Rallis, 1998; Strauss & Corbin, 1990). The *qualitative method* is an umbrella concept covering several forms of interpretivist inquiry that helps us to describe, interpret, and understand the meaning of family life and familial relationships with as little disruption of the natural setting as possible (Merriam, 1998). Various terms associated and often used interchangeably with the term *qualitative* are *naturalistic, ethnographic, heuristic/phenomenological, grounded theory,* and *case study research.* Because there is confusion about these terms, clarification is provided here to give readers a better understanding of these different methodological approaches.

TYPES OF QUALITATIVE RESEARCH

The varieties of qualitative approaches have often been labeled *strategies* (Denzin & Lincoln, 1994), *genres* (LeCompte, Millroy, & Preissle, 1992), and *methodologies* (Schwandt, 1993). A more thorough discussion of each can be found in Denzin and Lincoln (2000), Merriam (1998), and Strauss and Corbin (1990), to name a few. The following is an introduction to at least six types of qualitative methodologies often used in social science research.

Table 2.1 provides a summary of six distinct types of qualitative methodologies that share three common characteristics of interpretivist research: employing the researcher as the primary instrument for data collection and analysis, acknowledging the intersubjective nature of human meaning as well as researcher bias in interpreting data, and sharing the goals of understanding and describing patterns of human meaning-making in their natural contexts.

Many *basic qualitative studies* neither seek to develop substantive theory nor wish to capture a single case in detail. These common basic qualitative studies simply endeavor to discover, describe, and understand the process or object of inquiry (Merriam, 1998). In a basic qualitative study, data are often collected through interviews, observation, and/or focus groups, with the analysis identifying patterns in, within, and across cases to provide a description of these patterns. An exemplar basic study in family communication is Ferguson and Dickson's (1995) examination of children's expectations of their single parents' dating behaviors. In individual semi-structured interviews, children were asked to describe their feelings and expectations. These interviews were transcribed and analyzed systematically to identify themes. In this study, recurrent themes were identified within and across the cases. Discourse analysts will also capture talk and identify patterns of interaction within that talk. For example, Breheny and Stephens (2003) described the discourses used by mid-aged women to account for their own and other women's experience of menopause. These basic qualitative studies contribute to general understandings of phenomenon and are typically guided by research questions.

Ethnography is derived from the Greek *ethnos*, meaning "a tribe, race, or nation," and *graphos*, meaning "something written down." Thus *ethnography* refers to a written report about a group of people—or writing culture. In ethnography, culture is integral to the observation of behavior in naturally occurring settings, as well as the ongoing analysis of the data. Although the definition of culture is

TABLE 2.1

Common Types of Qualitative Research Studying Families

Type	Characteristics	Example
Basic qualitative study	• Includes description, interpretation, and understanding • Identifies recurrent patterns in data (e.g., interview, open-ended responses) in the form of themes or categories • May delineate a process	• A study of the discourse and narratives of victims of familial abuse. (Montalbano-Phelps, 2003) • Examination of how wives discursively represent their relationship with husbands who have entered a nursing home (Braithwaite, 2002) • Explored offspring's perceptions of how their parents communicated disappointment (Miller & Lee, 2001)
Ethnography	• Focuses on culture (broadly defined) • Interpretive descriptions of the shared practices, beliefs, and behaviors of some group of people and placing it in a cultural context	• An interpretation of how the concepts of "home" and "family" function in the life of a 29-year-old man dying of AIDS (Cherry, 1996)
Autoethnography	• A self-reflexive account that simultaneously produces and interprets a text from firsthand experience • Description of the practices, beliefs, and behaviors of a person or a group from an insider's perspective	• Reflections on growing up in a family culture where parent–child sexual intimacy and abuse were normative (Ronai, 1995)

	Is concerned with the essence or basic structure of a phenomenon • Uses data that are the participant's or investigator's firsthand experience of the phenomena	• A study of the meaning of interparental violence for adolescents (Goldblatt, 2003) • A study of stress and its perception in childhood (Robson, 1999)
Phenomenology	• Is concerned with the essence or basic structure of a phenomenon • Uses data that are the participant's or investigator's firsthand experience of the phenomena	• A study of the meaning of interparental violence for adolescents (Goldblatt, 2003) • A study of stress and its perception in childhood (Robson, 1999)
Grounded theory	• Is designed to inductively build a substantive theory regarding some aspect of practice • Is "grounded" in real world experience	• A framework for describing how families who have adopted special-needs children manage the complexities of this kind of family (Lightburn, 1998) • Families' responses in adapting to severe mental illness over time (Rose, Mallinson, & Walton-Moss, 2002)
Case study	• Is intensive, holistic description and analysis of a single unit or bounded system • Can be combined with any of the previous types	• A study of intergenerational messages across four generations of women in one family (Miller, 1995) • A research- and evidence-based book using a case-study approach to understand family issues and social problems (Peck & Dolch, 2001)

Note: Adapted from Merriam (1998).

oft debated, Chen and Starosta (1999) suggested that culture can be thought of as "a set of fundamental ideas, practices, and experiences of a group of people that are symbolically transmitted generation to generation through a learning process" (p. 25). An ethnography is a sociocultural interpretation of data collected through direct observation. In the field of communication, Conquergood (1994) provided a seminal ethnographic piece on refugee youth in Chicago street gangs. In this ethnographic work, Conquergood moved into a tenement in a notorious neighborhood called "little Beirut," and lived there for 5 years, observing, getting to know, interacting with, and examining the lived experience and symbolic links among youth in several street gangs. Another communication researcher, Gerry Philipsen, examines the system of rules that organize a speech community called *speech codes*. Philipsen's (1992) book *Speaking Culturally* identified a "Nacirema"* way of talking as the prevailing speech code in the United States. This kind of research is highly participatory and provides a rich portrait of the culture under investigation.

On the other hand, an *autoethnography* is to ethnography what autobiography is to historical biography. According to Ellis and Bochner (2000), an autoethnography is "an autobiographical genre of writing and research that displays multiple layers of consciousness, connecting the personal to the cultural. [Usually written in the first person], autoethnographers gaze back and forth, first through an ethnographic wide-angle lens, focusing outward on social and cultural aspects of their personal experience; then they look inward, exposing a vulnerable self ..." (p. 739). Several of the autoethnographic accounts that have surfaced in the past decade or so have made a marked impact on the study of parent–child relationships and family life. Ellis and Bochner's (1995) book, *Composing Ethnography: Alternate Forms of Qualitative Writing*, broke new ground in the promotion of autoethnographic writing, claiming that the practice emphasizes the understanding of individual identity within cultural, social, and historical communities and frameworks. This kind of qualitative inquiry offers a way for marginal or subordinate groups to represent themselves and challenge established knowledge. Ronai's (1995) work examined her childhood growing up in a sexually abusive household and illuminated, in a simultaneously poignant and repulsive fashion, how the statistics on childhood abuse cannot hope to capture the experience of living with sexual abuse. This kind of work provides a forum for the voices of insiders who have firsthand knowledge of a phenomenon of interest.

Although all qualitative research draws from the philosophy of phenomenology or the *essence* of experience (a phenomenon) in everyday life, *heuristic research* is a form of phenomenological inquiry that integrates the personal experience and insights of the researcher with the experience of research participants. The root meaning of heuristic comes from the Greek word *heuriskein*,

---

*Nacirema is American spelled backwards.

meaning "to discover or find," and the uniqueness of heuristic inquiry is the extent to which it legitimizes the experiences and insights of the researcher as he or she comes to discover and understand phenomena through shared reflection and inquiry with research participants (Moustakas, 1990).

The rigor of inquiry comes from systematic observations of research participants, in-depth interviews, and examination of the dialogues that occur between the investigator and the participants (Moustakas, 1990). Through these methods, the researcher gathers detailed descriptions, direct quotations, and case documentation. The heuristic process is abductive, moving fluidly from whole to part and then back toward whole once again. Although other qualitative methodologies may also move back and forth in an abductive manner, some lose the sense of the human participation in the research process. A goal of heuristic research is to retain the visibility and voice of the participants throughout the examination of the data (Douglass & Moustakas, 1985). Some examples of heuristic studies are Ambert's (1999) exploration of the effects of sons' delinquency on mothers and fathers, Lather's (1997) representation of women's experiences as members of the HIV positive/AIDS community, and Moustakas' (1974) work on loneliness and love.

Grounded theory is an inductive approach used to develop substantive theory regarding some practice or occurrence. Glaser and Strauss introduced this methodology in their 1967 book, The Discovery of Grounded Theory. Grounded theory methods consist of "systematic inductive guidelines for collecting and analyzing data to build middle-range theoretical frameworks that explain the collected data" (Charmaz, 2000, p. 509).

The goal in grounded theory is to move beyond patterns in the data, toward arranging them in relationship to one another, and thereby building a theory grounded in interpretive data (Merriam, 1998). This process of building theory is:

> not just to work with a single case, then proceed to the next one and treat it as a separate case, and so on. Rather, [in grounded theory] we want to know what this case teaches us about other cases. We want to move from the specific to the more general. Therefore we use a case to open up our minds to the range of possible meanings, properties, dimensions, and relationships inherent in any bit of data. (Strauss & Corbin, 1998, p. 88)

Family research includes several examples of grounded theory studies. One example is Sciarra and Ponterotto's (1998) development of grounded theory to understand adolescent motherhood among low-income Hispanic families living in high-crime areas. According to this study, participants became more dependent on and were more supervised by their mothers after their pregnancies, leading to greater stability and balance in their lives.

Finally, a case study refers to "an intensive, holistic description and analysis of a bounded system such as a single instance, phenomenon, or social unit"

(Merriam, 1998, p. 27). Though most case study research exists in the organizational communication literature, there are some notable examples in the area of family communication. For example, Holihan and Riley's (1987) study of a Toughlove parental support group and Miller's (1995) case study of one family with a tradition of suicidality. Another example of how case studies may be used in family research can be found in Peck and Dolch's (2001) *Extraordinary Behavior: A Case Study Approach to Understanding Social Problems.*

In summary, this chapter discusses six different types of qualitative methodologies often utilized when investigating family issues and family relationships. Although these methodologies are exclusive in approach, they share some of the common characteristics of all interpretive research. In the practice of qualitative research methods, these multiple approaches are often combined or triangulated in order to contribute to the depth and richness of understanding. This book uses exactly this kind of combined approach.

Denzin (1978) identified four basic types of triangulation: *data triangulation*, the use of a variety of data sources; *methodological triangulation*, the use of multiple methods to study a single problem; *theory triangulation*, the use of multiple theoretical perspectives to interpret a single set of data; and finally, *investigator triangulation*, the use of several different investigators in a study. The research in this book triangulates data, theory, and methods building on evidence from case studies, and phenomenological and ethnographic research, ultimately emerging as a grounded theory study that serves to identify key dimensions of negotiating the mother–daughter relationship across the life span as well as laying the foundation for a substantive theory of mother–daughter communication during this negotiation process. Information was gathered from multiple data sources, and multiple theories from several disciplines were employed to guide my interpretation of the data. Also, several methodological tools such as observation, interviewing, and journaling provided a view of maternal relationships and communication that proved to be multifaceted and many layered. In the end, the goal was to produce a heuristic account of intergenerational mother–daughter relationships and develop a grounded theory of maternal relational communication. I echo the words of Douglass and Moustakas (1985) when arguing that this kind of work "is concerned with meanings, not measurements; with essence, not appearance; and with quality, not quantity ..." (p. 42).

The reporting in this book is descriptive, interpretive, hermeneutic, and heuristically layered—descriptive, because detail is so crucial; interpretive, to determine the significance of what I have observed; hermeneutic, to achieve a meaningful interpretation by constantly moving among the parts (individual family members) and the whole (grandmother–mother–daughter relationship); and heuristically layered, to represent meaning simultaneously through the multiple voices of both the participants and myself as researcher/daughter/mother.

THE STUDY:
EVERY GRANDMOTHER–MOTHER–DAUGHTER
RELATIONSHIP IS CONNECTED BY TWO
MOTHER–DAUGHTER BONDS

Focus and Boundaries of the Study

The purpose of this study was to examine maternal relationships and provide a description and interpretation of how women experience these relationships and negotiate them communicatively. Given this purpose, I focused my observations on women as they interacted with one another in their own home environments, and I gathered their subjective perceptions of their own grandmother–mother–daughter relationships. To keep data collection relevant to the phenomena under investigation, I established these boundaries and criteria for inclusion-exclusion (Lincoln & Guba, 1985). For example, the boundary limiting this study to grandmother–mother–daughter relationships forced data collection to target participants who met this criterion, excluding other relationships (e.g., mother–son), and focused data collection and analysis on communication within maternal relationships. Other information, such as conflict in participants' professional relationships, was revealed. Although interesting, such information was not within the scope of this research project.

Theoretical Framework

A host of perspectives provide insight into grandmother–mother–daughter relationships, all of which provide a specific lens through which scholars can view these unique relationships. As indicated in chapter 1, many scholars within the disciplines of psychology, feminist studies, and communication currently advocate a relational approach to understanding women's relationships in the 21st century. This approach is inherently interdisciplinary and stresses connection and mutuality in personal relationships. Given my interest in exploring women's experiences of this connection and my curiosity about how communication processes mutually shape these relationships, a relational approach provided the initial theoretical framework for this study—a "lens" through which to view these relationships. Indeed, this frame guided, but did not limit, my inquiry, and functioned to inform my interpretation of the data gathered during my time in Elkwood.

Toward a Relational Understanding. Most contemporary theories of mother–daughter relationships focus on the connectedness between mothers and daughters, rather than the severing of this connection as emphasized in traditional Freudian theories. Object-relations theory stressed the need for the daughter's separation from the mother (Chodorow, 1978), whereas the self-in-relation theory emphasized connection rather than separation (Jordan, Surrey, & Kaplan, 1985; La Sorsa & Fodor, 1990; Surrey, 1991). Feminist scholars such as Jordan and Surrey (1986) argued that the term *relationship-differentiation* is preferable to the traditional term *separation-individuation* because of the need to view differentiation as a dynamic process within the relationship itself. However, clinicians La Sorsa and Fodor (1990) claimed, "Neither the classical psychoanalytic model nor the newer 'self in relation' model fully captures the total essence of what the issues are for the contemporary mother and daughter. What we need to do now is move toward a dyadic interaction model." (p. 605). This dyadic interaction approach is currently located in the theoretical underpinnings of the relational communication framework for understanding human dyadic interaction.

Relational Communication Framework. The purpose of this study is to examine women's experiences of their maternal relationships and to analyze patterns of communication that link these women across generations. A relational framework is particularly useful as a lens and is referred to in some literature as a framework that represents a consequential-cultural approach to communication in close relationships. Burleson, Metts, and Kirch (2000) defined this approach in the following manner: "All communication in a relationship is *consequential* .... Communication enacts the relationship; expresses images of the self, other, and the relationship; creates patterns, routines, and rituals; establishes and perpetuates shared codes and other meaning systems; and reinforces communal norms and rules. In short, communication in relationships creates and maintains a *relational culture*" (p. 246).

A relational approach to understanding women foregrounds women's lives as lived in relation with others, whereas a relational communication frame within that approach views communication as the lifeblood of relationships (Knapp & Vangelisti, 1996), as the mechanism by which relationships are developed and the glue that holds them together, and as the means by which they are dissolved (Guerrero, Anderson, & Afifi, 2001). Wilmot (1995) originally outlined and Guerrero et al. (2001) summarized the following principles that serve to provide the scaffolding for the relational communication theoretical framework.[6]

- *Relationships emerge across ongoing interaction.* This principle suggests that relationships form across repeated interactions. Guerrero et al. (2001) summarized this principle as "in part, relationships represent a collection of all the communication episodes in which two partners have engaged over time, and each episode adds new information about the relationship" (p. 19). At varying points in time, "turning points" in the relationship may lead to the negotiation and renegotiation of the relational identity.
- *Relationships contextualize messages.* How I perceive my relationship with you frames how I interpret any messages we exchange. This principle in-

---

[6]See Guerrero, Anderson, and Afifi (2001) for further discussion of these principles.

dicates that individuals must seek to understand behavior in its relational context. Messages convey different meanings, depending on context. For example, a terse demand to "pick up your clothes" delivered from a mother to a daughter may not be perceived in the same way as the same demand delivered by the daughter to the mother. Relationships and their surrounding norms, definitions, and practices frame communication behavior.

• *Relationship types overlap one another.* Relationships such as grandmother, mother, and daughter may seem to fit into distinct categories; however, this principle suggests that relational types are not always mutually exclusive. In fact, Wilmot (1995) indicated that the "boundaries [between relationship types] is often fuzzy" (p. 28). Depending on how each interactant defines a particular role, a daughter may function to "mother" her own biological mother and the mother may allow herself to be mothered by the daughter. Despite relationship labels, meanings of who we are to one another are continually negotiated and renegotiated.

• *Relational definitions and communication episodes frame each other.* This principle indicates that my communication with you affects how I will define our relationship and, conversely, how I define my relationship with you will affect how I communicate with you. As the relationship changes, our communication will also alter to reflect those changes. Moreover, if there is a change in the way we communicate, this may, in turn, shape how I perceive our relationship. In sum, our communication has the potential to both reflect and shape our relationships.

Within this framework, relationships are considered dynamic, enacted moment by moment across time (Milardo & Duck, 2000). These ongoing interactions serve to develop unique *relational cultures*.

Relational Cultures. Much like the meaning of culture in the broader sense, relational cultures "consist of shared meaning systems; characteristic interaction routines and rituals; norms and rules that organize, sequence and control behavior; and role structures that organize situated identities" (Burleson et al., 2000, p. 246). Moreover, these relational cultures "create, express, and sustain personal relationships and identities of partners" (Wood, 2000, p. 77). A relational culture emphasizes the notion of relational partners collaboratively creating a unique culture in an ongoing fashion, making modifications and redefining the relational culture over time. Partners' interaction is considered central to establishing this relational culture and also to establishing the relational identity, defined as who "we" are in the world. It is difficult, however, to define the "we-ness," specifically in the mother–daughter relationship, without addressing the balance between individual identity and relational identity and then contextualizing that balance within the larger family and social contexts.

Burleson et al. (2000) affirmed that scholars must understand that although any relational culture will be unique, all relational cultures exhibit features characteristic of other relationships in their class (e.g., mother–daughter, grandmother–granddaughter). Every particular relational culture will share some elements and be transferable to other relational cultures in its class and reflect larger sociocultural norms. Indeed, communication is embedded within a system of societal and local beliefs and practices that give rise to communication and then, in turn, are adapted through this exchange (Sillars, 1995).

Widening the theoretical lens to include relationships across multiple generations (grandmother–mother–daughter) does not distort the picture as much as it provides a slightly different vision of maternal relationships across the life span; indeed, every grandmother–granddaughter relationship is connected by two mother–daughter bonds. A relational approach using a relational communication frame serves to focus my inquiry on the ways in which women in these different relationships experience these different maternal relationships and also on how communication functions within and across these relationships.

Participant Selection

In order to assure valid and credible information, purposeful criterion sampling (Patton, 1990; Taylor & Bogdan, 1984) was used in this study. This mode of sampling is based on selecting participants who fit desired characteristics. One of the strengths of grounded theory research is the practice of extending and refining previous research on a phenomenon. Following the same general rules for data collection and analysis and assuming a similar set of conditions may extend theoretical explanations. Because this study was intended to build on my previous research findings, I entered the same Midwestern community used in Miller (1995) in order to maintain the continuity and homogeneity of the research sample. I enlisted the participation of grandmothers, mothers, and daughters whose lives were connected in a White, suburban community in the Midwestern United States. Although this selection restricts findings to women with similar characteristics, it was necessary to restrict sampling to this homogeneous group. In addition to reproducing sample characteristics from one study to the next, cultural similarity among participants is advisable because cultural and ethnic backgrounds tend to influence family dynamics and unique norms of behavior (Galvin & Brommel, 1999). Thus, I sought grandmothers, mothers, and daughters who shared similar ethnicity and socioeconomic characteristics. Additional criteria for participation in this study stipulated that the participants must be within the same biological family, live in close proximity within the targeted community, engage in interaction with the other family member participants at least one time per week, and be willing to allow me into their homes and lives for interviews and observations. The criterion of living in proximity is not anomalous, considering national data that report 50% to 75% of older adults lived within a half hour from their closest child (Lin & Rogerson, 1995). Therefore, purposive sampling resulted in a selection of 18 women who were biologically related, interdependent, living in close proximity with frequent interactions, and who were willing to participate. The list of participants is found in Table 2.2.

Although obtaining a sample of women from a wide range of developmental periods was not a specific goal, the following developmental periods across the life span were represented in this sample: Linda, Tabitha, and Scout represented women in late adolescence (16–20 years old); Kendra and Georgie were young adults (21–29 years old); Sam, Kelly, Katrina, Gina, Barb, Becky, and Morgan were all in mid-life (30–59 years old); and Sylvia, Diane, Rowena, Lois, Charlotte, and Meredith were older adults (60+ years old).

To determine if sampling procedures were sufficient, both the appropriateness and adequateness of the sample were assessed (Morse, 1997). *Appropriateness* refers to the degree to which the choice of informants and method "fit" the purpose of the study as determined by the research questions and stage of the research. The fit of any participant was determined by characteristics of her being female; self-reporting that she considers herself to have a relationship with her daughter, mother, and/or grandmother, interacting with the other family participants a minimum of one time per week; and her willingness to share her constructions about these relationships. For pragmatic purposes, all three participants in a given family needed to live within the same community. After initial consultation with each family member, I determined if each female met the selection criteria and was an appropriate candidate for participation in this study. Ultimately, a snowball approach was used, by which one woman recommended another woman in her community, who recommended another, and so on. Initial interviews were conducted until 18 women (six families) who met the selection criteria were recruited for participation in this research.

Adequacy refers to the sufficiency and quality of the data. To ensure adequacy, one assesses the relevance, completeness, and amount of information obtained. If the data are adequate, there are no "thin" areas and the resulting explanation will be complete (i.e., saturation of data). An outcome assessment of adequacy was based on whether saturation was achieved, and if the explanation made logical sense to the researcher and to the participants. Saturation within each relationship was sought in this study. Therefore, data were collected from each relational partner using multiple techniques. As Fitch (2000) pointed out, "talk *about* an event or relationship is much different from talk *during* an event or *within* a relationship" (italics added, p. 8). Nevertheless, one's analysis of meaning tends to occur naturally outside of direct interaction in the reflection on that interaction. Therefore, interview and observational data are utilized as complementary data sources in this study. In the end, there was ample data from multiple sources to achieve the criteria of adequacy.

Consent

The contact person in each family solicited the cooperation of her other family members. After a family agreed to an introductory interview, I met with all three

TABLE 2.2
Demographic Factors of Participants

Name	Family	Age	Education	Children	Marriages	RPB	Employment
Sylvia	1	82	High school	M = 1; F = 2	1	S, AOD, E	Homemaker
Diane	1	64	College	M = 1; F = 3	1	S, AOD, E	Homemaker
Sam	1	40	High school	M = 2; F = 3	2	S, AOD, E	Educator
Katrina	2	58	High school	M = 2; F = 3	2		Entrepreneur
Kelly	2	37	High school	M = 0; F = 2	4	S, AOD, E	Dance teacher
Kendra	2	21	High school	M = 1; F = 1	1		Homemaker
Rowena	3	72	High school	M = 0; F = 2	1		Homemaker
Gina	3	50	College	M = 1; F = 1	1		Volunteer coordinator
Georgie	3	25	College	M = 0; F = 0	0		Accountant
Lois	4	62	High school	M = 1; F = 2	1		Homemaker
Barb	4	40	College	M = 2; F = 1	1		Homemaker
Tabitha	4	18	College prep	M = 0; F = 0	0		Student
Charlotte	5	63	High school	M = 2; F = 1	1		Homemaker
Becky	5	43	Postgraduate	M = 0; F = 2	2		Educator
Linda	5	18	College prep	M = 0; F = 0	0		Student
Meredith	6	63	College	M = 1; F = 3	1	S, AOD, E	Homemaker
Morgan	6	42	2-year JC	M = 0; F = 4	1	S, AOD, E	Minister/educator
Scout	6	18	College prep	M = 0; F = 0	0	E	Student

Note: JC = junior college; Children M = male; Children F = female; RPB = reported problem behaviors; S = suicide attempt; AOD = alcohol or other drug addictions; E = eating disorder; Employment = employment at the time of the study.

women, discussed the overall project, gained consent, and arranged to attend certain events in their lives (e.g., birthday parties, church services).

The process of obtaining consent is one of the more harrowing aspects of a qualitative research design, and this study proved to be no different. In this investigation, I was concerned about family members denying consent, particularly the grandmothers in the sample. One of the grandmothers was more than 80 years old. I discovered that although sharing casual conversation and information about health were comfortable for them, in-depth self-disclosure about family relationships was not taken lightly. This generation of women, although familiar with the self-disclosive culture of the 1990s (Priest, 1996), was not reared within that culture of public disclosure. Moreover, I learned very quickly about my own sense of values and identified the resurgence of one of my own family themes—"respect your elders."

At the outset, I was reticent to infringe on an older person's privacy or offend her sensibilities in any way. With all of the women, but mostly with those older than I, I tended to frame the request to participate in a manner I felt would meet with approval. For example, I would begin my initial dialogue with a reminder that I had written a stage play about mothers and daughters. The conversation would then be directed toward my interest in mother–daughter communication across generations and then to our shared interest in understanding more about maternal relationships. Each woman would usually express her enthusiastic consent with a comment such as, "Certainly, and, boy, I have some stories to tell!" (Sylvia, OD-1, 2).[7] At the end of the process of securing consent I felt relieved that I had gained access to each family and was able to step through their door, literally and figuratively.

Data Collection

Interviews.   After the initial meetings to obtain consent, a private interview was scheduled with each woman. Retrospective information and current perceptions of grandmother–mother–daughter relationships were solicited during these face-to-face, semi-structured, formal interviews. The interview schedules were designed to solicit description, stories, and perceptions of personal and relational identity negotiation between mothers and daughters. Participants were encouraged to narrate the "story" of their relationship with their grandmother, mother, daughter, and/or granddaughter. This approach was based on recent research emphasizing the importance of narrative in understanding family process (Friedman, 1993; Gilligan & Price, 1993; Yerby, Buerkel-Rothfuss, & Bochner, 1995). I gathered participants' stories of their maternal relationships and used these as a starting point in my analysis. These

---

[7]To interpret this citation, refer to the following guide: name of participant; type of data (e.g., personal memo [PM], analytic memo [AM], observational data [OD], interview data [ID]); # of the memo, observational, or interview transcript; and the page number of the transcript.

narratives provided a basic structure from which to organize and synthesize relational events.

Each woman's initial interview was conducted within the first 6 weeks of my stay in Elkwood. Some of the women were hesitant at the beginning of the interviews, and later seemed to welcome the opportunity to reflect on their lives with an engaged listener. In the end, all of the participants spoke openly and articulately about their lives, and their thoughts, feelings, and relationships. An average initial interview lasted 2 hours and generated 21 pages of transcribed text.

Informal, unstructured, and conversational interviews were also conducted throughout the course of my fieldwork. These conversations were often directed at seeking the women's thoughts and feelings about specific interactions I observed, debriefing my own interpretations and collecting theirs. After a few months in the field, these informal conversations were also conducted to discuss emerging theoretical speculations, collect additional data, achieve verification of ideas, and refine the theory.

Artifacts. Participants in this study were also asked to provide family artifacts of their maternal relationship, and these included items such as *memorabilia, photographs,* and *video footage.* Katriel and Farrell (1991) and Meese (1998) explored the meaning of photo albums and scrapbooks as an artifact of life narration. Their studies suggest that the family photo album is a text performed for self and audience that reflects the cultural ideology of the family. Participants were asked to explain their artifacts. Five of the six participating families provided artifacts and explanations to me. Katrina's family did not participate in this form of data collection due to distractions associated with an illness in the family during the course of my fieldwork. The illness impacted the amount of time and energy the women in this family could donate to this study, and I did not want to pressure them to provide more time and information than they were comfortable supplying.

Those women who offered artifacts often shared interpretations of them with their mother or daughter. Charlotte's family was the only family in which all three generations of women were together when they described their family photo album. After each session in which a woman or women described their artifact, I documented my observations and any direct quotes into my field notes.

Observational Data. The systematic use of direct observation has been an important research tool for centuries, because observations provide researchers with the opportunity to witness the complexities of social interaction. In this particular study, observational data were collected over a period of 8 months of participating with and observing participants in their homes and community. In addition to the informal observations, an intensive 3-day observation period was conducted with each family. During this period, I resided at the home of one member of the dyad. The women interacted each day over that 3-day period, and I documented the *in situ* communicative interaction among the participants. Because I resided with Family #1 throughout the majority of my stay, they allowed me to observe them almost constantly for 8 months. Unfortunately, I did not have the privilege of observing Family #2 over a continuous 3-day and night period, although I did spend more than 30 days talking informally with these women and observing them in interaction during the daytime hours of my tenure in Elkwood.

The reality of this kind of research is that many of the rich data points are obtained during *informal* gatherings at which participants are active and the observer fades into the background. For example, I accompanied some of the participants on outings and participated in family meetings, interpersonal confrontations, and family celebrations such as birthdays. During this time of being *in situ*, naturalistic observation, I adhered to fieldwork guidelines suggested by Glaser and Strauss (1967), Taylor and Bogdan (1984), and Strauss and Corbin (1990). I learned early in my study about the delicate balance between participation and observation. Sometimes I observed from a sofa or a corner, whereas other times I participated in dinnertime conversation or went grocery shopping with participants. During these observational periods, I systematically documented the symbolic exchange (verbal and nonverbal) in any maternal relationship interaction that I had the opportunity to observe, and any incidence of a woman commenting on her own identity in connection to or apart from her maternal relationships. Using the conceptual boundaries of my study to direct my observations, the observational data collected in this research consisted of incidences of communicative interaction between women in a maternal relationship (i.e., mother–daughter, grandmother–granddaughter) as well as informal day-to-day commentary about their relationships with grandmothers, mothers, and daughters in the study. I sought to understand these women by soliciting and observing their everyday talk, actions, interactions, and recollections.

In conducting observational, interpretive research, I acknowledge that my documentation of interactions does not necessarily represent "objective truth." At times, there were conflicting versions of what occurred during an interaction or what "meaning" should be attributed to the particular interaction. Although infrequent, these conflicting perceptions occurred among the participants, as well as between the participants' perceptions and my own. Another strength of the grounded theory approach is the luxury of checking my perceptions with the women of Elkwood and also using current theoretical knowledge to inform my interpretations. Necessarily, then, I developed a collaboration with the participants throughout the research process, asking for their reactions to my observational notes as well as asking them to provide their own meanings and interpretations.

Field Notes.   Observations in natural settings can be represented as descriptions through open-ended narrative, through the use of predetermined checklists, or in field note format (Angrosino & Mays de Perez, 2000; Rossman

& Rallis, 1998). But no matter the format, the reporting of concrete events in fieldwork should begin at a low level of abstraction and then move toward interpretation (Pelto & Pelto, 1978). As Angrosino and Mays de Perez (2000) outlined research begins with raw observational data (i.e., she moved over to her mother, stroked her cheek and embraced her), in which the observer documents events as he or she observes them, taking nothing for granted. The researcher then moves into focused observation, wherein the observer's lens becomes more focused on the issues relevant to the goals of the study as determined before the study began (e.g., the *a priori* questions), or determined as relevant during the process of the inquiry. Flexibility is key to observational research as well as sensitivity to what participants think is relevant. The next step in the process includes subjecting the focused observations to interpretation (e.g., what does this mean?). Then, finally, the researcher systematically concentrates on organizing, comparing, and contrasting the observations in order to create higher-order observations of the data. These organizing observations then become the content of analytic memos.

The field note format used in this study is based on the process just described. My field note pages contained the location, date, and time of the observation in the right-hand corner. The page was then divided into three sections from left to right: analytic memo, description, and self-reflections. The description section would typically utilize a broad lens, taking in the details, actors, and actions occurring in the setting. The following excerpt stems from viewing a setting with this broad lens: "The beige walls were bare except for one photograph of a young child placed directly above the headboard of the double bed. The afghan was thrown onto the bed in a heap although the sheets were drawn up and tightly tucked into the mattress" (Charlotte, OD-3, 1). The broad lens was also helpful in mapping the homes of the participants and the Elkwood community. Mapping allowed me to chart objects (i.e., houses), space, use of space, and boundaries. Maps within and between houses were useful in interpreting the story of social relationships in the community.

Eventually I narrowed my observational lens to focus more specifically on the actors and activities relevant to the study's purpose. LeCompte and Schensul (1999) suggested that observational researchers document "whatever the informants say or do, items from their speech and behavior are selected for recording and documented with the researcher's purpose in mind" (p. 31). This focused, narrow lens forced me to sense what these women said and did that was pertinent to maternal relationships. Many of my field notes documented dialogue that occurred in natural settings and were transcribed as accurately as possible. Although I truly value the information that rigorous discourse analysis provides, my intention was not to document and transcribe dialogue with the precision necessary for discourse analysis. The intention of documenting episodes of dialogue was to get at the gestalt of the interaction, paraphrasing if necessary. Fortunately, however, I was able to document some conversations verbatim by recording interactions with a mini-recorder and by meticulous attention to dialogic detail during interactions. A sample note at this stage of the process follows:

> Charlotte, Becky, and Linda point to a photograph of a younger Charlotte holding [another grandchild] on her lap and Becky was pushing the wheelchair. The women describe an incident surrounding the photograph:
>
> Charlotte says, "Becky, you pushed me!"
>
> Becky replies, "Your chair tipped, Mom."
>
> Linda interjects, "You lost your balance, grandma. I don't remember, did [the baby] fall?"
>
> Charlotte says, "No, I threw her on the grass so she wouldn't get hurt. I had four broken vertebrae!"
>
> Becky rolls her eyes, "But we went on with the trip, didn't we Mom?"
>
> Charlotte offers an aside to me, "It's because I was used to pain by then."

Focused observations allowed me to develop sensitivity to verbal (e.g., use of accusing "you" and personal "I") and nonverbal (e.g., rolling of eyes) relational codes. I attempted to adhere to the following advice from Rossman and Rallis (1998): "to be a good qualitative researcher you develop sensitive eyes and ears, like an artist's or a detective's; this eye or ear detects the figure and the ground—the detail within the whole" (p. 157).

Another example of moving from a wide observational lens to a more focused inquiry occurred approximately 2 months into my fieldwork. At this point I had begun to document extreme levels of cohesion within certain relationships; therefore, I elected to focus specifically on the dimension of cohesion for two weeks. Turning to the Clinical Rating Scale (Olson, 1990, 1993; Thomas & Olson, 1993)—an empirically based family assessment tool—I utilized their established categories of relational cohesion to guide my targeted inquiry. I noted behaviors and comments, and interpreted and coded them into the following *a priori* categories: disengaged, separated, connected, and enmeshed.[8] Moreover, to enhance the credibility of these observations I conducted additional interviews with each participant to assess her perception of the relational cohesion in her maternal relationships. The accounts from the women were consistent with my observations and also added information about participants' satisfaction with their perceived levels of relational cohesion.

In addition to field notes, analytic memos were generated to document higher-order observations and interpretations of the data. The writing of analytic memos is the first stage of a qualitative analysis moving from documenting raw data to interpretation and speculation. Recall that in abductive research the investigator moves back and forth between data and guiding theory, build-

---

[8]For a complete description of these dimensions of cohesion, see Olson (1993).

ing on information already gathered and filling in any gaps. Hence, data analysis occurs simultaneously with data collection.

During this next phase of analysis, I moved beyond raw description toward analysis, integration, and ascribing my own interpretation (e.g., What are the connections between these two experiences?). Descriptive memos answered the who, what, when, where, and how questions, whereas analytic memos began to address the why question. My personal speculations were identified as observer's comments (OC). Often, I would have the opportunity to approach the participants of an interaction, share my observation with them, and ask them to articulate their feelings, meanings, and motivations. Whenever this occurred, I added these clarifications to my notes and provided the point of view (i.e., Sylvia's POV). This activity was conducted to avoid making inferences about intent, motivation, or feelings based only on observed behaviors.

Analytic memos also represented my thoughts and interpretations of data across actors and their activities. By moving back and forth between previously gathered data and current observations, I was able to selectively compare and contrast data. Ely (1991) suggested that analytic memos can be considered as conversations with oneself about what has occurred in the research process. The following represents an analytic memo I wrote after the initial semi-structured interviews with the participants:

> The expectations of perfection are bidirectional in families #1, #2, and #6 (see interviews with Diane, Sam, Sylvia, Kelly, etc.). Mothers and daughters alike articulate these expectations. Ultimately, I guess that if you expect someone to be perfect … sooner or later you will, in turn, criticize them for their faults. The "perfect mother" myth … is there a perfect daughter myth? (Michelle, AM-2, 4)

The entries are *about* the documented data. They themselves then *become* data, pointing in a direction for further investigation.

The third section of my field note page was reserved for self-reflective notes regarding the observation. Because I was the primary research tool in this observational study and wanted to provide a heuristic account, I was careful to document my personal biases, hunches, assumptions, and feelings as I proceeded throughout the investigation. These personal notes situated me (as a researcher, woman, daughter, and mother) in the research and also provided a baseline against which I could compare what actually emerged as the study developed. Bogdan and Biklen (1998) argued that reflective field notes should contain reflections on method, ethical dilemmas or conflict, the researcher's frame of mind, analysis, and points of clarification. Not only did these notes allow me to construct the multivocal, layered account in this book, but they also challenged my assumptions while conducting my research. A sample reflective note that served to do just that was one I wrote within the first month of my fieldwork: "Rowena just has nothing critical to say about (Gina or Georgie). I wonder what she is hiding?" (Michelle, PM-1, 6).

At the end of that particular week, I glanced back over my notes, caught my personal note, and then decided to amend it in the following way:

> Does she have to be "hiding" anything? I do not want to fall into the trap of *expecting* negative or critical comments about g–m–d relationships. I need to accept Rowena's perception of her relationship. Yet, while I won't expect negative comments, I want to be sensitive to cues that may contradict her verbal account of her relationships. The cues may or may not be contradictory. Remember that! (Michelle, PM-1, 7)

Self-reflective notes allowed me to bracket my own subjective biases (not rid myself of them), entering the world of my participants more honestly than if I had not written self-reflective memos. Staying conscious of my subjective connection with the research process also helped me to approach my work with these women "not as a person who knows everything, but as a person who has come to learn; not as a person who wants to be like them, but as a person who wants to know what it is to be like them" (Bogdan & Biklen, 1992, p. 79).

Trustworthiness

Inevitably, considerations of qualitative research inspire discussions of scientific validity and reliability. Scholars often see particular strengths of qualitative research, such as reliance on the human instrument and the flexibility of research design, as weaknesses (Merrick, 1999). Several authors have already broached the issue of scientific validity and reliability in qualitative research (see Altheide & Johnson, 1994; Becker, 1996; Lincoln & Guba, 1985, 1999; Mays & Pope, 2000; Merriam, 1998; Merrick, 1999; Morse, 1991; Wolcott, 1990), arguing that positivist terms such as reliability and validity are inappropriate and misleading when applied to qualitative research. I do not reiterate the debate in this discussion. What is important to articulate, however, is that the criteria used to judge merit of any mode of discovery are made explicit. I clarify my position on these issues as they pertain to this study.

As shown in Table 2.3, instead of the traditional criteria of validity, objectivity, and reliability, this research uses the *trustworthiness criteria* such as credibility, transferability, dependability, and confirmability to evaluate the scientific merit of this research. The credibility of this research refers to the accuracy of the information obtained in this study; that is, should we believe this information to be trustworthy? In this study, certain provisions were made to enhance credibility, such as using multiple methods in collecting data rather than a single method, extending the duration of my time spent in the community observing the same relationships rather than conducting a single observation of a larger cross-sectional sample, and finally, employing the use of respondent validation to verify the credibility and trustworthiness of the information.

TABLE 2.3
Techniques to Ensure Trustworthiness

Traditional Criteria	Trustworthiness Criteria	Criteria Met in This Study Through:
Internal validity	Credibility	**Extended engagement in the field:** • Ongoing, longitudinal data collection • Persistent observation (careful observation of the situation to determine salient factors and characteristics) **Triangulation of data types:** • Interviews • Gathering artifacts • Observations **Respondent validation:** • Formal and informal discussions of emergent findings with participants, verification, and adjustment of interpretations
External validity	Transferability (extent to which findings are transferable to other settings	• Data grounded in naturally occurring behaviors • Delimited claims to sample characteristics **Detailed (thick) description of:** • Concepts and categories • Structures and processes related to transactions
Reliability	Dependability Reduce reactivity	• Purposive sampling • Accurate records maintained for an audit trail (to accurately retrace the stages of the research process) • Self-reflection illustrated through personal journals of researchers disclosing biases • Protection of informants' confidentiality • Reduce reactivity by observing systematic change in family behavior over time • Reduce reactivity by functioning as a participant as well as an observer • Observing systematic change in family behavior over time • Functioning as a participant as well as an observer
Objectivity	Confirmability (clear exposition of methods of data collection and analysis for auditor confirmation)	**Meticulous Data Management and Recording:** • Verbatim transcription of interviews • Careful notes of observations • Clear memos on theoretical, methodological, and personal decisions • Accurate records of contacts, interviews, and observations

The transferability of this research refers to the extent to which the findings are transferable to other settings. By seeking a homogenous sample of women for this research, observing behavior in natural settings, providing detailed and nuanced descriptions of their relationships, and articulating patterns within relationships and across relationships, this particular study should provide adequate information from which to extrapolate and transfer information to similar maternal relationships among Caucasian, middle-income women.

Trustworthiness criteria demand that the results of a qualitative inquiry be dependable. Re-interviewing participants over time, while obtaining self-reports in addition to observational data, serves to minimize random errors that might occur in both investigator and participant performance and increases the dependability of the results. Moreover, purposive sampling, self-reflection, and accurate records (to retrace the stages of the research process) help to ensure dependable and trustworthy results.

The issue of reactivity also frequently emerges as a concern with qualitative research methods. However, evaluation studies of reactivity during naturalistic observations in private homes find little reactivity (Christensen & Nies, 1980). This reactivity literature suggests that family behavior is not dramatically altered by the presence of an observer (Bussell, 1994; Jacob, Tennenbaum, & Krahn, 1987; Weiss & Perry, 1983). Moreover, direct observations provide us with the opportunity to witness the complexities in social interaction that are not available via other methods.

In this study, I made certain that I functioned more as a participant than as an observer during the period of time in which I was earning the trust of the participants. Additionally, when I was taking notes during an in-home observation, I reduced the inherent obtrusive nature of the process by carrying a mini tape recorder and jotting observations on a field notepad while in the bathrooms of the homes. I would sporadically escape to the restroom in order to document an observation and then, at the day's end in the privacy of my room, document all other observations. Furthermore, the duration of my stay in Elkwood contributed to reducing reactivity and increasing the trust and comfort levels between myself and each woman over time.

The last criterion of trustworthiness—confirmability—refers to the clear exposition of how I conducted the research so that others might confirm the results. This was accomplished through meticulous data management and maintenance of accurate records. Interviews were transcribed verbatim, field notes were documented systematically, accurate records were maintained on each observation and interview, and decisions were documented and organized chronologically. These steps were taken to ensure that I, and others, could confirm my findings.

Data Management

Qualitative research often appears to require a mix of very different skills: efficient management of data combined with detailed knowledge and sensitive ex-

ploration, as well as the ability to create abstractions, identify patterns, and
probe the emerging patterns. Huberman and Miles (1994) emphasized, "A good
storage and retrieval system is critical for keeping track of what data are available" (p. 430). Therefore, the NUD*IST or "Nonnumerical Unstructured Data
Indexing Searching and Theorizing" program was used in this study to manage
data documents such as interview transcripts, field notes, unstructured conversations, and journal entries, as well as nontextual records such as photographs
and drawings. This software program is used extensively in qualitative research
and its merits are addressed in several publications, such as Barry (1998), Fielding and Lee (1998), Richards and Richards (1994), and Weitzman (2000). This
management and analysis program served as an essential tool in the data analysis for this study. Over the course of 8 months, the amount of data was volumi-
nous, and at times overwhelming.

Data Analysis

Analysis reduces data to a story that I can tell; interpretation tells the reader
what that story means. Analysis also organizes the piles of raw accumulated
data into smaller piles of summarized data (LeCompte & Schensul, 1999). This
process permits me to discover patterns and themes in the data and link these
with other patterns and themes. Themes are defined as "recurrent ideas" and/or
"a unifying idea that is a recurrent element in a text." In this study, a theme was
determined by the presence of one or more of the following: (a) if there was *recurrence* of behavior or an expressed thought (e.g., if two different statements
made a similar reference or suggested shared meaning); (b) if there was *repetition* of key words or phrases; (c) if there was heightened *consensus*, or agreement,
across participants; and (d) considerable *intensity* suggested an important con-
viction. Qualitative data analysis is an iterative process that begins during the
conceptualization of the study and proceeds through interpretation of the results. Locke (1996) described qualitative data analysis as a "recursive, process-
oriented, analytic procedure" (p. 240). This description is accurate in that the
data collection, coding, and interpretation often overlap. These overlapping
processes allow for a richer understanding of the data and for additional data
collection as necessary. While I collected more information, I moved back and
forth between data and theory as well as between relationships and families,
building on the information I had already gathered, making sense of it, and filling in any informational gaps along the way. Basically, the analytic process was
as follows: I made observations; I asked questions; I got answers; I then asked
more refined questions; I received more complete answers; I compared and contrasted the answers; I summarized and ordered data in order to establish patterns and linkages; I noted instances that clarified, modified, or negated what I
thought was "going on" in these relationships; and then I ultimately modified
and limited my speculation (adapted from LeCompte & Schensul, 1999).

Analysis of data entailed complete transcription of all interviews and notes, entry into the computer, followed by coding procedures outlined by Strauss and Corbin (1990) and LeCompte and Schensul (1999). The difficulty in articulating these procedures lies in the fact that this process begins from the first day of data collection rather than after the completion of data gathering. The recursive nature of this work requires one to sort, analyze, interpret, make claims, and then collect additional data to verify, refine, or disconfirm these claims. The following general procedures were utilized in this study.

Data Sorting. Data sources for this study were interview data (ID), observational data (OD), personal memos (PM), and analytic memos (AM). Most of these data were considered meaningful units for analysis, because they were already limited by my central purpose. Data management practices kept the data from these different sources separate. During the first few months of this study, this stage of the analysis was focused on primarily on the interview data, incorporating new data sources as they were gathered.

Open Coding and Assignment of Codes. Open coding involved "the naming and categorizing of phenomena through close examination of data" (Strauss & Corbin, 1990, p. 62). Open coding began by a careful reading of each data source, identifying units of data, and assigning each unit a conceptual label. For example, the following unit of data, sometimes referred to as a *data bite*, was assigned to a category that was provided a conceptual label of *recognition of achievement*: "the neighbors were *so* impressed [with my daughter's achievement]" (Diane, OD-5, 20). By situating this particular piece of information/data in the surrounding context of the statement, I noted that Diane was basking in the reflected glow of her neighbor's approval of her daughter's achievement. As it turned out later in the analysis, this recognition was central to many of the mother–daughter dyad's relational identities. However, at this stage in the analysis I merely labeled emergent concepts.

Comparing and Contrasting. The next step in the analysis included examining each unit of data assigned to conceptual categories, and then comparing and contrasting each for logical relationships and contradictions. The constant-comparison method (Glaser & Strauss, 1967) requires that each unit of data be compared to previous units to determine if it was similar to any other data or different from previous units. If any given unit of data was determined to be conceptually similar to an existing category, then it was labeled with that category code. If it was different, a new conceptual category was established and the data unit was labeled with the new category code. Additionally, efforts were made to label units with an *in vivo* code—a code using the language of the participants. This type of conceptual code allowed for the most accurate reflection of the participants' thoughts. These codes are first-order concepts; that is, ideas taken directly from informants' responses (Van Mannen, 1979). As you can imagine, this ongoing process generated numerous conceptual codes within and across cases.

Axial Coding and Ordering.   This stage marks a move toward data reduction. As the data were conceptually coded and compared, I sought to identify central categories (sometimes called *core categories*) that organized and represented key concepts. Categories, according to Strauss and Corbin (1990), are groupings of "concepts that seem to pertain to the same phenomena" (p. 65), and each category contains various properties or characteristics.

Remember that although core categories evolve from raw data, they are abstractions—products of analysis condensed into a few words that explain key dimensions of "what this research is all about" (Strauss & Corbin, 1998, p. 146). Axial coding allowed me to analyze relationships within and between concepts to create central categories, or *domains* as Spradley (1979) termed them. To help determine the relationship between concepts and identify domains, Spradley's (1979) semantic relationship questions were used (e.g., "X is a kind of Y," "X is a reason for doing Y," "X is a step in Y," "X is a place to do Y"). During this stage, a sample domain of salience was identified as *conditional acceptance* and it contained the following subcategories: maternal validation and approval, social rejection, maternal rejection, and conditions for maternal acceptance.

Aggregation and Identification of General Themes.   The next step in the process involves another level of abstraction where domains (and the subcategories within each domain) are collapsed into parsimonious groupings of broader, more inclusive themes. As a brief review, note that up to this point conceptual categories were identified and defined, and those categories similar to one another were clustered together into domains. In this phase of the analysis I examined the domains for possible relationships and aggregated into themes. These themes, although no longer specific to any one relationship or family, are derived from comparing data from each case and should, in a general sense, have relevance for, and be applicable to, all cases in the study (Strauss & Corbin, 1998). A theme is any cognitive principle, tacit or explicit, recurrent in a number of domains that consists of multiple concepts linked into meaningful relationships. The stage of aggregating and identifying themes ultimately generates groupings of meaning based on my interpretation of the data, and thus represents a second-order analysis (Van Mannen, 1979).

Many of the themes that emerged in this study fit within the structure and theoretical frame of dialectical theory. The structuring of key themes as dialectical tensions provided a flood of understanding into how these women experienced their maternal relationships and why this relationship has so often been characterized as complicated. The development of key themes assisted me in making sense of "what is going on here" and, aside from identifying dialectical tensions inherent in negotiating the mother–daughter relationship, informed my understanding of how communication processes functioned in the management of these tensions. In the end, the general themes applicable across all the cases in this study were dialectical tensions, relational cohesion, discursive practices, and problem behavior.

Additionally, throughout the analytic process I maintained ongoing documentation of coding decisions and my thoughts about any given code, category, or domain. This activity is called developing an "audit trail" (Glaser & Strauss, 1967; Strauss & Corbin, 1990). This audit trail became useful during later phases in the analysis.

Theoretical Coding and Modeling. Because the goal of much qualitative work is *discovery*, some studies terminate at the end of Step 5 and present findings of what they discovered from data analysis and interpretation. This study, on the other hand, unfolded in such a way that a substantive theory grounded in the raw data began to emerge. Thus, a few more steps were involved to complete this process. If theory building is a goal of a research project, then findings should be presented as a set of explanatory relational statements (Strauss & Corbin, 1998). These explanatory statements represent an interpretation of phenomenon and articulate how core concepts may be interrelated (e.g., "under these conditions …"). After determining the general themes underlying the patterns of maternal relationships in Elkwood, I pondered how these themes functioned in isolation and in conjunction. Chapters 4 and 5 provide discussions of key underlying patterns in the Elkwood maternal relationships, whereas chapter 6 offers a visual model of how these coalesce into a conceptual model for understanding intergenerational maternal relationships. Based on these patterns and model, I propose a grounded theory of mother–daughter communication. Although this theory is substantive and not a general theory, I argue that it may be transferable to other similar relationships. In the end, this process resulted in a conceptual model that illustrates the dynamic complexity of contradictions in these mother–daughter and grandmother–granddaughter relationships and a reasoned speculation about the connections among relational communication and women's problem behaviors.

Establish Boundaries. The final stage in my analytic process was to establish the boundaries of both the model and the theoretical speculation developed during the preceding stage. Once the overarching theoretical scheme was mapped out, the theory needed to be refined. Refining a theory consists of "reviewing it for internal consistency and gaps in logic, filling in poorly developed categories, and trimming excess ones, and validating the theory" (Strauss & Corbin, 1998, p. 156). During this process, I revisited each claim in the theory to assess if the nature and scope were clearly articulated and determine if each was fully developed. If any was underdeveloped I revisited all data sources to assess if something was overlooked and often returned to the women of Elkwood to gather additional information. Ultimately, I aimed toward and achieved *theoretical saturation* across all dimensions of this grounded theory. Theoretical saturation denotes that no new dimensions emerged from the data after adding new individual participants or new dyads, and that the analysis accounted for most of the possible variation in the data (Strauss & Corbin, 1998).

Additional activities in this stage are trimming the theory and validating the developing theory. Although interesting, some dimensions were undeveloped because they did not address the central purpose of the study, such as the women's work relationships. In this study, unless the data pertained to how work relationships related to maternal relationships, then data specific to women's work relationships were excluded from the developing theory. Validating a developing theory does not refer to testing it in the quantitative sense. Strauss and Corbin (1998) argued that theory emerges from data, but is in itself an abstraction. Therefore, it is important to assess if the abstractions fit the raw data. This is where the audit trail came into play. I provided an independent auditor with my developing theory and the audit trail, including the nature and scope of each domain, and decisions regarding coding, collapsing, and determining relationships. This auditor validated the emerging theory and assisted me greatly by pointing out points of imprecision in the theory development. Ultimately, however, as an interpretive study, this last phase reflects a final step toward clearly articulating my reasoned speculations.

This book tells the story of this investigation. Join me, if you will, on my qualitative research journey.

3

Grandmothers, Mothers, and Adult Daughters in Elkwood

The psychosocial interior of a family is where members meet and make a life to-gether. Individual selves confronting, engaging and being struck off from one another ....

—(Handel & Whitchurch, 1994, p. 4)

SETTING

In 1994, I packed my bags, kissed friends and family goodbye, and with my infant son boarded an airplane bound for a city in the Midwestern United States. As we descended through the clouds, I viewed a patchwork of earth below. Farmland. Wooded areas peppered with houses and small bodies of water. As we continued our descent, an increasingly suburban landscape sprawled below and beyond. Tract homes and housing developments, trees, sidewalks, and Lilliputian cars zipped along the freeways. The plane circled the airport once before landing.

After a 45-minute drive from the airport, I arrived in Elkwood,[9] where I was to stay for 8 months—exploring, learning, and sharing with a group of 18

---

[9]*Elkwood* is a fictional name for the town represented in these pages. Any resemblance to actual locations bearing this name is strictly a coincidence.

women who had agreed to participate in this study of family communication. I inhaled deeply and exhaled my nervousness as I sat in a car and watched the scenery pass by.

Elkwood also breathed. No, that's not right ... it *billowed* in the wind. As I entered the town of 30,000, I saw hundreds of trees blowing and bending. The sky was clear and houses along our route lined the streets in tidy rows. Passing a few solitary traffic lights, we moved deeper into the residential district where the roads became a little wider and the stop sign was the only mode of traffic control. Maneuvering our way through the town I entered the section where I was to live for the next 8 months. As we drove through the town, the homes became progressively more upscale and expensive. Most were two-story Tudor-style brick homes with well-manicured, winter lawns. Almost every door or window was adorned with large, symmetrical wreaths wearing red bows. There was no snow on the streets, but the wind promised a chilly stay for the first few months of my habitation.

Elkwood's character proved to be unique. Even though the homes were decorated in tasteful similarity, each house had a distinctive character. On the north side of town there was a new development of million-dollar homes. In fact, this community boasted more Ph.D.s and more wealth per capita than any other small town in America. The homes were large, but not ostentatious. Where one home was expansive, the next was unassuming in architecture.

The remainder of the north side was populated with rows of homes whose values ranged from $100,000 to $200,000. These lawns were also well manicured with somewhat uniform holiday decorations, but the houses were smaller in scale than the previously described homes, and were built from wood rather than brick. This north side blended into the central district of town by way of moderately priced housing. Although these homes may have been modest in comparison to the other neighborhoods, they were well maintained. Within these neighborhoods you could also find commercial enterprises such as a local grocery and café, town library, municipal buildings, and downtown retail stores.

Many of the façades of the municipal buildings reflected the history of downtown Elkwood. For example, stone pillars and marble busts of founding fathers graced the entrances to the halls of justice and a local bank. Yet, at the same time, modern enterprises peppered Elkwood. Eateries, coffee shops, and bookstore-espresso bars were located on virtually every street corner. There were moments during my stay when I walked through town to greet the pleasantly pervasive smells of coffee beans and baked goods emanating from the shops. According to local townspeople, business in the town's small business retail stores had suffered terribly with the recent construction of a local Wal-Mart. Still, these people were proud to announce that store's arrival as well as the location of a 14-movie cineplex theater. These new businesses signified to many citizens in Elkwood that they now lived in "a civilized community."

Below the downtown area was the south end of town. Here, there was clearly a sense of "the other side of the tracks" mentality, not only among the north-side population, but among the south-end population as well. The paint on these homes was often chipped and faded. Decorations consisted of a few scattered strings of lights. Older cars littered the streets and chunks of sidewalk created haphazard and dangerous walkways.

But for all of the energy the south-end expended trying to look and feel poor, there remained an aura of small town suburbia. There is a difference between urban plight and poverty with its stench of garbage and noisy activity, and this suburban lower socioeconomic neighborhood that strove to make a house (no matter how worn) a home. Perhaps it was merely the presence of the trees lining the streets and uneven sidewalks that skewed my thinking toward a Norman Rockwell frame of reference, but I sensed a physical strength of community in all parts of this town—upper and lower income alike.

Nevertheless, it was in the north side of Elkwood that I spent most of my days and nights during this investigation. I lived in a home there with one of the project's participants—Diane—and her husband and dog. They had a four-bedroom, three-bath home with an expansive lawn and a welcome mat that read "Welcome Friends and Family." It was here that I laid my hat, but it was in the homes and the lives of all of the female participants that I learned the story of grandmothers, mothers, and daughters, and how lives may be linked with velvet chains.

CAST OF CHARACTERS

Although their names are changed here and identifying data have been disguised to preserve the privacy of each individual, the women's voices represented in these pages are real. The following are composites—thumbnail sketches really—of the women who participated in this investigation. These sketches are presented to provide a glimpse into their lives, their relationships, and their interconnectedness across generations.[10]

Family #1: Sylvia, Diane, and Sam

Sylvia was the 82-year-old matriarch of this family. She was 5'4" and appeared frail, loving, and stern, and was, according to others, something of a hypochondriac. Her large, expansive home (approximately 5,000 square feet) was the vortex of the family. Everything there was meticulously kept, with several knickknacks carefully placed in each room. The household employed one full-time housekeeper, one full-time personal nurse, and one full-time groundskeeper.

Everyone in Sylvia's extended family of 2 children, 8 grandchildren, and 23 great-grandchildren tried to stop in to see "Gramma" one time per week. Family

---

[10]To protect their privacy, not only have participants' names been changed, but so too have information on certain physical characteristics and locations.

members would typically walk into the house without knocking, grab a cola, say "Hi," get some candy, and leave. Sylvia liked visits from her family members and she seemed energized by their attention. On the second floor of her home a huge wall was dedicated to family portraits and pictures of grandchildren and great-grandchildren, and these pictures extended into the foyer and two additional hallways. At the lower level, a huge wooden plaque containing the name of each great-grandchild written in calligraphy overtook one entire wall.

Sylvia expressed great love for and pride in her family. She made it clear to me that she and her husband provided well for their entire extended family and she felt responsible for each member's welfare—financially and relationally. I overheard Sylvia call a granddaughter who was not married and offered, "Phyllis has a nephew that owns his own house and isn't married. She's going to talk with him and see if he'll ask you out." The granddaughter's response apparently was "Gramma, you are so funny." Sylvia replied, "No, I'm worried about you. I want to make sure you find a nice man who can take care of you." Being "taken care of" was very important to her.

Sylvia grew up in the early 1900s when the prevailing cultural norm was for a husband to financially care for his wife and children. The wife was to physically care for the household and offspring. Sylvia adhered to and found comfort in this role, and maintained her marriage and family through poverty, prosperity, alcoholism, physical abuse by her husband, and her own multiple suicide attempts. According to Sylvia, her husband got violent only when he drank, and she stayed committed to him until his death, which happened during the last month of my fieldwork.

When asked about the experience of moving from relative poverty to wealth, Sylvia explained:

> I helped [my husband] to make money, we kept two men at our house as borders and I packed their lunches for them and gave them breakfast, then gave them their dinner at night. They paid room and board and I had no help, I did it myself. I would go down and pack their buckets and make their dinners for them every night and done the linens and done their beds .... My husband started drinking. Yeah, I don't care about one glass. But two, he would get in the habit of getting drunk; he would get mad, angry, mean. He was mean. That wasn't too much of problem because he was making a living out on the road. He would drink with customers and I didn't know it because he wasn't home from one weekend to the next.

> Never in my whole life, had I dreamed of having what we got now. And that's why it came—because we worked hard for it, and I just never thought about it. People used to say, "Oh you're so lucky," that used to make [my husband] so angry when they'd say that. I'd say, "Well, we worked for everything we got." People would say that to me too, "You worked for it, you deserve it."

Sylvia stayed with her husband because "that's what you did in those days." Sylvia also recalled that her husband dearly loved his first child, Diane. Nonetheless, when Sylvia gave birth to her second child, his desire for a son became clear: "He came running into the room [after the birth] and said, 'Well, what is it? What is it?' and I said, 'It's a boy' and he grabbed me by the throat and said, 'If you're lying to me I'll kill you.' "

Sylvia said that her husband was not overtly affectionate, although in the materialistic sense he bought her "everything she needed" and took care of her. She also expressed pride in her husband because he "took care of the rest of the family" (financially). Others perceived Sylvia as a loving woman, very dependent on others, spoiled with material items, and somewhat needy, requiring substantial emotional nurturance.

Her daughter Diane felt the sting of the gender preference in her household. At the age of 64, the pain accompanying "being the *wrong sex*" permeated her relationships with her own daughters and her granddaughters. Diane revealed that she always had and "probably always will" be making up for the fact that she was born female.

Sylvia was noticeably dependent on Diane for both physical and emotional support. Diane and other family members reported that, without fail, every time Diane was to leave on a vacation or other trip, Sylvia became ill or injured herself. Diane could remember only a handful of times in her adult life where she did not terminate a trip early to return home and care for her mother. Throughout her lifetime, Sylvia had made multiple suicide attempts, abused prescription drugs, and battled alcoholism.

Sylvia did not talk much with me about her addictions or suicide attempts, and said even less about her ideas about her daughter as an individual person. It appeared difficult for her to construct an image of her daughter—who she was or what she desired—beyond how this daughter affected her own life. According to Sylvia, Diane is described as "strong-willed when she wants to do something and I want her to do another ... she is loving with me, yes, I know she loves me ... I don't know, though, much about other things."

Diane lived next door to her mother and when she walked into a room you could sense her energy. At 5'2', she is pleasantly rounded, with an expertly styled blonde coiffure. Diane is educated and very committed to her family. She has a broad, open smile, exuding warmth, and I immediately felt comfortable in her presence. When I first entered her home, she hugged me and invited me in without hesitation. The fact that she accepted me into her household for an 8-month period conveyed to me a spirit of generosity. Moreover, I quickly felt at ease with her obvious affection for my infant son. Diane provided me with every convenience, and I immediately felt welcomed.

As I interacted and spoke with the members of Diane's family, I learned more about Diane. Although she was very gracious, loving, and prone to acts of kindness, others described her as insecure and ambitious, with a tendency toward passive-aggressive behavior. Diane also planned to commit suicide when she was in her 30s but had not "gone through with it." According to family members, Diane was an alcoholic like her mother, yet she perceived her alcohol use to be merely "social drinking" because "that's what we do around here." The relationship between Sylvia and Diane was fraught with tension. Although Diane "loved her mother without question," she said that she felt cheated by her mother. Diane articulated a sense of extreme obligation to care for her mother, yet did not feel nurtured in return. The tension that existed between Diane and Sylvia reverberated into Diane's relationships with both her daughters and granddaughters. One of Diane's adult daughters remembered:

> My mom fears my grandma's reaction to everything we do. She literally says, 'I'm afraid she'll get all upset and there will be a problem.' For example, my mom said to me 20 minutes after I got home from a trip, 'Did you return the call to gramma? You don't want her to get nervous.' She reminded me twice. Boy, do I feel like a child again when she does this, having to be told what to do and how to conduct my behavior with others. Of course, I don't say anything and I call grandma right away cause I don't want either one of them to get upset.

Sitting on a tall stool at a local café, Diane and I ate club sandwiches and chatted about her relationship with her mother. She said:

> I feel that my mother and I were close probably for the first 20 years of my life. I don't remember there being any problems in our relationship at all for the first 20 years, but I find it interesting when I don't remember any specific kinds of feeling that I have experienced with her. I don't remember feeling that protected or—well, I felt loved—but I don't remember feeling any real, real closeness, other than maybe like sisters or something, because she was so young when I was born probably. She just turned 18 in July, I think, and I was born in January. I started trying to remember specifics in my childhood, and I could only come up with two. I remember that I had a surprise birthday party when I was in the fourth grade. That's the one really good thing I can remember. Isn't that interesting?
>
> It seems like after I reached 20 years of age, I remember a lot of things. I didn't like the way that my mother treated my grandmother. She was not very nice to her. She demanded a lot from her, but I never saw her give a lot, and that always bothered me, so I was very protective of grandma. It seems like after I had my dental assistant degree was when I became the parent, instead of the daughter. I think before then I probably felt like a daughter, but it seemed like after that, I felt more of a parent. When I was 50 years old, the burden became too much and I just—I stopped a little bit—I mean, I tried to distance myself from that parent role. It has always bothered me that I have not been a child or a daughter. You know, that I haven't felt like a daughter. The only time I felt like a daughter was with my [maternal] grandma.
>
> I guess I would explain it as, if I had a problem, I would want to go to my mother and have her understand it, and I don't get that. If I have a problem, she always has a worse one, and I have to be there for her. I don't get the comfort that I would like to have as the daughter. I have tried really hard to give my daughters that comfort because I have missed it.

Solotaroff (1999) eloquently pointed out that central to each individual is his or her identity—his or her *story*. We "all start out in other people's stories, a character in a narrative that predates us. From the moment of our birth, the players in that narrative are busy telling us who we are" (pp. 17–18). Not particularly happy in the role in which she was cast, Diane struggled to write her own narrative. Central to this emerging narrative was the characterization of herself as a good parent, one with the utmost concern for her children. On numerous occasions she indicated that it was through parenting that she found fulfillment:

> The way I perceived [my first-born daughter] was she was an ideal child. [She was a] very well-behaved girl, a good student, and talented. A tremendous amount of love went out to her; she was everything that I always wanted. I always wanted children, and when she was born, it was like I was totally fulfilled. I had a little girl. I can remember thinking I wanted a boy for my husband, but I really wanted a girl, so when she was born I was absolutely thrilled that I had my little girl to mother and play house with and the whole bit. I don't know, it was just, I don't ever [*extended pause*] and I love all four of my kids … but, I don't ever remember feeling so much love for a child as I felt for her. She just was everything. [My daughter] perceived herself as being outgoing and not being accepted and not being loved and, you know I just couldn't see this because of the way I felt about her. I never saw that. It is really difficult when I hear her say things like that, because I still can't see her in that role, the way she sees herself, because of my perception of her.

Diane lived vicariously through her children. She reveled in their successes and wallowed in their failures. She proudly professed that she was very willing to "go to bat" for her children. When her first-born child announced her pregnancy as a 17-year-old youth, Diane was provided with an opportunity to go to bat for her daughter. She remembered:

> Back in those days, if you had a child when you were in high school, you could come back in school but you were not allowed to participate in the extracurricular activities. You went to school, you came home and that's all you did. I went to the school board, and they knew she had been gone that first part of the year. She had the baby in November of her senior year, so she was coming back to school after that. And I went to the school board and told them that I thought it was time that these rules should be changed, and they changed them. So I'm responsible for everybody being able to participate in other activities from then on.

She took pride in providing assistance to her children, whereas her children viewed that assistance more often as control. All of Diane's daughters said that Diane was "controlling to a fault" and she did things for her children irrespective of what they desired. Insidious maternal expectations colored the maternal relationships at all levels in this family, and Diane's daughter—Sam—was particularly vocal on this point.

Sam was Diane's 40-year-old daughter, a thin, attractive blonde, 5'8", with a smile that literally glistened. In fact, when first meeting Sam I was taken aback by her smile. Sam immediately wanted to hold my son, provide him with visual stimuli. She seemed very comfortable around children and had five children of her own. Sam was artistically talented and put those talents to work by tastefully decorating her home and filling it with her sketches. One room in her home was designated specifically for arts and crafts.

I saw Sam to be a committed mother who struggled to come to grips with her maternal relationships. She suggested to me on numerous occasions that while on one hand she felt very controlled by her mother and disliked by her grandmother, she wanted to provide her children with a supportive, nonintrusive environment. She vehemently expressed a need to give her children the freedom to experience life without her shadow looming above them. This did not stop her from expressing delight at the following incident:

> I remember when I was away on a trip and [my daughter] decided to have a party while I was gone. I just had this *feeling* that something was amiss. So when I got home I didn't say "Hi!," I said, "What happened?" She screamed, "How do you always know these things?" She's convinced that when she was little and had her tonsils out I had the doctor plant a microphone in her throat.

This "psychic" connection between mothers and daughters revealed itself in several ways during my time in Elkwood. To disentangle connection and control was, however, not so simple.

Sam had experienced many challenges in her life, had given birth to five children fathered by three different men, been the victim of domestic violence and rape, was diagnosed with an eating disorder, abused illicit substances, and attempted suicide on more than one occasion. During my time in Elkwood she participated in ongoing therapy and was actively exploring her maternal family relationships. She had a heightened awareness of her relationships with her mother, grandmother, and her own daughters. One day she told me the following:

> A sense of "family" was instilled by my Gramma. Family sticks together—even if your family's a schmuck! Even so, that's your family; that's your blood. This is what I say to my kids, "You'll have different friends throughout your life, you'll have different friends in grade school, junior high, high school and college, and out of school. But, your family will always be there, always be there. They're not going to change."

> And we always did a lot of things together as a family, you know, picnics and stuff with grandma and grandpa. Then when we became adults, and there was like these crises and all this stuff happening, the one thing grandma said kept us together was, we're a family, we are family. You know, you could see the pain in her because she didn't want to see any division. I think our whole side of the family is very sensitive and caring. Those are all things we learned, like from my mom. Somebody's sick, you'll take a meal, somebody needs help, and you'll do that. You'll drop everything and help somebody, which is what we saw.

Sam's commitment to the idea of family transcended her own household. She chose a career as an elementary school teacher and often referred to her students as part of her extended family. She would often go the extra mile for her students, contributing her time and personal resources for their benefit.

Each woman in Family #1 was demonstrating deference to the older females in the family unit while struggling for her own acceptance. Economic and emotional ties bound Sylvia, Diane, and Sam together as they shared a common devotion to the sacredness of "family."

Family #2: Katrina, Kelly, and Kendra

Katrina, Kelly, and Kendra also experienced a plethora of challenges in their lives. Katrina was a petite, slender, 58-year-old woman. Her typical attire consisted of jeans and sweaters that hung loosely about her frame. Her hair was stylishly cut in a windblown sort of way. During our first visit, I noticed that she had a hesitant manner, not sure whether to smile, touch, or share emotions too quickly. After spending some time with members of this family, I began to characterize Katrina as doggedly independent. Her story included pride in the fact that she depended on very few people, she owned her own business, and she felt most comfortable making decisions on her own without the input of others. Her education was limited to high school, and this fact contributed to the pride she felt in developing a successful business. Katrina had been married twice, but for the past 25 years had functioned as a single mother to her five children.

There was an aura of contained energy and bustle whenever I was around Katrina. She appeared much younger than 58 (but then again, I asked myself how much energy is one *supposed* to have at 58?). She worked an average of 10 hours per day and reserved her time away from work to be with her family. The time she spent with her family was devoted to activities such as watching her children and grandchildren in their individual pursuits, going to see films, and inviting family to her home for meals.

Katrina framed her terminated marriages as "great failures." There had been no divorces in her family prior to her first divorce. She recalled: "[During my divorce] my mother, in her usual way, issued a famous quote, she said that she, well, 'she just wasn't going to take sides,' and I say if your own mother doesn't take sides, who's gonna?"

Katrina felt much stronger and more independent than her mother and wanted to give her children everything she did not have, "… and I don't mean financially or money wise. I just wanted them to always be able to come to me." It appeared, however, that this desire to be depended on might have been the catalyst for a large chasm in her relationship with her daughter Kelly.

Kelly was 37 years old with long, thick, tawny hair and a charming way of throwing her head back while enjoying a full-throated laugh. She was approximately 5'6" and, like her mother, possessed an abundance of physical energy.

She was openly affectionate with others and expressive about her feelings, motivations, and perceptions. This openness and affection seemed in stark contrast with the difficulties she had experienced in her lifetime. Kelly had been divorced four times and battled both cancer and substance abuse. Yet, what had apparently "gotten her through it all" were her two daughters—Kendra and Kyle.

Once, on a cool spring day, Kelly and I were walking together in downtown Elkwood, heading for a local pub for a late lunch. The sun was bright, but the chill in the air was palpable, so I pulled my sweater closer to my body, and Kelly placed her arm about me to provide additional warmth. As we walked into the pub I felt comforted by her presence and part of my comfort, I assume, was due to the fact that Kelly was the same age as my older sister. I suspect that some aspect of my sense-memory was stimulated by this "sisterly" hug. Yet, Kelly was warm and had an aura about her that tended to "key everybody up." The energizing effect that Kelly possessed was apparent when watching her interactions with others. While in her presence, people seemed to laugh a bit louder and move a bit faster. Kelly exuded enthusiasm when talking about her daughters, conversing with her daughters and friends, or engaging in her favorite pastime—dancing. Kelly was equally effusive when sharing her feelings about the tensions between her and her mother.

> I have a real thing with my mother. My daughter [Kendra] gets on me when I get down on my mom. She says, "Mom, you're doing it again." My mother and I are both very strong women. Both control freaks. She takes charge, in control. She's judgmental and harsh with people. I'm not. As a parent I'm not like her. I'm a very warm person. My mother is cold. She really doesn't show emotion. I give hugs a lot and so does Kyle. I cry in front of others, show emotion. Mom never hugs and she is downright cold.

Kendra, Kelly's daughter, was 21 at the time of this study, petite like her grandmother, and verbally expressive. Kendra would more often than not correct, argue with, or chastise her mother regarding her behavior or attitude. It appeared to me that Kendra was an assertive woman and expressed a strong commitment to her own two children. The events of her mother's teenage years indelibly marked both her and Kelly's relationship.

Kelly had become pregnant with Kendra when she was 16 years old, during the early 1970s when teenage pregnancies were often hidden. Katrina shared the following information one morning with me as we sat sipping hot cocoa (with marshmallows!):

> Kelly wanted to get an abortion and I don't believe in that and so I moved to Elkwood. It was kind of an excuse. I wanted to move out of town and get on with my life anyway, and so I sent her to Pittsburgh to live with my brother and his wife. So she helped them with their little girl and took classes to get her diploma. She

finished her schooling there and when she was about 6 months pregnant she was getting pressure from everybody about what to do. I was saying no abortion, you either raise the baby or you adopt it out, that's your choice.

Nevertheless, Kelly decided to get married to the baby's father when she was 6 months pregnant. When Kendra was born, her father enlisted in the Army and Kelly and the baby moved in with Katrina and her other children. Soon Kelly began to feel abandoned. She filed for divorce and then began experimenting with drugs. Katrina recalled:

> She [Kelly] thinks he deserted her. Well, he wanted her and he wanted the baby, I mean, there was never a question of that. So anyway, I was working in Elkwood, and she was scaring me to death. I was running home at noon to see if the baby was safe. I thought, I didn't know where it was going to end, because Kelly would take the baby out ... and leave her with other kids while she'd go swimming. She's a teenager, she's a kid, and she'd put Kendra in the tub and I was afraid Kelly wouldn't watch her. And we had steps and I could just see the baby, I mean, I was just scared to death this baby wasn't being watched. So then she got in with a bad crowd and she got on drugs and she was living with me. She and the baby, and then I had my three younger ones, and they were happy in Elkwood.

> Kelly then decides she wants to leave when Kendra was 8 months old. Well, I said, "You can go but you can't take this baby with you." I mean she was in ... I mean terribly, into drugs at that time, so that's how I came to get the baby.

Katrina was awarded legal custody of her granddaughter and reared Kendra as her own. Kelly had always harbored resentment toward Katrina because she believed her mother had *taken her baby from her*. When Kendra reached the age of 5, Kelly remarried and had another little girl, Kyle. Kelly eventually moved back to Elkwood with her husband and Kyle, and her mother offered to share custody of Kendra, "You know, you have another child and so before she [Kendra] starts to go to school, if you want to give it a another try and so forth ... why, now would be the time." Katrina shared:

> So, it was time for me to make the break. I thought if I don't do this now, why I'll never be able to. So I took her furniture and her clothes and everything over to Kelly's. We said we'd try this on a 3-month basis and I talked to the judge because it's really more than most people can handle themselves anyway. The court had given me custody, so anyway, it was approved and she had her for those 3 months while she worked in the restaurant with me. So we were all in too close proximity, and she'd come everyday and tell me about her drinking husband who was partial to Kyle and didn't like Kendra and everything, and in my mind she was saying help me I can't do it, I can't keep her. So at the end of 3 months I took Kendra back.

Katrina retained full custody of Kendra. Years later, the discussion of this experience still opened wounds and Katrina maintained, "I did what I thought I had to do." The tension between mother and daughter had waxed and waned throughout the years, with both receiving counseling and therapy about their issues. Despite this tension, certain life experiences (e.g., Kelly's cancer) had drawn them momentarily closer. Katrina often remarked about how she had grown to admire her daughter as an adult. One evening she confided:

> When she was going through a horrible, horrible time [cancer], her public face is … well, my mother would say, "Oh she's just so nice, she's so fun, she's so happy." I'd say, "Mother, she's suicidal! She's so miserable, and this was what she was showing." I wish that people couldn't read me so well. I wish that when I'm depressed or unhappy, I could act happy like that. I mean, I really admire anybody that can put on a happy face like that, and she's great at it.

Kelly concurred with the assessment that she was very unlike her mother. After losing custody of her first child to her mother, experiencing four divorces, fighting a yearlong bout with breast cancer, losing all of her hair, and finding that her grandson had been born with a serious heart defect, Kelly maintained a persistent animosity toward her mother. Kelly believed both she and her mother were control freaks, yet "that," she maintained, "was the extent of our similarities." Kelly viewed Katrina's custody of Kendra as reflecting directly—and negatively—on her as both a mother and as a person. Moreover, compounding the tension was Kelly's jealousy and resentment over Katrina's act of "taking my daughter away from me." Kendra addressed Katrina as "Mom" from the first year she had custody and Kelly pointed out with obvious resentment, "My mother perpetuated this charade [that she was Kendra's mother] the first year."

Kelly, who at the time of this investigation was by now a young grandmother, argued she would never even consider taking her granddaughter away from her own daughter:

> Even if my daughter weren't competent I would try to reunite my grandchild with her mom. My daughter was taken from me because I was not a competent person. I am constantly being punished for that incompetence. So, I try and compensate. I want to be the best at everything, to show everybody and myself that I can be competent.

Of Kelly's two girls, Kendra participated in this study. Her participation was less than I wanted, because she had a 5-month-old son who had been in and out of surgery for the duration of my fieldwork. Yet, in my interactions with Kendra, I noticed an underlying tension between her and her mother that did not exist between her and her grandmother. She appreciated her mother's help during the recent medical crises with her son and admired her mother's courage during her bout with cancer. Nonetheless, she resented her mother for "abandoning" her as an infant. She indicated a belief that her mother was self-centered. She said, "If I'm sick, she's sicker … she relates everything to herself." In one breath she admired her mother, proud that she inherited Kelly's artistic talents, and in the next breath would call her mother selfish and controlling. Presumably, when

Kendra gave birth to her first child, she "gave it to Kelly royally." She confronted her mother and said, "How could you ever give up a baby? Look at this baby! How could you do what you did?" Katrina believed this episode was the first time Kendra had confronted her mother about the abandonment issue.

Dissatisfaction with mother–daughter relationships permeated every level of observation conducted within this family culture, although this claim may be confounded by the fact that Katrina was both Kendra's grandmother and mother figure. Nonetheless, as an adult, Kendra framed her relationship with Katrina as a grandmother–granddaughter relationship. Kendra saw Katrina as her grandmother, who offered her unconditional support. Yet, she freely admitted her grandmother did not provide the same allowance to Kelly.

This was a family of complicated and fascinating women who appeared to both adore and abhor with equal intensity. These women, despite their differences, persisted in the maintenance and development of their relationships and expressed a strong sense of the importance of their family in their lives.

Family #3: Rowena, Gina, and Georgie

Walking into Gina's home for the first time, I observed three females with expertly applied makeup and crisply ironed designer clothes. My first thought was that this family had won the genetic pool in God's lottery. In fact, Rowena and Gina had been beauty contestants in both district and state competitions. It was truly amazing to me (and still is) how one woman can be intimidated by another woman's looks. Nevertheless, I have to admit that when meeting these women, I was intimidated. I became hyperconscious of my own dress and style, feeling somehow smaller in my typical uniform of jeans and loose-fitting shirts (I had just had a baby, for goodness sake, couldn't they give me a break?!). Within a single week, however, I have to admit that I began to dress a little nicer and actually put on some makeup.

Rowena, at 72 years of age, was a stunning woman. She often could be seen gardening wearing high heels and stockings, and never seemed to break into a sweat. Oh, pardon me—I was informed that women do not sweat, they perspire. (I know it is a cliché, but I *was* corrected.) My involvement with this family heightened my own sense of femininity and colored my initial perceptions, but I soon learned there were multiple dimensions to these women's maternal relationships. Their story was a tale of strong and proud women who had powerfully entangled relationships with one other.

To an onlooker, Rowena appeared to be mannerly, stately, and a proud woman. She had been widowed for 30 years and lived independently in her own home next to her daughter Gina. Rowena's home, to my discerning eyes, was immaculate. She employed a housekeeper and a groundskeeper, but she could be observed gardening in her heels on any given warm summer day. She was self-sufficient and financially independent. Apparently, when her husband was alive, she was his "right hand" in the family oil business until his death. She mourned her late husband and expressed deep satisfaction with her relationships with her daughters and grandchildren. She shared, "I feel very uncomfortable bragging about my family. [But] when my girls were born I decided they were going to college. I encouraged that, even though back then we had no money. It was instilled in us all the time to invest and save and I handed that down to my daughters."

The only disappointment Rowena expressed was for another daughter, Rachel. Rowena was dismayed that the younger of her two daughters filed for divorce from her husband of 10 years. Rowena did not approve of the divorce, but "[my daughter] couldn't live with a fellow that drank all the time."

Rowena identified herself as an independent personality and took pride in the fact that she once assisted her father and her husband in their family businesses. Curiously, she framed her past work history as "not a working woman." "I never worked. I worked in my store, you know, and worked all the time. But, I never worked [for pay]. I just felt that I could do almost anything. You know, if I had to, I would have gotten a job. But, I didn't have to."

Nor was she an effusive person. During my 8 months in Elkwood, I never heard Rowena criticize or even directly compliment her daughters or granddaughter; yet her pride in them was evident in the way that her face lit up in their presence and in the way that she reveled in their attention: "My daughters are nice to me, both of them. And they think I'm special. I'm not very special but they think I am. I know Gina tells me, I suppose, once a week. And Rachel does too. But, Gina's always telling me 'What would I do without you, mother?' "

Rowena's eldest daughter, Gina, was equally as stately as her mother. At the age of 50, she appeared to be about 40 years old. (Perhaps my eyes weren't as discerning as I thought!) From what members of her family shared with me, Gina was an ambitious woman, dedicated to her community and to her family, and an active philanthropist in the Elkwood community: "I believe that you need to give to your community and I try and teach my children that, too. I try and do the most I can and I get a great deal of satisfaction from my work in the community. Not the attention, mind you, the satisfaction has more to do with contributing something positive … of worth, something worthwhile."

Gina indicated that her mother significantly shaped her view of the world. She and her husband purchased a home next door to her mother because she wanted to "get as close as I possibly could get to my family, without moving in." She explained:

> My mother was, you know, the big influence in my life. I looked up to her. And I respected her. And she was—quote—"a lady." And to this day I still look up to her. She just was a type of gal that came out of a very small town and had great goals. She was a great worker and a good cook. She liked to do everything. She was very strong, even though she looked fragile.

Gina referred to her mother as "a lady" and suggested that manners and respect were the hallmarks of her childhood socialization. Her mother's involvement in the community was deemed very important, and her own contributions to the community were central to how Gina defined herself. She was involved in the PTA, a local women's club, and myriad philanthropic causes. Gina believed that she learned valuable lessons from her mother. She said, "I learned to be involved and to always be dressed up. My mother was always dressed up. I mean, she always looked nice. I've always tried to present a nice picture."

Gina seemed to wear a perpetual smile. She pointed out that during her academic years, although grades were not of great importance to her, being well liked was. Central to the ongoing narrative of this family was the importance of presenting a "nice picture." Gina's home was large and expensively decorated. Leather-bound photo albums were dated and filed chronologically along bookshelves, and photographs of her family covered almost the entire surface of her refrigerator.

Gina had two children—Georgie and Jeff. During my time with this family, Georgie was a thin and muscular 25-year-old, with long brown hair, and a vociferous nature. Words fell from her lips in a torrent. Georgie was occupied with preparations for her impending wedding, and most of the pictures on Gina's refrigerator were of Georgie and her fiancé, as well as also of her son Jeff and his wife. It was striking to me how much Jeff's wife looked like Georgie, and how Georgie's fiancé looked so much like her own brother, Jeff. Georgie found humor in the physical similarities and she was pleased that her sister-in-law looked like her because, as she said, the girl was, "more like a sister than a sister-in-law." There were also several newspaper advertisements posted on their refrigerator, featuring Georgie as a model. Missing from the display of photographs were pictures of Gina and her husband. The photos on this refrigerator were a tribute to Gina's children.

Although Gina could be seen with a smile on her face at all times, Georgie presented a picture of a woman who was comfortable with expressing negative emotion. Planning a wedding is often a frustrating experience for many women, and Georgie, I suspect, experienced no fewer irritations than others who prepare for that blessed event. It was interesting to note that most of Georgie's frustrations involved logistical issues inherent in planning this large event, rather than relational issues with her mother. This is interesting to me, because during my time investigating mother–daughter relationships, I have discovered that wedding preparations can be one of the most stressful and exciting experiences of the adult mother–daughter relationship. In fact, as Zax and Poulter (1997) pointed out, the ritual of planning a wedding can be one of the more stressful events for mothers and daughters and marks a significant transition in the relationship. In Gina and Georgie's case, the wedding preparations appeared to be just one more event that they worked on side by side in almost total agreement.

Georgie and Gina were satisfied with their mother–daughter relationship, and this was demonstrated in their ritual daily luncheon. They were best friends and appreciated that friendship. Gina said:

Georgie was so easy as a child. She was next to perfect. I'm not kidding you. I can't point out one thing that I was even disappointed in. Jeff wasn't quite as easy. I *like* Georgie. I like her personality. I think she's a good person. I never had to be embarrassed of her, I've always been proud of her. I've learned about friendship from her. We have a special bond between us, and I have it also with my mother, and she had it with her mother. We like and respect each other.

Gina believed that if there was one thing that defined her relationships with both her mother and daughter, it was *respect*. She was taught and, consequently, taught her daughter to treat others with respect. Georgie agreed that respect was a core dimension that defined her relationship with her mother. She said:

My mom and I have always been very, very close. I've always looked up to my mom. You know, she's been a good role model to me and everything, and I think that's a lot of the reason why we've been so close—'cause I've always watched her and seen what she's done and been proud of her for things that she's done.... A lot of people respected Gina Miner's name, she has a lot of friends.

Georgie also had many friends. In high school, she had been active in student government and cheerleading. During college, she had been involved in a sorority, and she was currently employed at her father's place of business processing car sales in the accounting department. Georgie grew up in an environment where her mother and grandmother were "always [participating] in modeling schools and beauty pageants." This family culture required "ladylike behavior" where Georgie was to "always be a lady, always act, look and present yourself ... like a nice, classy lady in front of other people."

Georgie considered her relationship with her mother and grandmother to be very special. She admitted that her friends often asked her what the ingredients were to creating such special, conflict-free maternal relationships. She said that when she got these questions she would merely shrug, laugh, and respond with an "I don't know!" "Maybe," she told me, "it is because they [my mother and grandmother] have always been supportive. I can't remember any time when they have never been supportive of something I wanted to do."

This family appeared to be emotionally close and connected to each other. Each woman expressed extreme satisfaction in her relationships with the others, and the hallmark of their family was an embodied sense of pride.

Family #4: Lois, Barb, and Tabitha

When Lois first stepped into her daughter Barb's house on the day we met, she came bearing homegrown vegetables. As she whisked in through the doorway, she commented on how nice the yard looked, asked about the football game that night, and declared she really wanted to try and make it to the game. Without taking a breath she noticed me and exclaimed, "Well, heellllllllooo!"

Lois was a graying, spritely, 62-year-old woman who brimmed with energy, ready to propel forward in any direction. During a 1-hour period on a rainy spring day, she managed to bake cookies, set three appointments for the next week, unload her dishwasher, pay her bills, and discuss football with her grand-daughter. Whenever I talked with Lois, my rate of speech increased and I felt like I had to keep up with her sense of energy and enthusiasm for life. She appeared to wear her affection for her family on her sleeve. She said, "I always say that I love my children dearly and the very same. I wouldn't love one more, I couldn't, and I remember my mother always telling us that she never loved one more. That's the one thing I felt about my mother, always you are loved."

Lois's daughter Barb is an attractive, 40-year-old blonde, about 5'9", who—like her mother—virtually *oozed* affection for her family. Her manner was much more reserved than her mother's, however. Barb was gracious; she offered food and drink, creature comforts, and assistance with my infant. Her style was also soothing to me—soothing in the way that she calmly handled any mishap, such as a spill on the carpet or her son's angst at losing a football game. When others were fraught with tension, Barb displayed the ability to decrease that tension a few notches while simultaneously encouraging reason.

When Barb's extended family gathered, they gathered at her home. Her home was inviting with its hand-embroidered pillows lining the overstuffed couch. High, vaulted ceilings and white walls opened up the space and allowed me to focus on a few select areas of color—fresh-cut flowers in a rose-colored vase and a throw rug with a multiplicity of rich colors. Little placards of framed needlepoint quoting scriptures lined the walls. Barb had wanted to be an interior decorator, and although she never achieved that goal professionally, she decorated her family's and friends' homes.

Barb's daughter Tabitha was 18 at the time of this study, completing her senior year of high school, and involved in several school sports. Tabitha struck me as a confident, helpful, and cautious young woman. She was cute in a tomboy fashion, neither identifiably feminine nor masculine. She lived at home with her mother, father, and younger brothers, and expressed admiration for them. She also volunteered to care for infants in her church's nursery and in others' homes.

A sense of "family" was very important to all three generations of women. Barb suggested she and her sister had learned about family from her mother's example. She said that her mother had a close, loving family that "never had been known to have a disagreement." In fact, she added, "My mom has many sisters who all still get together for lunch."

Lois concurred that her relationships with the members of her own family of origin had influenced her sense of what a family should be. She explained:

Wednesdays were the day that me and my sisters would go home and take my mother out to lunch, we took her out and then we'd play cards together. This was our fun thing. We just had so much fun. We often said that when we left, we never left having talked about any one because my mother just would have never had time for that. So you'd go and you'd have a good time and you leave and you feel good. That's what I like about my family. I just don't think we ever had time to be critical of others.

Barb believed the strength of her family was derived from "faith and prayer, being positive and upbeat," and finally, "laughing and goofing around together." There seemed to be a strong ethic of giving to others within this family. Barb emphasized that giving was *not a job* but a pleasure for members of her family; they did for others joyfully and willingly. Barb offered the following interpretation: "As a matter of fact, I think that's part of the reason my mom's a rather happy person all the time, because she's such a giver and she doesn't do it to get anything out of it. Just the desire to do it, you get blessed because you've done it."

Tabitha was also identified as a giver, as well as an entrepreneur. She coordinated the only "youth booth" at a local crafts fair and apparently was "darn good at it." Her attitude toward her mother and grandmother was both assertive and respectful. She suggested that her mother "is scattered and I have to keep her on track" and her grandmother is "a great 'ole gal. She is taking me on a trip to Florida this year and I think it is time to get spoiled rotten!"

When referring to her daughter, Barb would say with a chuckle, "That is my Tabitha. She has a mind of her own. You gotta love her." Tabitha talked about her *weird* brother and how he had an aquarium that he loved, and that he wanted to major in marine biology in college. But, she added with exasperation, "He is afraid of water! Go figure." Tabitha was forthright in her opinions, and Barb admired this assertiveness in her daughter: "She's got great verbal skills and she's not intimidated by people at all, men, women, you name it. Other people always intimidated me. Not her! She's got confidence."

Barb's sister, Steph, was a contrasting character in this family. Although she was not in the original pool of women recruited for this investigation, she asked if she could add "her two cents worth." She would bound into a room, filling the space with spirit and intensity. Steph was younger than Barb by a few years, 5'3"?, dark, and claimed that she always had to live in the shadow of her *perfect* older sister. In her talk, Steph admitted that she was defiant and reckless as a teenager and was more vocal in reproaching her mother than was Barb. While growing up, Steph apparently felt competitive with Barb, particularly in the area of trying to please their father. Steph perceived Barb as "perfect" and discussed the difficulty of trying to live up to that standard. Steph seemed career driven. She said that she spent her life focusing on "what I could DO rather than necessarily striving for perfection in who I am." She was a self-admitted workaholic in a helping profession.

Steph expressed more dissatisfaction concerning her relationship with Lois than did Barb. She vocalized how she thought her mother saw her and her sister: "She thinks Barb should be stronger and she thinks I should be quieter, that's what I think. I hear that message from her a lot. That [Barb's husband] is so strong, so Barb needs to be stronger, and I'm too mean to my husband and my kids. I'm too outgoing and too demonstrative and too talkative. But she sees my husband as perfect."

Tabitha demonstrated her affection for her aunt uninhibitedly. She admired the members of her family, although her younger brother vexed her. She perceived this younger brother as "nerdy," yet she revered another brother who was a star football player on his high school team. She believed that her mother was a bit scatterbrained and provided the following examples: "I had to remind her of this appointment today. She always forgets things or messes them up. She needs me to keep her straightened out" and "My mother talks too much."

Tabitha and Barb were generally very playful with each another. The only episode I witnessed between these women that hinted at situational dissatisfaction occurred a few months into my fieldwork:

> Barb asked Tabitha, "You have to admit, that yesterday was not a real nice day for you, was it? And why was that?"
>
> Tabitha looked sheepish and replied, "Well because of being forced to go to my inane piano lessons."
>
> "Because I made you go, right?" added Barb.
>
> "Yeah," admitted Tabitha.
>
> I entered into the conversation and asked Tabitha, "So you had to go to piano lessons?"
>
> Barb informed me, "I make her take piano lessons."
>
> Tabitha said, "I just got all frustrated."
>
> "You didn't want to go but you had to?" I asked.
>
> Tabitha answered, "No, I didn't have to go, it was just ... well, I can't play and it's a waste of money."

In the end, Tabitha continued to take piano lessons and Barb continued to support her daughter, encouraging her that she *could* play and offering assurances that the money was well spent. Tabitha, although not always enthusiastic about her piano lessons, seemed to be mollified and indicated, "She [my mother] thinks I can play, but that's her opinion. But, I guess I can't get any worse!" She continued with her piano lessons throughout my stay in Elkwood.

With Barb as a grounding force, each member observed in this family was deeply committed to one another and attempted to live their lives in a manner that "honors family." Even when differences between women provided relational tensions, a "powerful sense of family" provided the backdrop for interactions.

Family #5: Charlotte, Becky, and Linda

"I don't think that we've had a healthy mother–daughter relationship over the years. So, if I could have a different relationship, I don't know whether it could

be a good one. I don't know if that potential is even there." These words were
spoken by Becky (age 43) as she described her relationship with her mother
Charlotte. Charlotte was in her mid-60s and wheelchair bound. She resided in a
nursing home/independent living complex. Charlotte's apartment did not have
pictures of her children or grandchildren on the walls or on her dresser. On her
end tables she displayed school photos of the children from her church who
helped her with her wheelchair. I initially asked about those photos, assuming
they were her grandchildren. She explained their significance to me with no information regarding the absence of photos of her immediate family members.

Charlotte was a formidable, opinionated woman. In my initial meetings with
her, I dared not question her opinions or appear to empathize with others who
might not have been in her favor. Overall, however, Charlotte was—to me—a
woman imprisoned by her physical limitations. She was aggravated by her im-
prisonment; she said, "My body has betrayed me. That's all there is to it. But, I
manage—somewhat."

When Charlotte visited Becky's house, she had to be lifted and carried from
her wheelchair to a room in Becky's house because the house was not wheelchair accessible. Becky proclaimed that the movement "is good for her [Char-
lotte], but hard to do." The role Becky played in her own and her mother's story
was that of *dutiful daughter* for her disabled mother. She expressed the following
to me during one interview: "To be dutiful. Do the right thing. Yeah, I am still
the dutiful daughter. I'm the only caregiver in my family. I'm really disturbed by
that. I mean it's horrible. It makes me very angry. I'm very angry with my brothers. They're taking no responsibility. They are very far away—South Dakota
and North Dakota."

Becky believed her mother expected more from her than she currently gave.
Her frustration with that was evident, and she thought those expectations colored her entire relationship with her mother. She suggested her mother was
chronically disappointed in her. One weekend, while strolling to a neighborhood park, I asked Becky, "So, you think your mother was disappointed in you?"

She replied, "No. I *know* that. She says that, even now. In subliminal, round-
about ways, um, she'll say it to other people in front of me. That I'm not there as
much as I need to be for her or should be. And that other daughters do this for
their mothers. Those are the messages that I'm hearing."

Becky indicated that even though she saw her mother on a regular basis, they
did not *do anything* together. She confided, "To be honest, nothing beyond the
superficial level of doing things with her." Apparently, she learned selflessness
from her mother, and now as an adult she admitted to being tired of this selflessness. She said:

> As a child and throughout I think her expectations of me have been to be selfless.
> Everyone else is first. And I've broken that finally in the last 15 to 20 years. Even
> my grandmother—and this is so vivid for me—looking, as a child, when I was
> looking in the mirror at myself, primping or whatever I would do—that was *very*

wrong. To be that self-centered and to be that focused on the surface and um, it was a big issue. But I was caught doing that.

In line with her convictions that one should not be selfless, Becky stressed the values of assertiveness and self-sufficiency to her own daughter, Linda. Linda, age 18, was constantly on the go. She was in her senior year of high school, involved in tennis and student government, an honor student, and had been voted prom queen the previous April. When I initially met Linda, she seemed very sweet and shy, was somewhat quiet, and was reticent to share her impressions with me. However, as time went on, I came to know Linda a bit better, and discovered that she had some very clear ideas about her relationships with both her mother and grandmother. She "respects and appreciates her mother and grandmother" and indicated that their relationships were based on that respect and trust. During the latter part of our time together, Linda said, "I like to have everything kind of laid out and organized. I have a plan. But, that is one of the things that drives me crazy about my mom, 'cause my mom, she just kind of goes with the flow."

Linda was cognizant of the tension between her mother and grandmother. One afternoon, she shared the following interpretation:

> My mom likes to think that people aren't really angry, that she isn't angry, she is just hurt. She always says that. She never yells at my grandmother or anything, but I know that so many times when my mom was upset with my grandmother she wants to yell. But, she likes to talk things out. Sometimes, though, I think mom maybe wants to get too much out of the conversation. More than my grandma is willing to give.

This family was interestingly different from most of the other families by virtue of the different quality of the mother–daughter relationships across two generations. The fractured relationship of Charlotte and Becky was very different when compared with the level of cohesion experienced in Becky and Linda's relationship.

Family #6: Meredith, Morgan, and Scout

Meredith was a 63-year-old woman with silky dark hair that was frequently bound in a clasp at the nape of her neck. She lived in a 3,000-square-foot home with her husband and two dogs. She was a registered nurse, although she had not been a practicing nurse for over 15 years. She had been married for 42 years to the same man, and she was in charge of most of the decisions in their household.

She was a strong woman and admitted to her share of life challenges. During her lifetime, she had battled an eating disorder and as a young woman had attempted to take her own life. Meredith's daughter, Morgan, was 42 years old, had four children, and had been married for 21 years. She was always impeccably dressed with skillfully applied makeup, and frequently and enthusiastically shared her beliefs about her Christian faith. Morgan's faith was reportedly her "lifeboat" after a turbulent adolescence and young adulthood during which she had experienced substance abuse and recovered from a suicide attempt.

Morgan's daughter, Scout, was an 18-year-old high school senior with waist-length golden-red hair, a wide gap-toothed smile, and a heart-shaped face with a perpetually perplexed expression. She did not wear any makeup during my visit, and she would consistently express annoyance over her mother's habit of using "tons of makeup." Scout did not have a history of suicidal ideation or substance abuse, nor did she report any inclination toward other problem behaviors. Her immediate plan was to enter a premedical program at a nearby university the following fall.

The women in this family expressed a strong sense of who they were as a family. That is not to say that they were satisfied with that identity. They clearly voiced their dissatisfaction with their maternal family relationships, while with the same breath expressing how important family was to them. In practice, these women spent considerable amounts of time each week visiting and participating in activities with each other.

Meredith expressed extreme frustration that her own parents failed to recognize her career achievements. This frustration and disappointment was woven tightly into the fabric of her personal narrative. She believed her mother and father did not value her as a person. Consequently, as a mother, she perceived it to be "her mission" to affirm her daughters' achievements and to encourage them throughout their lives.

Admittedly, she did not like change. She adhered to structure and made certain that "things would go" as she "expected them to." For example, she admitted:

> I can go with change. I'm rigid in a way, but when my kids get married, I think I can adapt to that and I try to let go and not interfere. But it does bother me when there is a big change. I guess I am more rigid than I thought. Yes, I want things to stay the same. I don't want my kids taken away from me when they get married. I know things won't stay the same when my kids get married, but I want them to.

She was forthright when reflecting on her own behavior and proud that she influenced her family and extended family with her love and attention. She told a story about staying up late into the wee hours one night, talking with her sister-in-law. She said:

> We would sit up and talk until all hours of the morning, and she said something that really surprised me. It also made me feel very, very good. She said that I scared them to death when I came into the family because they are not a touching family and she said, "I can't remember my dad ever holding me, ever kissing me, or ever touching me, and my mom certainly never kissed me." She said, "you walked into

the family and you're hugging and kissing and none of us had ever done that! We eventually did because you did." But, she said, "I have worked and worked and worked at it and I'm finally able to do it." She said, "I can hug my kids now, I can kiss them."

Meredith took pride in the influence she had on her husband's family. When asked about forming images of her own family (her, her husband, and her children) she exclaimed, "Of course, my husband had nothing to do with molding who we are as a family. He loves his kids, but he takes no responsibility for that. He doesn't want to make the effort. So I have to." She perceived that molding her family was her responsibility. She felt obligated to influence and control family functioning, provide her children with expectations for their behavior, and give the necessary encouragement to meet those expectations.

Meredith was also a consummate hostess. She was often concerned about whether I had "everything I needed." Additionally, she had an "open door" policy that implied I was welcome at her home any time of the day. Place settings at her table were always lovely, including napkin rings, mimosas, and vases of fresh flowers from the garden. During one meal at the beginning of the investigation, she told her adult daughter where to sit, "No, that place is for Michelle." I sensed that her adult daughter "obeyed" her mother's directive out of habit rather than respect.

Obtaining Meredith's approval seemed crucial to the functioning of this family. Her daughters and granddaughters sought to keep her happy because this apparently was easier than having to deal with her when she was unhappy. For example, on one occasion, her granddaughter, Scout, had made a gourmet dinner for Meredith the previous night. Scout informed me that Meredith was, "overdoing it with the success of my cooking thing. She [Meredith] is praising my cooking to everyone. Making constant comments." It seemed that Scout admitted that her grandmother's bragging was meant to make Scout feel good. Yet, Scout's reaction was to feel embarrassed. She said that it "brings attention to what I *did*." She added, "I don't like feeling like I have to perform to keep her happy." Morgan interjected, "She [Meredith] knows it all. Her stamp of approval or disapproval makes a difference in this family."

Morgan struggled with her firm dedication and obligation to her family of origin while attempting to nurture healthy relationships within her own household, which consisted of four daughters, her husband, and herself. Like her mother, Morgan was also described as "the hostess with the mostest." Morgan identified herself as lacking a positive self-concept and that suggested she tried to be *perfect* so she could feel better about herself. When discussing Morgan's self-image with Meredith, Meredith claimed that she envisioned herself as affirming Morgan as a person "every chance I can get." Morgan saw her mother as a loving but controlling woman who "makes you feel crappy if you don't reach her standards." Morgan often commented that she feared she would pass on this trait to her daughters; thus, she wanted to participate in this study to learn more her interaction with her daughters.

Morgan and her husband were both in the Christian ministry, and she believed her relationship with God was partly motivated by her need to feel unconditional acceptance. She revealed the following during a conversation about perfection and failure:

> When I don't do something up to somebody else's expectations, I feel disapproval from them. To me this equates with lack of love. And I don't know where that came from or how that happened. I know it obviously happened within my family.
>
> But, you know it's something that I constantly am telling myself. That I can make a mistake and they're still gonna care. And, so I tested, I'm allowing myself because of God in my life, I've allowed myself to have Him. Geez, I'm crying now.

Morgan did not want to perpetuate this perceived conditional acceptance with her own daughters. When asked how she was actively addressing this concern, she shared the following story. Apparently one of her girlfriends had placed Morgan "on a pedestal." She could do no wrong in this friend's eyes until the day arrived when Morgan did something to blemish that image:

> All of a sudden I couldn't be a friend anymore. Because I disappointed her, I let her down. So, my girls have had to walk through that experience with me. And so through that, what I've tried to do is be positive in affirming in a way that let them know that you have to look over other people's faults and not be negative. Not be negative about [this friend]. Meaning, not talk about her, to not blame her. I mean, because that happens, I think, that you perpetuate it, you blame. It's their fault. If they hadn't done this, if they'd been different, blah, blah, blah. It's always the other person, you know, and you have to do that to make yourself feel better. So, I think my girls are learning from watching me go through it and how I respond.

Morgan's daughter, Scout, believed that she had learned a lot about life from her mother. Although she and her mother "butted heads" frequently, she respected her mother's courage in dealing with her self-esteem problems and saw her grandmother as accountable for many of her mother's issues. Scout shared with me the following during a walk we took around her neighborhood:

> Not to be mean or anything, but all of us girls in the family just sorta know when [Meredith] approves of you and what you're doing. She's always showing favoritism to [two other members of the family] because of what they do. My Mom's not making a lot of money, she's not doing what [Meredith] thinks that she should be doing and so you know, I think my Mom struggles with that a lot. She is always trying to please [Meredith] but she can't always. My Mom's not like that because I know how much she hates it, so she tries not to be like that with us.

Yet, both Morgan and Scout expressed frustration with each other because they were so "different from one another." I witnessed several conflicts between these two women during my 8 months in Elkwood, yet all were apparently forgotten within a few days. The moments when this family was in harmony with one another were typically filled with laughter and camaraderie. Their conversations included laughter, overlapping speech, completing each other's sentences and thoughts, and an "in-group" speech pattern that I eventually had to decipher.

Meredith was the cog in the wheel of this family, holding it together during the rough times and continually enforcing family rituals and forging opportunities for family unity. Overall, this family culture consisted of images that overlapped and blurred continually. In the end, however, the feeling of tension amid the push and pull for alliances, self-esteem, and approval was palpable.

POSTSCRIPT

The preceding descriptions in no way represent these women in their totality. It was my intent to introduce them, giving them some voice in painting their own picture. I entered their worlds and family cultures, and came to understand their relationships over the 8 months in Elkwood.

What I did not expect at the beginning of my fieldwork was that the families who volunteered to participate in this study would be so fascinatingly complex. Nor did I anticipate that the lives of women in three of the families would be so fraught with multiple challenges (e.g., substance use, serial divorce, attempted suicide). Interestingly, women in only three of the families had experienced the bulk of these challenges, whereas there was a glaring absence of these problems among the women in the other three families. This sampling of families provided me with the opportunity to not only provide a descriptive account of the maternal relationships in these families, but also to investigate any connections within and across families pertaining to communication patterns and problem behaviors (e.g., substance use, eating disorders). This book seeks to provide description, interpretation, and a heuristic account of communication within the grandmother–mother–daughter relationship. In addition, due to the composition of the families in this study, I have an added opportunity to further explore the patterns of communication within and across families who exhibited various degrees of problem behaviors.

I am indebted to the women of Elkwood. Although their names and identifying information have been changed to protect their confidentiality, they will clearly know their own stories and the role they played in forming the story that is this book. Unfortunately, since the time I was last in Elkwood, three spouses of these women have passed away, and I am sad to report that Rowena, Lois, and Sylvia have also passed away. The deaths of these women is a loss not only to their families, but also to those whose lives were touched by their generosity and honesty. I truly applaud the strength of all of whom shared their stories with me, and I hope that this informed interpretation does justice to their complicated lives and relationships.

II

The Action

4

Contradictions

... the daughter is for the mother at once her double and another person.

—(Simone de Beauvoir, 1974, p. 38)

"Mother, I do not know you. Mother, I never knew you."
"Daughter, you knew yourself. Without knowing, you knew me."

—(Tillie Olsen, *Tell Me a Riddle*, 1961, p. 7)

"[My mother and I] lived in a kind of symbiosis. Without striving to imitate her, I was conditioned by her."

—(Simone de Beauvoir, 1974, p. 41)

"Tell me about your relationship with your mother" I said to Morgan. She paused, her face a study in concentration—the water ran in the background as her daughter took a shower in the adjacent room—then she shook her head and replied, "I'm not sure how to answer that. It's complicated."

Indeed, it is complicated. As I sit and try to write this account of mother–daughter relationships across three generations, I am stumped. I ask myself how I can faithfully represent the complexity of the maternal relationships I witnessed for 8 months, while at the same time presenting my interpretations in a coherent fashion. My mind wanders to a section of a poem by Amy Lowell (1916), entitled "Patterns":

I walk down the garden-paths,

And all the daffodils

Are blowing, and the bright blue squills.

I walk down the patterned garden-paths

In my stiff, brocaded gown.

With my powdered hair and jeweled fan,

I too am a rare

Pattern.

I see patterns within and across the relationships of the women in Elkwood, yet I sense that if I reduce their experiences to mere "categories" I run the risk of obscuring the voices around me while focusing on my own authorial, academic voice. Yet, I am reminded that researchers gain perspective through distance and by pulling back from data enough to see the patterns within. As Carbaugh (1989) suggested, I seek to "build a room" to house my understanding of women's maternal relationships. Just as a physical room requires a floor, ceiling, and walls, this room of comprehension requires the distinctive yet interdependent characteristics of description, interpretation, theorizing, and explanation. This chapter begins with a description and interpretation of key themes resonant in these data. These themes are structured within a framework of relational dialectics in order to offer a description of maternal relationships as comprised of an array of dialectical contradictions.

THE DIALOGUE

The process of interpreting information compiled across time is an informed, interdependent act. I pointed out in chapter 2 that this process is informed by and interdependent with many others—other scholars who have studied personal relationships, the participants, and myself from the multiple standpoints as woman, mother, and scholar. This polyvocality has served to guide my interpretation and led me to where I am today, venturing forth to join in the dialogue and thus building on and extending the relevant foundational theories. As Bakhtin (1981) might have characterized it, my authorial voice is inseparable from those scholarly voices that have come before mine, and my voice is connected to theirs. Thus, I draw on multiple theoretical ideas to discuss and explain what I saw and experienced in Elkwood. This writing contains an assortment of women's voices—grandmothers, mothers, and daughters—that contribute to the ongoing dialogue among women, mother, daughters, scholars, teachers, therapists, and so on.

Chapter 2 introduced the relational theoretical framework that served as the initial guiding structure for this inquiry. As I quickly learned, this framework was useful to observing the uniqueness in each dyad's relationship, but also assisted me in seeing connections among and between women's maternal relationships.

As I documented my field notes, images began to appear—patterns—like pencil rubbings over the narration of their lives.

How did these women experience their maternal relationships? To answer this guiding question, interview and observational data were analyzed and aggregate themes were structured within a framework of *dialectical contradictions*. The contradictions identified here represent the complexity of maternal relationships and are applicable to every case in this study. Variability did occur across relationship type (e.g., mother–daughter, grandmother–granddaughter) and relational points in time (e.g., mid-life mothers–young adult daughters, elderly mothers–mid-life daughters), and this variability is discussed within the larger discussion of this and subsequent chapters.

Personal relationships at any given point in time reflect the cumulative effects of previous interactions. Keeping this in mind, it is imperative to realize that my observations began "mid-stream" relationally. Each grandmother–granddaughter and mother–daughter relationship had a significant "story" before I began poking and prying. Clearly, many events had occurred in each relationship to shape it into the form I eventually examined. By getting to know each woman both separately and in conjunction with her grandmother, mother, and/or daughter, I was able to get a sense of the dynamic nature of how they experienced and managed their relationships on a daily basis, and to also gain a glimpse into their perceptions of how that experience had affected them across the years.

As Morgan pointed out in the earlier excerpt, the mother–daughter relationship is complicated. It is also characterized by myriad contradictions. The following dialogue between Diane and Sam illustrates an utterance of such a contradiction:[11]

Diane stated, "I do the best I can [as a mother]."

"Yes, you do," Sam replied.

Diane looked at me and stated with a bit of incredulity, "But it isn't enough."

"What do you mean?" asked Sam.

"It's not enough and much of the time it's too much," responded Diane.

"Yes, well, it's tough to determine how much is enough and how much is too much," admitted Sam.

I interjected with my own question, "Too much what?"

Diane said, "Too much ... I don't know ..."

Sam answered, "Too much direction, love, attention, expectations ...."

---

[11]Those who study the way human conversation actually is expressed (e.g., through transcription) realize that "real talk" is awkward, incomplete, and ungrammatical (Pearce, 1989). The focus of this analysis is descriptive, qualitatively interpretive, and not focused on discourse analysis; therefore, conversations and personal narratives are reported in this book edited for grammar, but retaining awkwardness and incomplete sentence structure.

Diane continued, overlapping Sam's speech, "Guidance, advice … too much … *input*."

"Yeah, but it's needed at times," deferred Sam.

Diane considered this with a "Hmmm" as Sam added, "And not needed most of the time" [*laugh*].

Diane looked at me and asked, "See what I mean?"

Sam looked at her mother and said, "No, I appreciate it, ya know … but like when I was 12 it was warranted and now it sometimes seems intrusive. Shoot, just last week your advice was needed. Remember when I needed you to help me with the plans for the fundraiser?"

Diane thought about this and responded, "Um hmmm."

Sam continued, "But today I didn't need you to tell me what to cook or not cook for [my son]."

Diane once again appealed to the sidelines. "See what I mean? I never quite know what they want from me" [*smile … sigh*].

Managing relational contradictions emerged as very salient to understanding the maternal relationships in Elkwood. According to the *dialectical perspective* (see Montgomery & Baxter, 1998), all relationships are constantly changing and fraught with contradictions. These contradictions are social rather than cognitive phenomena. In this study, it was the ongoing management of those relational contradictions that provided the backdrop for the enactment of the daily dramas.

DIALECTICAL PERSPECTIVE

Scholars such as Baxter and Montgomery (Baxter, 1990; Baxter & Montgomery, 1996; Montgomery & Baxter, 1998) and Rawlins (1992, 1994) are among those who have fully developed the dialectical perspective and argue that relationships are constantly changing, never completely stable, and characterized by contradictions. Within this perspective, contradictions are relational phenomena. These authors further argue that communication is the mechanism used to manage these relational contradictions. A dialectical perspective complements the relational approach used in this study, and offers a possible infrastructure for organizing several salient domains identified as characterizing the mother–daughter relationship. Regrettably, because much of the work on dialectics has focused on romantic relationships (Baxter, 1990; Baxter & Montgomery, 1996) and friendships (Rawlins, 1992, 1994) rather than parent–adult child relationships, more development is needed to adequately illustrate the fundamental relational contradictions identified in grandmother–mother–daughter relationships.

Relational dialectics assert that persons in relationships manage opposing interdependent forces that stand in dialectical association with each other when one force is defined in terms of the absence of the other, yet they form a coherent unit or whole. Montgomery and Baxter (1998) explained that dialectical scholarship requires scholars to pick up strands of other dialectical studies and begin to weave among them new strands of findings to develop a more complete understanding of the complexity of forces that shape personal relationships. In the case of grandmother–mother–daughter relationships in Elkwood, I discovered relational forces that were, as Kelly expressed it, "a bitch to contend with!"

DIALECTICS IN ELKWOOD GRANDMOTHER–MOTHER–DAUGHTER RELATIONSHIPS

In 2000, the National Center for Health Statistics estimated that the average age of women who became first-time grandmothers was 47. With an increased life expectancy over the last century (Mancini, 1989; Nussbaum, Pecchioni, Robinson, & Thompson, 2000), Fingerman (2001) pointed out that this has provided grandmothers, mothers, and granddaughters greater opportunities to experience their relationships throughout later stages of the life course.

Many mothers and their adult daughters continue to sustain warm supportive relationships through later life stages (Davey & Eggebeen, 1998; Fingerman, 2001). Nevertheless, when interviewing women for the past decade about their adult mother–daughter relationships, I have heard over and over again how "complex" and "ambivalent" maternal relationships are, and have read numerous academic texts containing this same characterization. A text written by Fingerman (2001) about the mother–daughter relationship integrated the characteristics of complexity and ambivalence into its title, claiming that the mother–adult daughter relationship is *A Study in Mixed Emotions*. The consistency of this characterization heartens me and validates my belief that a dialectical approach to understanding maternal relationships may be the most insightful for scholars, practitioners, and women in general. I argue that the complexity of these relationships is best unraveled and simplified by viewing them through a prism of relational contradictions, and I intend to convey these contradictions not as abstracted labels, but instead as lived experiences.

Many of the contradictions that characterize the maternal relationships in this particular study are held in common with contradictions that characterize personal relationships in general. Social scientists have recognized that certain patterns of relational contradictions are common across personal relationships. Conville (1998) termed these *conventional dialectics*. The conventional dialectics of stability and change (Altman, Vinsel, & Brown, 1981; Baxter, 1988; Brown, Werner, & Altman, 1998), connection and separation (Miller, 1995; Miller-Rassulo, 1992), and open and closed (Altman et al., 1981; Dindia, 1998; Petronio, 2002; Rawlins, 1992) also emerged as fundamental to understanding maternal relationships in Elkwood. The commonality of these patterns of dialectics across relationship types is promising and suggests foundational dialectical challenges in interpersonal relationships. Table 4.1 lists the key relational contradictions functioning specifically in maternal relationships in Elkwood, and the conceptual definitions of each type. This listing is rather static, however, and does not visually represent the complex, overlapping domains of contradictions.

When first talking with Scout, I asked her to characterize her relationships with her grandmother and her mother. The request resulted in some colorful stories and wistful looks. After talking for about an hour she paused, looked confused, and asked, "Does this seem like we have a split personality to you? We are all domineering and controlling, whatever; but also very connected, close, loving, giving, and caring. Is this contradictory?" This comment makes perfect sense when viewing her relational experiences through the lens of dialectics. The dynamic tension experienced by these women was not *between* being connected and controlling; the tensions were located within two separate domains of contradictions—*connection-separation* and *dominance-submission.* For this family, the typical centripetal (or dominant) relational forces at play within each binary opposition were "loving emotional connection" *along with* "dominance." These forces did not negate each other; they were distinct but nevertheless part of the "knot" of forces that shaped these maternal relationships.

Textually or visually representing dialectical tensions across relationships is a difficult task. The difficulty lies in capturing the complex centripetal (dominant) and centrifugal (countervailing) forces at play in a given relationship, let alone across multiple relationships. Moreover, this difficulty is compounded by the inseparability of the contradictions themselves. A contradiction refers to

TABLE 4.1

Relational Contradictions in Maternal Relationships

Dialectical Poles	Definition
Stability-change	Contradiction of maintaining constancy or familiar patterns alongside variation and unfamiliar patterns
Connection-separation	Contradiction of maintaining both a "me" and a "we" in the relationship
Open-closed	Contradiction of desiring to both share feelings, ideas, and information with her partner—affording her open access—and to keep information restricted, private, and concealed from her partner—restricting or closing access
Real-ideal	Contradiction that exists when juxtaposing the day-to-day "reality" of a partner with the idealized version of who we think she "should" be
Powerful-powerless	Contradiction that exists when two partners simultaneously control and relinquish control of valuable resources

the dynamic interplay between unified opposites that are interdependent (Baxter & Montgomery, 1998). Yet, Montgomery and Baxter (1998) also suggested that instead of a dualistic, dichotomous conceptualization of relational contradictions, scholars are better served to conceptualize these contradictions as a *knot*—interwoven and interdependent. Montgomery and Baxter also called on the metaphor of *jazz* to illustrate the dynamic complexity of relational dialectics. Jazz represents a musical genre that "is identified by its inclusiveness and its improvisation; coordination of unique, sometimes discordant voices happens in the service of spontaneous, creatively synergistic music" (Montgomery & Baxter, 1998, p. 156).

As a result of living with these data and trying to make sense of the maternal relationships in Elkwood, I concur with the idea of using metaphor to represent this dialogic complexity. I can conceive of how dominant forces within any given relationship serve as progressive chords that guide the improvisation of managing countervailing forces. To represent this, I propose a metaphor of my own. For me, the image of a braid may be the most applicable metaphor for the dialectical contradictions identified in this study. When disentangling this braid one strand at a time, there are "anchor" contradictions that provide the common threads through which all other dialectical oppositions and their related dimensions are woven.[12] The anchor contradiction in a relationship refers to the dominant forces that may characterize a relationship at any given point in time. These dominant forces are features of all dialectical oppositions in the maternal relationships, pulling with centripetal force and affecting the other dimensions of the relationship as they pull with their centrifugal force.

To illustrate this, consider the dialectical contradiction of connection—separation—and recall Scout's characterization of the women in her family as "connected, close, loving, giving, and caring." In talking with these women and observing them in interaction, connection emerged as the dominant force defining relationships across three generations. Thus, this centripetal relational feature of connection (anchor strand) is countered by an array of centrifugal oppositions of disconnection that co-exist within the braid, such as connection-autonomy, connection-selfishness, connection-apathy.

Montgomery and Baxter (1998) proposed the concept of "dialogic complexity" to refer to the "multidirectional and spiraling" nature of interwoven contradictions functioning in concert with the dynamic flux of movement within each dialectical opposition. In my interpretation, the interplay of all these forces is simultaneous and ongoing throughout the life span of women's maternal relationships. I contend that to understand maternal relationships, scholars need to be able to examine and explain the possible range of associations among these forces.

---

[12]For those who do not know how to braid, the protocol is to take one or more strands to provide a central anchor for the braid, then weave a strand on either side over that strand and continue adding strands over and over while weaving the anchor strand throughout.

DIALECTICAL FORCES

The role functions of maternal relationships are much more distinct when a daughter is a child; the relationship revolves around basic physical care and socialization of the child. But as Fingerman (2001) aptly pointed out, things change when both women are adults. Role functions are not so clear. The voices of women in this study represent the voices of many who, while in the midst of their relationships with grandmothers, mothers, and daughters, tried to explain and make sense of them. Although these women reflected on the narratives of their lives with grandmothers, mothers, daughters, and granddaughters, they were simultaneously writing the story. The representations included in this book depict a slice of the story, a page here and a page there, often slowing the motion down and isolating the story elements a frame at a time.

Burgoon and Hale (1992) stated that relationships manifest patterns of themes that reflect the relationship at any particular point in time. The following reminiscences begin to illustrate the themes that emerged during my time in Elkwood:

> My relationships with my daughters are both wonderful and terrible. It's hard to be a mother yet it would be terrible not to be a mother. My relationships with my daughters have been harder now that they are grown up. With them getting married, moving out and all. I really don't think I have a problem with letting them go. I sometimes feel guilty that I want them to have their own life and be happy. I know that was hard for my mother—to let us go. Even today she still tries to control our lives. (Sam, Family #1)

> My mother never really wanted a girl. I know that. But when I had my own daughters. I was delighted. Well, my first daughter ..., you see, I had to marry her father. She was what you might call a "love-child." No, now that I think about it, she was probably my chance for escape. I was 16. A baby having a baby.

> Oh, but I thought I was so smart ... going to get away from my mother, start my own family, so what if I had to drop out of high school? I didn't need school. I needed to be needed. My mother was actually happy about it. I had a *man* to take care of me—to mother that was everything. My father left us for another woman when I was 11. I haven't seen him since. So, there I was, 16, feeling abandoned by both parents, and feeling very alone. [*She smiles.*] Then I had a daughter, someone to play house with, dress up like my own little doll. Someone I could mold to be another me. I loved it. I've been married three times, and it has been my daughters that have kept me going. (Excerpt from Miller, *Two of Me*, 2000)[13]

> Right or wrong, I gained much of my identity through my children. As I've gotten older I've really grown. Mothering is intense, like being too close to the trees and

---

[13]*Two of Me* is a play based on personal interviews with over 50 women concerning their mother–daughter relationships. All excerpts are based on actual accounts and illustrate the themes in this book beyond the experiences of the women of Elkwood.

not seeing the forest. As I've gotten more distance, I've learned that I'm not my children—or my husband for that matter. I am not my granddaughter so I can just enjoy her. Being a grandmother, especially as they have grown older, is very relaxed, because with age and experience comes the benefit of wisdom in dealing with a relationship with my grandchildren. I see my grandchildren as a gift of my labor thus far. Of course, not having to be a 24-hour-a-day parent makes it a lot easier to enjoy the gift! (Katrina, Family #6)

Moving along the life span from daughter to mother to grandmother requires modifications to one's story—adjustments to both relational and personal identities. Although most narratives suggest that life-span transitions from daughter to grandmother involve a process that is rewarding and "worth it," other stories suggest frustration with this process. Regardless of how they were evaluated, these maternal relationships were dynamic. Dialectical theory begins to capture this dynamism and provides continua on which to assess relationships at any given point in time. The contradictions identified and discussed here represent the recorded and interpreted experiences of a handful of women in Elkwood[14] and spanned mother–adult daughter as well as grandmother–adult granddaughter relationships.[15]

STABILITY-CHANGE

Stability refers to maintaining constancy or familiar patterns, whereas *change* refers to variation and unfamiliar patterns. Indeed, as women move through their life span their maternal relationships experience periods of stability and change. Although certain aspects of their relationships may be undergoing change, others may exhibit constancy. As these relationships changed across the life course, the contradictions themselves (e.g., openness-closedness) shifted and adjusted to accommodate relational modifications. Consider the following comment by Linda: "I've always been very open with my mother, I can tell her anything about everything. But, I'm at a stage in my life where I want to do things on my own and not depend on her so much to do things for me." Her mother added, "Just

---

[14]The generic *women* will be used henceforth to avoid the more cumbersome wording of *women in this study.*

[15]Each claim that I make in describing and interpreting these findings is *my own perception* of how the data should be described or interpreted. I have elected to add this footnote for the reader to avoid awkward wording throughout this monograph such as "In my opinion" or "it is my contention that ...."

because [my daughter] is exploring the world on her own doesn't mean that we are less open and honest with each other. I think I know pretty much what she feels about things and what she does during the course of any given week." As Linda transitioned from adolescence into young adulthood, she adjusted the balance of inclusion-exclusion in her relationship with her mother, excluding her from everyday activities while simultaneously including her mother through shared disclosures and openness with one another.

Stability and change are contradictory concepts, yet they existed simulta- neously at different levels (individual and relational) and across time. The women of Elkwood managed fluid change and relative stability in their mater- nal relationships on an ongoing basis, although some relationships experienced periods of significant change that proved to be pivotal to relational adjustment. In fact, relationship evolution itself is in part a function of the stability-change dialectic. Many relational researchers argue that nonfamilial relationships re- quire variation and changes across time (Gottman, 2000), but that little work has been conducted to understand if the same applies to parent–child relation- ships. Adolescent research refers to individual developmental changes of youth and often suggests that parents must be flexible in adjusting to these changes. However, less research has focused on the mother–adult daughter relationship to explore how variations at both the individual and relational levels shape the life span of this relationship.

Points of change that result in the recalibration of maternal relationships may be considered relational "turning points." These turning points often re- quire minor adjustments to the relationship itself and some major redefinitions. Some relationships examined in my study, however, experienced more change and relational adaptation than did others. Morgan, for example, felt that her re- lationship with her mother was "erratic, like a roller coaster, up and down all the time, depending on what's going on in our lives." Whether change occurred er- ratically or predictably, all of the maternal relationships I observed in Elkwood—especially as they moved along the life course—experienced periods of relative stability and periods of sudden and/or gradual change. Moreover, I also found that when change was *resisted* and women did not adapt, the rela- tionship would experience a period of "growing pains." The next section illus- trates some of these growing pains and demonstrates the importance of relational turning points as experienced by the grandmothers, mothers, and (grand)daughters in Elkwood.

Turning Points

When I asked women to retrospectively consider the turning points in their ma- ternal relationships, the contexts of the stories changed but similarities surfaced over time. Mothers and daughters tended to recall more relationally conse- quential turning points than did grandmothers and granddaughters. However, frequency information is not especially informative given that most of the mother–daughter relationships were maintained over a span of many more years than were the grandmother–granddaughter relationships. What I believe is of significance are the types of turning points reported and women's perceptions of how their relationships changed as a result.

Turning Point: Pregnancy and Childbirth

Landmark events in women's life course development such as menstruation and marriage may necessitate a redefinition of maternal relationships, but pregnancy and childbirth emerged as critical turning points for mothers and grandmothers. Pregnancy is a time of early attachment to a child. Gina shared, "First when I knew I was pregnant I prayed for a girl. Another boy would be nice, but I really wanted a girl. I talked to her every day in my womb." This sense of beginning a relationship with an unborn child resonated in women's stories. Daughters' births are defining for both the relationship and for the woman's individual sense of self. Morgan shared, "The birth of my daughters defined who I was." Mothers also pointed out that this "special" relationship with daughters often changed upon the birth of a younger sibling, Diane said:

> [My son] was born so quickly after Samantha was born that my time with her was cut short. Then he was sick so I spent a lot of time in the hospital and missed seeing her grow. I'll never forget when I came home from the hospital one day and she was walking! I hadn't even been aware she was balancing herself. I saw that and I sat down and cried.

As Samantha (Sam) recalled this period of time in her life, she claimed that her mother's unavailability actually strengthened her relationship with her grandmother. One day Sam shared, "[My grandmother] was the one that took care of [me and my older sister]. I remember sitting on her lap, she read us books, and she'd rock us to sleep."

For grandmothers, the birth of a grandchild is often "a defining moment—a grand passage" (Sheehy, 2002). Many women indicated that the birth of a grandchild "gives us another chance" and "I don't have to be on the front lines anymore, I can just watch the show." Sheehy also quipped, "It's when your childless daughter passes 35 that your inner grandmother begins to experience mild panic!" She added, "Grandchildren soften our hearts. They loosen the sludge of old resentments and regrets; it's a chance for reconciliation between our children and ourselves" (p. 7). According to Sam, "Lord knows my mom and me have had our problems, but I depend on her a lot to help with my kids. Not so much the day-to-day stuff, but the 'what should I do when this stuff happens!' " Lois mentioned a shift in her relationship with her daughter from spectator to involved partner once her daughter began having children: "I was able to be less of a spectator in [my daughter's] life and play a more active role once my grandchildren were born. She needed and I think [*laughter*] wanted me to be there for her and provide some help."

A turning point for many women in their relationships with their daughters was inclusion of the new grandmother in the birthing process. Whereas older women often relied on their mother's midwifery, younger mothers had a choice to include their own mothers in the birthing process. For many grandmothers, this experience marked a shift in both her relationship with her daughter and in her new role as grandmother.

Not all women were thrilled by the prospect of becoming a grandmother. Generally this was a positive event, yet there are contextual variables that determined how this event shaped maternal relationships. Diane (Family #1), for example, welcomed the birth of her first granddaughter, but the circumstances of her own grandmother's death—1 hour before the birth and in the same hospital where her second granddaughter was born—influenced her initial relationship with her new granddaughter:

> My grandmother was always there for me. It was just an absolutely perfect relationship. When my first granddaughter was first born, it was like I had this role to live up to, and it was easy because I had such a good model to go by.
>
> When my second granddaughter was born, it was very, very difficult because of the death of grandmother 45 or 40 minutes before she was born. I kind of removed myself from [the second grandchild] for a long time because it was too much of a symbol of that death and it made it difficult.

A daughter's pregnancy may also be experienced negatively—even shamefully—under conditions where a daughter is either a legal minor and/or unmarried. Miller (1995) reported the experience of a pregnant teen daughter in the early 1970s who was sent to live in a residence for unwed mothers. When visiting her home for the weekend, she was required to hide on the floor of her mother's car with a coat thrown over her to avoid being seen by neighbors. This kind of reaction was not uncommon during this period in U.S. history; nevertheless, it was still consequential for many maternal relationships. Families #1, 2, and 6 were all faced with adjusting to the pregnancy of adolescent daughters in the 1970s and 1980s. Katrina said:

> Well, since Kelly was my second 16-year-old to get pregnant, I had a real problem with it, and the handling of it. My oldest married the boy, but Kelly wanted to get an abortion. I don't believe in that. So, I told her that was not an option. I picked up and moved my family to another town and I sent Kelly to live with my brother and his wife in a nearby city … she resented me for it. (Family #2)

Morgan (Family #6) was also a pregnant teenager who believed that her mother "made her" give up the baby for adoption. Although Meredith does not agree that she forced her daughter into any kind of decision, Morgan nonetheless—25 years later—framed this decision as a turning point in her relationship with her mother. Sam also identified her teenage pregnancy as having long-standing consequences for her relationship with her mother:

> Getting pregnant, and having my daughter in high school, had a major impact on my relationship with my mother. Both my mom and my grandmother told me that no man would ever want to marry me cause I had a child. But I married Jack.

> My mom wanted me to go to college and marry a man who would take care of me, have a successful job, have wealth, and be beautiful. [*Sigh*]. But, I failed her. I got pregnant in high school, didn't go to college, and married a man who was abusive.

The teenage pregnancies in this sample occurred in the 1970s and 1980s. Since that time, vast changes have occurred in the cultural norms surrounding single motherhood, pregnancy, and women's sexuality. Nonetheless, during my third month in Elkwood, Morgan's 35-year-old sister Ali came home to stay with her family for a while after going through a divorce from her husband of 10 years and a failed relationship with another man whom she had met during her marital separation. Ali was 13 weeks pregnant. Yet, Morgan's reaction to this when first talking with her sister was not to ask, "How are you?"

> Instead, she asked, "Did you tell Mom yet?"

> Ali responded, "Yes."

> Morgan pushed her French fries around in her ketchup for a moment and then asked with a pained expression, "How did she react? Did she have a fit about how she's gonna explain this [to others]?"

> Ali, visibly annoyed by this suggestion, lifted her chin, inhaled and said, "This is my issue to explain, not hers. It's my baby—not hers."

Morgan later told me that her mother was "really disappointed" and took it personally that her sister Ali was pregnant "out of wedlock." Apparently, Meredith exclaimed, "First you [Morgan], then [another sister], now Ali! Where did I go wrong?" About 1 week after this comment was made, Ali shared with me that she was shocked by her mother's reaction. Ali was "thrilled to have this baby after so many years of trying to have a child" and she wanted her mother to be happy too. She argued, "It's not like I am a 17-year-old teenager. I have a job, I have a life, and I can take care of this baby very well, thank you!" Events that might serve as catalysts for change in the mother–daughter relationship were typically not considered catalysts for change in the grandmother–granddaughter relationship. When a daughter's pregnancy or childbearing strained the mother–daughter relationship, grandmothers frequently provided the social and emotional support for the granddaughter and great-grandchild. This often strengthened the bond between grandmother and granddaughter. In the case of Morgan, in her early 20s she eventually went on to marry a man and then proceeded to have four children in a short period of time. She pointed out that it was her grandmother rather than her mother to whom she felt most connected at this time in her life. She said:

> This is not a thing against my Mom, but when I needed her the most, when I had my kids, when they were little, she didn't have time. My grandmother was there, all the time, constantly. I mean if it wasn't for my Grandma, when all my kids were little, I'd have never gone out. Because she took me to the mall, she took me everywhere. I mean it didn't bother her to have all those children around you know. When someone is that close to you that much, I mean I was close to her before, but that really cemented for me our relationship and stuff, and we did everything together. Really, she was like my best friend during that period of time.

By obtaining legal custody of Kendra as an infant, Katrina merged her role as grandmother into that of mother. This created a change in Katrina and Kelly's mother–daughter relationship and also added a new dimension to Katrina's relationship with her granddaughter. When Kendra, as a toddler, began to address Katrina as "Mom," the boundaries between grandmotherhood and motherhood became blurred. Over the years, Kendra and Kelly "worked out" their relationship, but when Kendra's daughter was born recalibration was necessary among these complicated relationships. Kendra in her role as new mother confronted her own mother about "abandoning" her when she was an infant. The birth of her own daughter reopened old wounds and required both mother and daughter to adjust to new perspectives of one another.

Turning Point: Changes in Proximity

Affirming what Golish (2000) discovered in her research on turning points in parent–child relationships, women indicated that changes in *proximity* functioned as turning points in maternal relationships. When daughters moved away for short periods or "back home" (literally back into the household or back to their town), this physical proximity was sometimes tied to relational connectedness. Yet, for others, when a daughter or granddaughter moved physically away it provided the necessary distance to see the other person in a new way:

> She is such an individual. Since she has been away she's no longer like a daughter, she is acting like my friend. (Morgan, Family #6)

> When I got away from home. That's when I really could see myself and myself in relation to her differently. Growing up I was real small, within a family of heavyset women. My older sister was a little bigger, and I was just exceptionally small. Anyway, my mother always treated me as sickly and I didn't know I was not sick until I was 16 and got away from home. She had designated me the sick one or the sickly one and all I had was like my tonsils out and a broken arm, and maybe some headaches. The headaches were probably from being nervous and I just think that had

to be her influence on me because when I left town I was not sickly and I was quite healthy and I'm fine. So, I had to get away from her to see the influence, the bad influence, she had on me. (Katrina, Family #2)

Daughters who got married and moved from their parents' homes and mothers who remarried and/or relocated "forced change in the relationship," and this required a certain amount of adjustment for mothers and daughters. After Sam divorced and returned to live "back home" with her mother temporarily, Diane remarked, "When you got married, in my heart I felt that I had lost you. Now I feel like I have you back." Later, Sam shared the following with me: "That comment really shocked me. I don't think she ever lost me. My God, I just lived a little bit away. What happened was that someone else had my full attention, and she didn't want to share me. She never lost me, we just had to figure out a way that she could share me."

To stay connected to grandmothers, mothers, and daughters, women sometimes purchased homes in close proximity. Among the participants, three of the families owned homes next door to one another and the other three had residences within 15 minutes of one another. At the time of this writing, Scout had married, had her own daughter, and had moved to a city approximately 2 hours from Elkwood. This autonomous living did not last long. Within 6 months of this move Scout's siblings had all moved to this city and taken jobs. Morgan and her husband followed suit and found a home within 10 minutes of Scout and her family, and they are currently looking for housing for Meredith.

Turning Point: Violating Expectations

Expectancy violation theory (Burgoon & Hale, 1988; Burgoon, 1978, 1993) suggests that in personal relationships members have expectations that may be violated by their partner. How that member reacts to these violations may have consequence for the relationship. Violations may heighten arousal and uncertainty in the person perceiving the violation. As Burgoon and Hale (1988) indicated, even when an unexpected behavior is perceived to be better than the expected behavior, a positive violation has occurred. For example, Becky, when experiencing a positive violation, exclaimed, "I actually made it through one day with [my mother] without her making a complaint! What a wonderful change of pace." Her surprise was due to the perception that her mother would ordinarily complain about something during the course of their visit. A violation of that expectation resulted in a positive interpretation of her mother's behavior and—that day—she felt good about her relationship with her mother.

Minor violations occurred on a monthly, weekly, or even a daily basis in some relationships, and grandmothers, mothers, and adult daughters adjusted to them in a variety of ways. However, a host of perceived violations functioned as key turning points in the mother–daughter relationship. The pivotal turning-point violations reported by the mothers and daughters in Elkwood were collapsed into two categories: *transgressions* and *acts of devotion*. Transgressions are actions that violate the taken-for-granted rules of the relational culture; acts of devotion are actions that imply that the relationship goes "above and beyond" what was expected (Guerrero et al., 2001).

Transgressions as Violation. Transgressions were the most frequently reported turning points reported by both mothers and daughters (at all ages) and the least frequently reported by grandmothers. Women expected their maternal relationships to provide them with both emotional and instrumental support. Instrumental support included practical forms of assistance with activities or tasks such as helping with household tasks, assisting with errands, or providing financial aid. Emotional support included behaviors such as expressing love, providing encouragement, empathizing, and offering and accepting advice.

This expectation did not really abate until the relational partner became incapacitated (i.e., by frailty or illness). When the expected support was not forthcoming, the stability of the relationship was compromised, forcing the dyadic partners to adjust. Transgressions were closely tied to managing the dynamic tension between resentment and forgiveness. A resentment that occurred as a result of a transgression might fester and become toxic if that resentment was sustained and asserted itself as a dominant force in the relationship.

Women's adult maternal relationships often reflected cumulative effects of previous transgressions. In fact, some transgressions were recalled 20–50 years after their occurrence, and consequently affected the entire course of the women's adult relationship.

Sam, at the age of 40, suggested that her mother's lack of support for her career aspirations as an adolescent not only affected her own life course, but was also a turning point in her relationship with her mother:

> I wanted to be a nurse. I didn't want to be a registered nurse [RN], because I thought all a registered nurse did was paperwork. I wanted to be hands on with the patients. That's what I really wanted. Of course back then [in the 1970's] Mom thought that career opportunities were only for those people who were RNs. But at that time I wanted to go to vocational school to become an LPN. And that was the career choice that I made. But … my mom wouldn't sign the paperwork [required for me to go to the vocational school]. She said that if I wanted to be a nurse, I had to go to college and be an RN. Of course, she was the mom so she was always right. Ha! She still is. So anyway, I didn't go to vocational school. Instead, I got pregnant in high school. I guess I showed her. [*smiles*]

Sam and Diane experienced a continuous struggle to manage the interdependent forces of dominance-submission in their mother–daughter relationship. The transgression just described was not the first to have shaped Sam and Diane's relationship, but it was fundamental to Sam's perception of her mother as having inordinate power in their relationship.

Daughters often felt entitled to their mothers' emotional support. When that support was not forthcoming, this occasionally undermined a daughter's perception of security in the relationship. In the following excerpts, Katrina talks about her mother's reaction to her daughter's divorce and Sam reveals her sense of betrayal:

> My mother, in her usual way, issued a famous quote; she said, she "just wasn't going to take sides [between my ex-husband and me.]" I say if your own mother doesn't take sides, who's gonna?! (Katrina, Family #2)

> I vividly recall when I was 12 I told mom [Diane] that my friend's dad was "feeling up" his own daughter, me, and another friend. I knew it was sick, so I told my mom and she said, "Well then you can't go back." But then she invited him to a dinner party, like, the next week. I went back to my room thinking *I can't believe she's doing this!* (Sam, Family #1)

Sam indicated that even at the age of 12 she recalled feeling "insecure in my relationship with my mom." But, she said, "I always knew that she loved me."

In some relationships, mothers reported becoming emotionally dependent on their daughters when the girls were quite young, and instead of providing daughters with needed emotional support and nurturing, they *required* that support and nurturing. *Parentification* refers to a role reversal in which the offspring is placed in the position of having to parent his or her parent (Boszormenyi-Nagy & Spark, 1973). Parentification of daughters in this sample had long-lasting effects on the dynamics of mother–daughter relationships. Diane reported a history of early parentification. Sylvia had made multiple suicide attempts during Diane's youth, and hence Diane always felt obligated to care for her mother's fragile emotional health. Finally, at the age of 20, Diane admitted being resigned to a relationship with her mother where she was the parent rather than the child. She said, "It seems like after about the age of 20 I admitted to myself that I had become the parent, instead of the daughter." Several months into my fieldwork, she shared:

> When I was 50 years old, the burden of being my mother's mother became too much and I just, I stopped a little bit. I mean, I tried to distance myself from that parent role. It has always bothered me that I have not been a child or a daughter. I haven't ever really felt like a daughter [with my mom]. The only time I felt like a daughter was with my grandmother. (Diane, Family #1)

Diane expressed on numerous occasions that she never intended to repeat this pattern of parentification with her own daughters or granddaughters, and had made extensive efforts to avoid "being needy" while retaining her control as matriarch in the family for three generations. She consciously provided her children and grandchildren with emotional, financial, and instrumental support, but required their capitulation to her control in return.

As discussed further in this chapter, Families #1, 2, 5, and 6 contained the most distressed maternal relationships. Although these women were closely connected to one another emotionally and through proximity, issues of dominance and power in these relationships were central to understanding their maternal ties. Perhaps the nature of their interconnectedness highlighted control issues, but the Elkwood matriarchs wielded a substantial amount of emotional power over their adult daughters and granddaughters. The need for maternal approval in these families often was overwhelming, and disapprovals were regularly interpreted as rejections. Perceived rejection from a maternal relative was universally framed as a transgression, especially in families whose identities were tied to being loving and cohesive. One day Morgan sat quietly in her rocker while I breast fed my infant son. The air was dry; the quiet of the day lulled us into conversation. We chatted about family and about mothering, and Morgan confided in me her frustration about the way her mother had handled certain transgressions. She said:

> Several years ago my daughter, Shana, won an award for something she did in college. My mother [Meredith] took her out to a fancy restaurant to celebrate. Shana hugged my mother and thanked her orally, but she never sent [my mother] a thank-you note. Anyway, a year ago both Shana and Scout were honored [at a local community organization] and my mom took Scout out to celebrate but she made sure that Shana knew she wasn't included as punishment for her faux pas [not sending a thank-you note for the previous dinner]. This has shut Shana off from her grandmother and I don't know if they will ever mend it.

It was not only daughters who perceived lack of support as a relational transgression. Mothers also expected reciprocal support from their daughters, especially as they moved into mid-life. All mothers would call their daughters at least weekly if the daughters hadn't already visited with them. These calls were often "just to talk" and served to connect women during periods of time in their day or their weeks when they felt disconnected from each other. Gina and Georgie (Family #3) lunched together every day, visited, and shared their day. For women who expect this support as a standard relational practice, however, violations were sometimes framed as transgressions.

Charlotte (Family #5) indicated that "My daughter should be the one to care for me. It's hard for me to get around and I depend on her." Yet, Becky was employed full time and had her own family to care for; she felt that the time she had available to assist her mother was limited. Charlotte often complained to Becky that her expectations were being violated ("*Other* daughters take their mothers to lunch at least once a week"), but because Becky believed she was doing "all" she could "humanly do" to assist her mother, these transgressions—by nature of their regularity—became a defining feature of their relationship. Charlotte consistently interpreted her daughter's behavior as transgressions, and Becky assumed her role as transgressor.

Mothers also recognized that daughters' transgressions could function as key turning points in the mother–adult daughter relationship. Many of these events were related to inclusion-exclusion dialectics; for example, daughters not coming home or spending time with mothers during vacation periods, spending time with in-laws or spouses and not including their mothers, not permitting their mothers to be either present or to visit during an event, not sharing some information with their mothers, or outright deception. By and large, however, the key violation that these mothers recounted across different points in time was the transgression of not "being there" when needed.

Proximity alone did not necessarily lead to frequency of contact in maternal relationships. As in the case of Charlotte and Becky (Family #5), issues of availability, access, and offering support became more salient as mothers aged, grew increasingly frail or ill, and became more dependent on other family members. Yet, "not being there" functioned as a key turning point between healthy mothers and their adult daughters, too, with the most powerful violations occurring with mid-life daughters and older mothers.

As I walked into Diane's family room, I drank in the sunlight and the smell of vanilla. There was always some luscious smell in her home. However, that day in her home Diane was sitting alone and looking forlorn. She had something to share with me about daughters not being there for their mothers, and she sadly told me the following:

It's just that I feel so alone sometimes. Everyone is doing their own thing and they don't have to time just to stop and say hi, to help out around here a little bit. I mean, it is really hurtful. I called Sam just last week to touch base and tell her how depressed I've been feeling. But, she was very abrupt on the phone and didn't have time. I hate to impose, but, hell, I'm always there for them, aren't I? I haven't called her since and now she is angry with me because she thinks that I have no right to be mad at her. I think I'll just make plans with [my other friends] for this weekend. Maybe talk with [a friend who is a counselor] instead. [*Pause*]. It just hurts. (Diane, Family #1)

Lois felt a similar rejection and need to be able to depend on her daughter:

I always thought that I would eventually move down to live near her [another daughter who lived out of town]. But now, I have to seriously rethink this. I mean she really hurt me by not being here for my birthday. She says that it is too long of a drive. But I have driven down there many times for less important things. I have needed her for other things in the past, too, and she has just not been there for me. I just don't know if I can depend on her to be there for me and I am not going to find that out after I move down there! (Lois, Family #4)

Some women seemed to hoard their resentments about past transgressions and merely added new ones to their list. When talking with my husband about the strained and sometimes acrimonious nature of certain maternal relationships in Elkwood, he asked, "They're all adults, why don't they just move away

from each other?" This is an easy question to ask because we live in a mobile society that prizes autonomy and individualism; the question reflects a philosophy
of relationships wherein if people don't get along they can just leave.

For a moment, his comment made me stop and speculate about his philosophy toward relationships. I mean, if we started having problems would he just
move away or leave? This possibility was not even feasible to me—the strength
of our ties to one another and our "roots" run much deeper than this philosophy
suggests. The strength of family ties is not something to be underestimated. The
adult women in Elkwood, however, may have had the means and the opportunity to distance themselves from their maternal relationships. These relationships often endured and remained closely connected. Meredith and Morgan,
for example, freely characterized their relationship as full of resentments. They
also expressed incredible devotion to each other and "to family." Morgan
bluntly acknowledged, "[My mom] may be a pain in the ass, but she is my pain-
in-the-ass mother!"

Thibaut and Kelley (1986) defined a nonvoluntary relationship as "a relationship in which the person is forced to stay even though he [or she] would pre-
fer not to" (p. 169). Although some mother–minor child relationships may be
characterized as nonvoluntary, when daughters become legally independent of
their parents they have an opportunity to voluntarily maintain or terminate
mother–daughter relational ties. Older generations of women may not have
had the resources or opportunities to terminate family ties, but many contemporary women are not restricted by tradition, resource, or opportunity. Although not included in this study, there are women in the United States who
have elected to sever their mother–daughter relational ties. For those women,
this book may not resonate. The women in Elkwood—despite their ambiguous
relationships—elected to sustain, nurture, and continue to manage their maternal relationships into adulthood and across generations. These women's experiences were mixed but they all perceived their maternal relationships as
voluntary and central to their own identities. However, some also portrayed
them as "sometimes barely tolerated."

These women did not terminate their maternal relationships due to transgressions; indeed, they saw them as valuable and irreplaceable. However, in response to transgressions they did create relational *boundary* structures and
managed boundaries in different ways. Boundaries can be seen as borders de-
marcating areas of self, other, and self-in-relation. In maternal relationships,
boundary structures were erected at a variety of levels (e.g., generational
boundaries, role boundaries, boundaries around specific activities and
information).

Boundary areas also became sites of border disputes, especially as women
managed their maternal relationships across the life span and adjusted to a variety of changes. Boundaries served to protect the integrity of the individual and
the relationship. As the individuals and relationships changed, boundaries were
typically renegotiated. Some women also interpreted boundary disputes and vi-

olations as relational transgressions. Depending on the perception of the actual transgression, boundary violations could function as a significant relational turning point.

A boundary dispute occurred during my fieldwork that affected not only Diane and Sam's relationship but also Diane's relationship with her granddaughter. This dispute illustrates seemingly innocuous boundaries between the mother role and the grandmother role and how the borders around role functions can assume mythic proportions, leading both partners to vie for control.

There was an informal gathering at Sam's home; I was present. Excitement was high because Sam's daughter's wedding was coming up and plans were afoot. The day before, Sam had confided in me that she was frustrated with her mother because, as she put it, Diane "thinks she is the queen mother of wedding preparations."

During the picnic, Sam, her daughter, and Diane began discussing wedding plans. Although I did not overhear the discussion, according to Sam her mother "made some judgmental comments" about what Sam and her daughter "shouldn't be doing" and what she "should be doing" concerning the wedding. Sam later reported to me that she was "tired of her mother always needing to be in control" and she was "sick of trying to please her."

Thus, Sam said to her mother, "Butt out!"

All of the guest's heads turned and our conversations fell silent.

Sam handed her mother an etiquette book and demanded, "Here. Look in here and see where it says the mother of the bride *must* do this!"

Diane stormed out of the room, calling Sam a "little shit."

Sam called after her, "Yeah … go cool off."

After about 20 minutes Sam exited the room and joined her mother in an adjoining room. This room was a glass-enclosed porch; thus, I was able to both see and hear what transpired.

Diane continued to swear at Sam and then Diane punched Sam in the chin. Sam told me later that her first instinct was to think, "I could knock her flat." So, she raised her hand and slapped her mother across the face. Diane called Sam a "bitch" and a "goddamn shit" and stormed out of the house.

The guests were visibly upset. Sam proceeded to go upstairs to her room, and her husband was left to clean up both the physical and emotional mess. I joined in the work and assisted him in the physical clean-up efforts. Then, after all people had left and the house was tidied up, I went upstairs and found Sam lying on her bed talking with her daughter.

I stepped inside the room cautiously and asked, "How ya doin'? Can I join you?"

Sam's daughter answered, "Sure" as Sam shyly smiled.

"Do you wanna talk alone … ?" I asked.

"No, we've been talking," said Sam's daughter.

I asked, "About what?"

"This afternoon's entertainment," Sam replied.

"Oh."

Sam's daughter added, "I tell you what. I am not going to let this ruin things for my wedding. *Period.* I love my grandmother, but I have totally lost respect for her. I don't care if she doesn't even come to the wedding now."

I didn't have a whole lot to say in response to this comment, so I merely nodded my head and looked out the window.

This was a unique episode of interaction between Diane and Sam. Sam and her daughter disclosed that "Sam always gives in" to Diane and that Sam's daughter expressed admiration that her mother actually "stood up to [Diane] for once." She said to her mother, "I'm proud of you." Confronting a maternal figure was often a difficult task. Despite the adult status of the women, the hierarchical role structure of maternal relationships often persisted, with daughters situated in the subordinate position.

When talking about this episode at a later date with Diane, she admitted that she was wrong to have let the situation get out of hand the way that it did. She claimed that she was "trying to help out" and that if Sam and her daughter were "going to join forces against her, then she would do what she was told and just butt out." As it turned out, this incident successfully created boundaries around the role functions for the mother of the bride and the grandmother of the bride. With no additional challenges to those borders, Diane was invited to the wedding and all went smoothly.

Acts of Devotion as Violation.   Not all violations were negative. Several events and actions—although not as colorful—were interpreted as positive violations. Acts of devotion are surprising acts that serve to intensify feelings of connectedness between women. The women sometimes expressed shock when a granddaughter, mother, or daughter said or did something that strengthened the maternal bond. For instance, when Linda was completing college applications, she surprised her mother by writing an essay that placed her mother as the protagonist: "When she was applying to various colleges and filling out applications. She had to do scholarship applications and she talked about me. I had tears [in my eyes]. She was very eloquently talking about how her mother influenced her and this career choice with the homeless" (Becky, Family #5).

Other acts of devotion included a mother "going to bat" for her daughter and losing her own position in a community group as a result, and a daughter taking her vacation time at work to spend time alone with her mother, "even though I wasn't sick or nothing big was going on. We just hung out." These seemingly minor acts seemed to have a significant impact on women's perceptions of their relationships. Tabitha pointed out, "Knowing that she is on your team, really on your team no matter what, is important. These little things just make you sit back and think more about what you just take for granted all the time."

Acts of devotion were not just relational currencies or "little things" women did to demonstrate the importance of the other in her life. However, acts of devotions may truly have changed the course of a relationship. When a relationship was in disrepair or experiencing instability, acts of devotion may have conveyed a willingness to put forth the effort to engage in relational work.

Cooley (2000) argued that repair in parent–adult child relationships is seldom a focus in contemporary research. This study pointed out the need for additional research efforts on repair and also suggested a beginning point. As mentioned earlier, I found that when violations occurred, women tended to negotiate new boundaries and adjust old ones to accommodate the changing relationship. For many women, the act of establishing new or negotiating changes in boundary structures was "an act of healing" and indicated "a profound change" in how mothers and daughters related to one another. Negotiating the erection, fortification, or omission of existing relational boundaries—especially when a relationship was experiencing instability—was a formidable challenge. Yet, doing so appeared to serve as an act of devotion.

A significant turning point for Sam and one of her daughters was when Sam decided to fortify a stronger border between her own identity and her self-in-relation to this daughter. The following account was taped during an interview with Sam, who was discussing how she might have been a contributing factor to this daughter's suicide attempts:

> Every time she tried to commit suicide, she would call me on the phone or would come over and tell me, um, I would be called—every time—and it all revolved around me. So [after receiving counseling and was told I needed to do this], one day she came over and I'm like, "I got this great news for you. I want to tell you what I've done wrong." I said, "And none of this is your fault because I've done this to you." I said, "Do you know what I've done? I let you out of the crib because you grew up and I put you in a bed. But what I did was put side rails on the bed and I never took them off. Because I didn't ever want to see you fall and get hurt. So I kept those rails up, and you can do whatever you want, but those rails are up there so you don't get hurt."

> Then I turned to her and said, "You know what I'm going to do now? I'm taking the rails down. And you're gonna fall and you're gonna get hurt, and I know it's going to be hard on me, but I can't do anything." I said, "It's my fault. You want to be an adult, that's what you've been asking me for, and I wasn't letting you because I kept those bumper rails up so you wouldn't get hurt." I said, "Today I'm taking them down."

> I said, "From now on, you're right, when you try to commit suicide, I'm not coming over. I'll be more than happy to call and get you help, but it's the decision you made, and as an adult, now you're gonna have to carry it out." She's like, "What?"

I said, "Honey, this is so good, you don't realize I'm letting you go. I'm finally going to let you go." And I said, "I love you so much, and this is the hardest thing in my life I ever had to do, because I want to keep you safe." I said, "I'm letting you go. Don't ever look at this as a negative, this is the first time I'm letting you become the adult you want to be. And I've said I'm taking these down." God has shown me all this and it was time because I was the one who didn't take the railing down. [My daughter] had been asking me to take them down, she'd been kicking, but I kept them up. And I think that was the turning point in our relationship. And she's never yet, never once tried to commit suicide after that. Never.

This narrative struck me as particularly potent as I listened to it and then again when transcribing her words. This amazing connection between mothers and daughters literally defines some women's sense of self. Cloud and Townsend (2002) stressed that personal boundaries define human relationships. For these women, boundary management served a central function in negotiating and re-negotiating their maternal relationships. Although her daughter did not ini-tially see this fortification as an act of devotion, Sam perceived it as both one of devotion and one that changed the course of their relationship. Subsequent dis-cussions with both Sam and this daughter reflected a joint narrative portraying this boundary-setting episode as a pivotal moment in their mother–daughter relationship.

Turning Point: Seeing the "Woman" Behind the Role

Many women also reported a moment in time or an event that served to move one away from seeing a grandmother, mother, or daughter in her *role* identity, to-ward viewing her as her *personality* identity—as a "woman" with unique strengths and weaknesses. Nydegger (1991) termed this process of beginning to view parents as individuals rather than just parents as *filial comprehending*. Ado-lescents tend not to think of their mothers as individual people with lives apart from mothering, but this point of change occurs for many women in young adulthood and certainly by mid-life. A reframing occurred for the women in Elkwood. This required women to see their maternal relationship partners in "a different light."

The turning point, however, was interpreted positively or negatively depend-ing on its context. Gina remarked that when she was in high school she began to see her mother in a new way. She had always respected her mother, but during her high school year she began to notice her as a woman with: "… a lot of musi-cal talent. She would practice and perform, you know, like at church, and all the weddings and the funerals. So, I just always looked up to her and saw her for who she was. I think this is where we really started moving into being friends" (Gina, Family #3).

Gina experienced this turning point in high school, but some women do not experience it until young adulthood: "Just recently I've been able to focus on the good things of her, actually leaving home and being able to get along with her, more like a friend. We're really close and that's cool and everything like that, but also, like, there was a time when I couldn't stand her" (Scout's sister, Family #6).

In adulthood, many women begin to see their mothers as sexual beings. This new view of their mothers may have been inconceivable to them when they were younger. For example, one day when she was rummaging though her mother's drawer for a pair of warm socks, Morgan was aghast when she happened upon a vibrator.[16] As she said, "This was *not* for the purposes of giving herself a back massage, if you know what I mean. *Yuck!* My mom is my mom and I do not want this image of her stuck in my mind. It forever changed how I think of her." This reaction was similar to Diane's, who exclaimed the following about sharing information about sexual behavior with her mother, "I don't want her telling me about her sex life. I have a sex life, she doesn't!!"

Seeing a mother as a sexual being may be a more difficult adjustment than viewing a daughter as a sexual being. Mothers know that their daughters' sexuality is imminent once the daughters begin menstruating, but events such as unexpected physical developments (e.g., a daughter developing very large breasts) or consideration of daughter's sexual preference may function as turning points. The process of beginning to see a daughter as an individual woman with a unique body (not in the image of her mother's) or with unique sexual preferences (rather than any expected preference) requires a certain amount of redefinition of the mother–daughter relationship. There is evidence from other studies that children who begin to see their mothers as unique women apart from their maternal roles—achieving "filial maturity"—may experience fewer tensions in that relationship (Fingerman, 1998b, 2001; Nydegger, 1991).

Turning Point: Caregiving

Caregiving is defined as any form of assistance provided by one party for another, but much of the literature on caregiving focuses primarily on providing care for individuals with chronic illness (Kahana, Biegel, & Wykle, 1994). The most common caregiving dyad in Western culture is a daughter providing care for her mother (Cicirelli, 1992). It is not surprising, then, that much of the research on mothers and their mid-life daughters is focused on the role reversal that occurs when daughters shift into the caregiver role for frail mothers. This reversal casts the late-life mothers (typically around the age of 70) into the role of cared for and nurtured—the daughtered (Fingerman, 1998a). For some women, the transition into the caretaker role is a "natural" course of events and perceived as just another phase of the life course, but others encounter this turning point with resistance. Diane felt that she "was never fully able to be a daughter, and now [that my mother is not physically strong] I really can't be. I want to, you

---

[16]I would like to thank Meredith for her sense of humor and good nature by allowing me to use this story here.

know, depend on her. But, she depends on me more than ever now. The rules really haven't changed much. I just have less choice now."

Transitioning into the role of caregiver is a crucial turning point for many older mother–mid-life daughter relationships. The dynamic tensions associated with that care are discussed in further detail throughout this chapter. Nonetheless, the caregiver role is not reserved exclusively for this point in time in maternal relationships. The onset of sudden illness or economic hardship for younger women may also stimulate the renegotiation of maternal relationships.

Mothers care for their daughters from infancy throughout the life span. Many mothers perceive this life-long provision of care as integral to their relationship with their daughters (Ruddick, 1989). Fingerman (2001) pointed out that both mothers and daughters derive joy from providing care across the generations. She argued that this care strengthens bonds that link families together.

Katrina, Kelly, and Kendra had their fair share of contending with illness. As each challenge was presented, these women joined forces to assist with caregiving. Despite the dynamic tension between resentment and forgiveness that was consistently being negotiated by Katrina and Kelly, Katrina willingly assisted Kelly when she battled cancer in her early 30s. Katrina shared the following account: "Kelly's husband was on the way out at that time. He showed his true colors through her illness because he was not supportive. So, I took her for treatments and stuff, and I also took her to the [regional] clinic to get a second opinion. We kind of put down our boxing gloves and dealt with each other a bit differently during that time [in her life]" (Katrina, Family #2).

Then Kendra's son was born with severe health problems. This event required Katrina and Kelly to join forces across generations to provide assistance to Kendra:

> I think [Kelly's illness] made us real close. We're kind of like, maybe all families are, but we're all there for any emergency. When [Kendra's son] was born, that was another thing that definitely brought us closer. It was like we had to work together and it was the first time that I felt that Kelly said to me "I need your help" and didn't want to shut me out. She really clearly said to me that we don't have to do it separately, and that sort of thing. (Katrina, Family #2)

Caring for children may, for some, seem like an extension of basic mothering. However, when relationships are strained, the care may prove to be healing for both the illness and the relationship.

Granddaughters also provided care for their grandmothers. Caretaking tasks typically fell into the domain of "daughter's work." However, granddaughters pitched in and helped when necessary. The responsibility for the care of grandmothers fell onto granddaughters' shoulders when the relationship between mother and grandmother was strained or if the mother was emotionally unavailable to provide care for her own mother. Scout often helped her grandmother as much as possible because it was getting increasingly difficult for her grandmother to do things on her own. Scout said, "My mom gets irritated with her 'cause she thinks she does stuff for attention, but I don't mind [helping out]."

Realizing that grandmothers would not "always be there" seemed to forge new connections and new appreciation for the intimacies shared between younger and older women. In addition, for some—like Sam—who experienced distance in their relationship with their grandmothers, a grandmother's illness may create changes in the basic definition of that relationship. One day, Sam shared the following as we were planting flowers in her garden. Sprinkling mulch over the bulbs she had just planted, she admitted, "I always thought of my Grandma [Sylvia] as our rich aunt. Never really as a grandmother, 'til now that she's old and she's sickly and she needs us. Now she's my grandmother. But when she was running around and being social and stuff, like, she never seemed like a grandmother to me" (Family #1).

Grandmothers and Granddaughters. Grandmothers and granddaughters in this study exhibited relatively stable relationships across time, tending to adjust somewhat seamlessly to gradual changes that occurred rather than experience pivotal turning points that required substantive recalibration of the relationship. The birth of a granddaughter initiated the relationship, family illnesses or crises often brought them closer, developmental milestones were observed from afar, emotional/instrumental/financial support typically flowed from the grandmother to the granddaughter with gradual changes occurring that led toward a more egalitarian exchange of support occurring as the granddaughters aged. Grandmothers would require more support from their granddaughters if their own daughters were unwilling or unavailable to provide that support. Still, daughters, rather than granddaughters, were the ones expected to provide the support for their own mothers.

In these relationships, stability did not necessarily equate with harmony. For example, Sam and Sylvia reported that their relationship had remained relatively stable across the years, but this stability was reflected in a constant and familiar pattern of respectful contact, if not emotional closeness. Both Sam and her grandmother recalled a nurturing relationship when Sam was an infant and toddler, but as Sam matured this relationship became more distant as each woman focused much of her attention on the maintenance of her own mother–daughter relationship.

Events that provided catalysts for renegotiation of the relationship between mothers and daughters did not seem to have the same effect on grandmother–granddaughter relationships. As Rowena pointed out, those women who share the space in between grandmothers and granddaughters provide a buffer in the grandmother–granddaughter relationship so that "each little thing doesn't become defining." Many mothers, on the other hand, admitted that their daughters defined them at least partly as women. Katrina provided insight when she pointed out, "I am not my granddaughter, so I can just enjoy her."

The mother–daughter relationships in Elkwood presented a range of experiences. All mothers reported that their daughters were welcomed, cherished, and wanted pregnancies even if they were not necessarily planned. With the exception of Kelly and Kendra, mothers provided physical care and assumed the primary responsibility for their daughters' socialization. Mothers and daughters in Families #1, #2, and #6, along with Charlotte and Becky in Family #5, represented relationships with the most instability and erratic change in their relationships over the life course. Generally, however, even after substantive changes these women remained emotionally connected.

CONNECTION-SEPARATION

… the daughter is for the mother
at once her double and another person.
—(Simone de Beauvoir, (1965, p. 56)

Scholars who study maternal relationships often claim the essential task of daughters is to form a unique identity separate and distinct from that of their mother (Cooley, 2000). As discussed in chapter 2, issues of integration and fears of "becoming just like my mother" are central to understanding the mother–daughter relationship and permeate research and popular accounts.[17] In the stage play titled *Two of Me*, a central character whines:

> I don't want to be like my mother, I just want to be liked *by* her. My mother was so obsessive … with me … with the house … with everything. She even ironed the sheets! I always had to clean up the slightest mess. Always had to floss in between my braces and wash my face with Noxema, couldn't eat chocolate (makes you break out, ya know). I was really a sight then. Thick glasses, big braces, skinny, no makeup. No chocolate! They even called me "Mona-ugliness" at school. I was the new kid. We moved out here from Harvey, that's in Illinois, you know. Junior high can be hell when you're new and ugly. But my friend Carla never seemed to notice. She fixed me up right away … makeup lessons … new hairdo … tight cut-offs. She even convinced me that it was okay to cross a forbidden street to cruise through the mall …. That most likely, my mother wasn't in the bushes watching. Ah … such liberation. Of course, my Mom started calling me a slut … and you know I showed her. Got myself a Mexican boyfriend … and then, pretty soon, I got myself a miscarriage. [Pause] It's funny how things turn out. I'm grown up now, have my

---

[17]See the film or read the book *How to Make an American Quilt* by Otto Whitney for an illustration of the classic struggle between integration and individuation.

own apartment ... am really set in my ways. [*Smiles*] I ran into Carla again the other day and we laughed and we talked and she said, "It's okay, at least YOU don't iron your sheets." ... *But I do!!* (Blaine, 1990)

Aragno (1998) also dramatically illustrated the need of her daughter to differentiate herself from her with the account of the girl flinging herself on the floor and issuing the battle cry, "Die so that I may live!"

This is, of course, not news. Fingerman (2001) reported that in her sample the "strongest mother–daughter ties in late life seem to involve a careful balance of positive and negative feelings, of connection and autonomy ... the balancing act in this tie involves a careful mix of closeness and distance" (p. 50). Greek myths such as such as the story of Persephone and Demeter warns of too much about the closeness between mothers and daughters, offering cautionary tales about mother–daughter kinship (Levinson, 1992). Literature has historically admonished women not to give into the pull of mothers' influence and has encouraged women to carve out their own unique identity separate from that of their mother. An identity is what makes one uniquely individual, a collective set of characteristics by which a person is recognizable or known. Who are we as women, separate from our mothers? For many women, using mother and grandmother as referents is actually part of the process of carving out a unique identity. As Edelman (2000) wrote, both grandmother and mother "define the terms *mother, daughter,* and *woman* for me" (p. 10).

Connection-separation is considered one of the hallmark dialectics of all personal relationships—not just maternal relationships—because, by definition, relationship implies interconnectedness. Thus, viewing the tension inherent in this dialectic from a relational framework, it is not so much managing the tension between "me" and "her," but rather managing the balance between "me" and "we."

Connection

In most modernist identity scholarship, personal and relational identities are presented as separate. *Personal identity* is defined as the process and manner in which individuals define themselves and understand their selfhood—who "I" am (Adams & Marshall, 1996; Archer, 1994; Jackson, 1999). *Relational identity* is defined as the process and manner in which relational partners define themselves in relation to each other and understand their unique relational qualities—who "we" are (Acitelli, Rogers, & Knee, 1999; Wilmot, 1995; Wood, 2000). A relational identity is suprapersonal; it transcends the two individuals involved. Personal identity theorists have historically focused on adolescent individuation from parental figures, arguing that until separation from parents is truly resolved, and the "I" becomes more important than the "we," one may never become an individuated, autonomous individual (Surrey, 1993).

Over the past decade, however, scholarship has begun to acknowledge the interdependence of the construction of a new story, the development of individuality *within* the context of relationships (Adams & Marshall, 1996; Hecht, Collier, & Ribeau, 1993; Wilmot, 1995). This paradigm shift is critical when considering its application to understanding mother–daughter relationships. Much of the past identity and mother–daughter relational research has been limited to Western and European cultures, where the ideology of individualism and autonomy is stressed (Gergen, 1991; Gilani, 1999). Wilmot (1995) pointed out that as we broach the 21st century, identity theorists are moving away from the paradigm in which individuals are cast as islands loosely connected by relational threads toward a paradigm of the embedded self, or self in relation. Embedded selves are cocreated within the context of relationships. This is critical to understanding the relational ties among grandmothers, mothers, and daughters.

Within this new relational paradigm, the struggle to manage the dialectical tensions of differentiation and connectedness—differentiating from mother while staying emotionally connected to her—is a life-long process that is never wholly resolved. This developmental picture depicts healthy autonomy and elaboration of self while remaining in connection with relational partners (Cooley, 2000; Guisinger & Blatt, 1994; Jordan, 1993; van Mens-Verhulst et al., 1993).

Autonomy is often characterized as this isolated entity, casting the autonomous individual into the role of a person who is self-governing and not subject to the control of others. However, within a relational paradigm, *autonomy* refers to *the ability to assert individuality within the context of relationship* "in reference to relational obligations, control attempts, rules, or emotional processes" (Peterson, Madden-Derdich, & Leonard, 2000, p. 194). There is emotional, behavioral, and value autonomy. *Emotional autonomy* refers to governing one's own feeling separate from others, *behavioral autonomy* refers to governing one's own personal conduct and behavior, and *value autonomy* refers to making judgments and choices about one's own personal belief system (Peterson et al., 2000). Hence, instead of viewing separation from mother as a daughter's fundamental developmental goal, the relational paradigm argues that separation and connection are *both* basic to the mother–daughter relationship. The goal is not to achieve total separation, but instead to manage the dynamic tension between these seemingly contradictory needs. The trick, however, is to move toward an autonomous self while *remaining connected* to the relational partner.

The desire to separate oneself from one's mother does not resolve itself once a daughter develops into adulthood. In fact, as my experiences in Elkwood demonstrated, there was a constant movement between both connection and separation across the life span.

For some of the women I worked with, the stability of that "we-ness" provides solace. Morgan, for example, shared the following insight: "I don't know how, but sometimes we both 'just know' how the other feels. When to stay away, when to comfort, even when to confront. This telepathic sensing of her really has established a true sense of uniqueness in our relationship" (Morgan, Family #6). Lois echoed a similar message: "We have a special bond between us, and I have it also with my mother, and she had it with her mother. We like and respect each other."

Some of these women appropriated their own daughters in order to heighten their relational connection. McMahon (1995) called this "the appropriation of others into the sacred realm of the self" (p. 21). *Appropriation* refers to taking possession of or making use of something exclusively for oneself (*American Heritage Dictionary of the English Language*, 2000). McMahon argued that *propriation* is a neglected construct in relationship research and is an important process because it suggests that mothers may appropriate daughters as constitutive of self. Through this process, the daughter becomes sacred "through [her] association with self " (McMahon, 1995, p. 22).

While folding laundry one day with Meredith, we talked about her relationship with Morgan. She remarked, "When I had her, I found me." This sense of completing oneself as a woman was mentioned only when discussing the birth of a daughter, rather than when discussing the births of sons. "I know it's probably not healthy," Katrina remarked, "but I judge myself by how good she has turned out. I live vicariously through her sometimes. To be honest, I am praised for her successes and judged by her failures. It really is, and I'm not kidding, it's like [my daughters] are an extension of me." This entangled sense of identity was validated in the minds of many of the daughters. Sam indicated, "Mom was Amy Vanderbilt reincarnated, or at least she wanted to be. It made her look good when we were good. So, *I* was good to make *her* look good."

All daughters pointed to the central importance of her mother in her life. Although Scout was embarrassed when telling this story, the following nicely illustrates a daughter's desire for connectedness with her mother:

> I know it's silly, but I thought I was adopted for about 2 years when I was little. From the time I was … uh … 4, I think, to when I was 6 years old. [*Smiles*] My older sisters told me when I was 4 that my parents found me in the gutter with the rats eating my toes and that my parents felt sorry for me so they took me in. My sisters warned me that if I ever acted up that they would send me back to the gutter. [*Laughter*] I didn't say I was a smart kid. Just impressionable! My parents had a copy print of the *Mona Lisa* on their wall and my oldest sister told me that was my real mother. I would sit up nights looking at her and one day I took a chair over to the print and I kissed her smooth cheek. It wasn't until my father saw me staring at the print one day that he asked me why I kept looking at it and I told him. He laughed and cleared up the misconception. [*Sigh*]. That night as my mother slept on the sofa I crept to her side, kissed *her* smooth cheek, and it smelled of rose water. I will never forget that smell or that moment of absolute love. (Scout, Family #6)

Some daughters expressed pride in their physical similarities and identification with their mothers and grandmothers. Identification is a means of connecting yourself with another person by attributing to self the characteristics of the other person. Some of the women shared:

> I think I am like my Mom. She's always there for people even when they're not there for her you know, like, someone to talk to and a good friend and in that way I think I'm like her. I see myself as like her. (Linda, Family #5)

> My mother was sort of regimented, you know, and always took vitamins, and did all the right things. I mean, it was sort of unreal, you know, when you look back. But, she always looked very nice. And I just thought, to do that at almost 90. I'm going to, and hopefully I have. I always try to look fairly nice like she did. To present a nice picture. (Gina, Family #3)

> Whenever I went to my grandmother's house, her sheets were starched and ironed. And it felt good. My mother does that too. I'm not that good. My mother–in-law is here now, and like I have flowers in her room, and when my father-in-law comes to see us, I put an ash tray and candles and stuff in his room. And then I always [get] things you pick up for free and keep in a basket, so when guests come, you've got it for them. I want to be like my mother in that regard. I *am* like her in that regard. (Barb, Family #4)

In addition to seeing self as connected to mother or daughter through common characteristics, identification also requires a belief that other people likewise acknowledged the commonalities. Georgie said, "… anywhere I go with like my mom and my grandma, and my aunt as well, I mean, people stop us and ask us oh, are you related, and you look alike and you're all so, you know, nice looking, and we've been told that for years and years. So it's made me feel really good, actually" (Family #3).

Much of the time women were astutely aware of the characteristics they shared with their mothers, yet sometimes they were unaware of other connections that repeated across generations. One morning I drove with Becky to drop Linda off at her job as a summer camp counselor for mentally challenged teens. The following conversation occurred en route:

> Becky said, "You know, as a teenager I volunteered in a residential center for the mentally retarded. So did your grandmother. Back then they called them institutions and they were awful, just awful."
>
> "You did not!" exclaimed Linda.
>
> Nonplussed, Becky continued, "Yes, I did."
>
> "Then how come I never heard about it?" asked Linda.
>
> "I don't know, I hadn't really thought about it until now," replied Becky.
>
> "Wow. I didn't know that," Linda announced and then turned to me, "That's kind of bizarre, isn't it? I'm thinking of working with the homeless or mentally chal-

lenged as my career and I didn't even know both my mom and grandmom did the same thing."

She sat pensively for a moment, then declared "Awesome."

Other family members were also quick to note similarities among the women in their family across generational boundaries. Many men admitted that their wives were "scarily" like their mothers-in-law. Some interpreted this similarity in a positive fashion and others in a negative fashion. In fact, many daughters who valued the emotional connection they had with their mothers and grandmothers sought to separate themselves from identifying with and having others identify them too closely with their mothers.

Clearly seeking to separate her own identity from that of her mother, Sam enacted the following scene when she and I were shopping at the grocery store. Another shopper waved hello to Sam and said, "Hello Diane." Sam waved hello and walked past the person. Her face flushed and her lips pressed tightly together.

She complained, "I hate that."

"Hmmm," I eloquently responded.

"That happens all the time and I hate it."

"What does?"

"I am just a clone of my mother. If they don't think I'm her it's always like 'You're Diane's daughter.' Yes I am …. 'I can't remember your name.' So I came up with a response, 'Yes I am, and you know I just get so excited how much I look like my mother because I was adopted and I think they did such a good job matching us together.' And most people go, 'No you're not!' So that's what I tell people all the time when they say you look so much like you mother. Isn't that great?"

In the struggle to define self, some women felt they had to differentiate themselves from their mother. Kelly provided the following insight: "I look like my mom. I think that's another reason for not wanting to be like her; a lot of times people don't want to be who everybody associates them with."

Grandmothers and granddaughters found that establishing a unique identity while staying connected in relationship to mothers was less important than it was for mothers and daughters. Even into daughters' mid-life, the tension between mother–daughter connection and separation was palpably taut, whereas grandmothers and granddaughters appeared to negotiate a slacker tension early on in their relationship.

Grandmother–Granddaughter Connection.   Most grandmothers and granddaughters did not reflect the "You are me" identification that characterized some mother–daughter relationships. Rather, grandmothers' identification with granddaughters was a more loosely tethered connection of "You came from me" and *I cannot wait to see where you are going.* According to Bosak (2000), connections across generations between grandmothers and granddaughters are far less psychologically complex than are mother–daughter relationships, and grandmother–granddaughter relationships connect grandmothers to the flow of life, providing a legacy. As Katrina pointed out, "Mothering is intense, like being too close to the trees and not seeing the forest … being a grandmother is … very relaxed."

The grandmothers in this study were unified in their expression that grandmothering is more relaxing than mothering because grandmothers do not have the primary responsibility for rearing the child on a day-to-day basis. Grandmothers and granddaughters did not perceive this lessened responsibility as impeding their relational connection—it merely loosened the connections to a more comfortable level. Although some mothers and daughters might become enmeshed with each other, most grandmothers and granddaughters tended to get merely entangled (Edelman, 2000). Generally, granddaughters did not have to struggle for their independence from grandma because they already had it!

Granddaughters expressed appreciation that their grandmothers were there for them, often in ways that their mothers could not be. Morgan said that her grandmother "gave me the unconditional love that I needed all my life. She accepted me just like I was and loved me even if she thought my choices were wrong." Diane also stated that her maternal grandmother was the one who "loved me no matter what and was the one who provided support."

Grandmothers sometimes arranged activities to do with their granddaughters in order to nurture the relationship. For example, Lois took her granddaughter on a special trip with her each year; Rowena and Georgie lunched daily together, even when Gina could not join them; and Meredith took Scout on a shopping expedition once per year that they designated as "their time." Katrina indicated that "I can devote more quality time to [my grandchildren and great grandchildren] since I only have them for a certain amount of time. So, I try and make it special." Edelman (2000) argued that grandmothers typically aren't involved in the "two-steps-forward, one-step-back jig" that mothers and daughters dance (p. 84). Therefore, the grandmother–granddaughter relationship usually lacks the strong sense of ambivalence and power struggles that often occur between mothers and daughters.

The connection between grandmothers and granddaughters, however, seemed to be moderated by the mother in between. Sometimes this moderating effect strengthened the bonds between grandmother and granddaughter. For example, Morgan explained, "My mother wasn't always very approachable. So, I liked just spending time with my grandmother, not even saying anything, just being together." Diane also experienced a strong bond with her grandmother in reaction to a mother whom she perceived as distant: "I didn't like the way that my mother treated my grandmother. She was not very nice to her. She demanded a lot from her, but I never saw her give a lot, and that always bothered me, so I was very protective of grandma. So, we got to be very close."

Mothers could also actively discourage a connection between grandmothers and granddaughters. During the time when Kelly was redefining her relationship with Kendra as she grew into adulthood, Kelly asked Kendra to "stay away" from Katrina so that Katrina did not influence their developing relationship. Katrina maintained a loose connection with Kendra during that time, whereas Kelly and Kendra tethered themselves more closely. Moreover, mothers would inadvertently affect the connection between grandmother and granddaughter when voicing their own unresolved conflicts with their mother. Witnessing their mothers' continued struggle for independence from grandma seemed to have an effect on the grandmother–granddaughter relationship. Sam admitted that, "I felt more intimidated by my grandmother than loved. Since my mom was scared of her ... or at least that is how I saw it ... kinda bullied by her ... I never made any effort on my own to develop a relationship."

At times, the grandmother's or granddaughter's own behavior led to the loosely defined connections between grandmother and granddaughter. Linda indicated that although she loved her grandmother "because she is [my] grandmother" she found her grandmother's treatment of her own mother "unfair." At times she did not think it was worth the effort to "keep my grandmother happy, 'cause she is not going to be [happy]." Sylvia argued that although she, too, loved her granddaughter, Sam's mistakes and choices had created a distance between them, weakening the already loose connection.

Generally, however, the grandmothers of Elkwood provided nurturance, support, someone to share activities with, and unconditional love for their granddaughters. Granddaughters also provided reciprocal support, someone to share activities with, and unconditional love for their grandmothers. Although granddaughters provided grandmothers with less nurturance than grandmothers provided them, in the end they seemed to provide more hope. As Morgan said, "Your children are perfect, but your grandchildren are perfection."

Separation

Although the connections among grandmothers, mothers, and daughters can be especially entangled, family research over the past several decades has discovered that to grow into emotionally healthy women, females must come to terms with their mothers and move toward individuation and autonomy even as they remain emotionally connected to their mothers. As indicated in earlier chapters, historically the field of psychology has cast daughters' movement toward individuation as a process occurring during adolescent development. Nonetheless, these data support the claim that managing the dynamic tensions between connection and separation is a life-long relational issue, never to be actually resolved.

From the theoretical perspective of dialectics we might predict that for young women such as Linda and Scout, a dominant force in the relationship might be to separate from their mothers and strike out to carve unique identities in the world. However, we might also predict separation as a dominant force for mothers in mid-life as they strive to define their own identity apart from their adult children. La Sorsa and Fodor (1990) argued that mid-life mothers age 34–55 with young adult daughters are confronting a crisis of both separation and self-definition. These scholars suggested that mid-life mothers may be experiencing issues of aging, mortality, an end to fertility, and asking themselves this question: Beyond mothering, who am I?

This Elkwood data revealed that for mid-life mothers the struggle to separate occurred across multiple domains. Mothers reported seeking emotional connection with daughters far into mid- and late life. Although most women reported a dominant tension toward emotional connection rather than emotional autonomy, they also revealed a need to pull away from their maternal influences specific to values and behaviors. Sam, for example, was transitioning into mid-life during the time of this study. The following interview excerpt illustrates how, although remaining emotionally connected to her mother, she also actively considered differentiating from her mother in terms of values and behaviors:

> You know, I love her dearly but she drives me nuts. I mean, none of your furniture is going to come visit you in your grave. It's people. They won't say, "Oh, gee she was a good person to let me sit on the good couch" or "She wiped her shoes before she came onto my floor," people are going to come [to my funeral] because "She was really neat, she was fun, she cared about us." That's what I want when I die. What would somebody put on my headstone … "She was a great housewife, or she was a good friend?" I want to be a good friend; I don't want to be [a] housewife. I don't want to be Miss Clean and Miss Perfect; I just want to be a good friend. And be a good wife, good mother, and good sister. (Family #1)

Analyses of these women's experiences reveal two different interpretations of a woman's differentiation—as direct retaliation against her relational partner or as a normal process of establishing a unique personal identity. These contrasting interpretations are part of a larger, more crucial pattern that emerged in these data. The patterns of connections linking these women seemed to be divided into two distinct groupings: (a) those that were so extreme in cohesion—*enmeshed*—that they perceived the process of differentiation as threatening to the relationship, and (b) those that were moderate in cohesion—*connected*—and perceived the process of differentiation as a normal one that offered no particular threat to the relationship.

Enmeshment

Relational cohesion is viewed as a dimension on a continuum from enmeshed (i.e., a high degree of connectedness with demands for consensus and loyalty, and members are expected to think and act alike) to disengagement (i.e., a low degree of connectedness; members are highly independent, emotionally and/or physically separate; and members have little effect on one another; Olson, Sprenkle, & Russell, 1979). In the general population, most relationships fall somewhere along this continuum. Based on the assessments conducted in this study, I established that 8 of the 18 mother–adult daughter relationships as enmeshed, and I list these in Table 4.2. As described previously, I focused my fieldwork on assessing relational cohesion for several weeks. Based on observational coding using *a priori* categories developed by Olson (1993) and by conducting individual interviews, I categorized all mother–daughter and grandmother–granddaughter relationships into the following two categories of relational cohesion: enmeshed and connected.[18]

TABLE 4.2
Families, by Cohesion and Problem Behaviors

Family	Relationship	Cohesion	Problem Behavior
Family #1	Sylvia–Diane	Enmeshed	Yes
Family #1	Diane–Sam	Enmeshed	Yes
Family #1	Sylvia–Sam	Enmeshed	Yes
Family #2	Katrina–Kelly	Enmeshed	Yes
Family #2	Kelly–Kendra	Enmeshed	Yes
Family #2	Katrina–Kendra	Connected	No
Family #3	Rowena–Gina	Connected	No
Family #3	Gina–Georgie	Connected	No
Family #3	Rowena–Georgie	Connected	No
Family #4	Lois–Barb	Connected	No
Family #4	Barb–Tabitha	Connected	No
Family #4	Lois–Tabitha	Connected	No
Family #5	Charlotte–Becky	Connected/Enmeshed	No
Family #5	Becky–Linda	Connected	No
Family #5	Charlotte–Linda	Connected	No
Family #6	Meredith–Morgan	Enmeshed	Yes
Family #6	Morgan–Scout	Enmeshed	Yes
Family #6	Meredith–Scout	Enmeshed	Yes

[18]I suspect that none of the relationships emerged as disengaged or separated by virtue of the participant selection criteria. This finding, thus, served to validate the sample characteristics.

The connected relationships in this sample were characterized by their emotional closeness along with their loyalty expectations for members. These families also tolerated moderate levels of emotional distance. Involvement in each other's lives was encouraged and togetherness was emphasized over separateness, yet personal distance was respected with a demonstration of distinct generational boundaries. Time together and shared activities were important in these relationships, but time alone was permitted. Families #3, #4, and generally #5 were interpreted as connected relationships. Becky and Linda's and Charlotte and Linda's relationships appeared to be connected. My sense of Charlotte and Becky's relationship was that it navigated a precarious balance between enmeshment and connectedness. Charlotte demanded very high involvement from Becky, requiring loyalty and control. Although Becky admitted she complied in her younger years, she said that she was engaged in ongoing attempts to establish discrete boundaries in her relationship with her mother. Becky explained, "At this point in my life I have to live my own life and not live the life that she expects of me." Becky often talked to "herself" (although I was present), mentally validating her own strength in sustaining distance between her mother's expectations for connectedness and her own. I heard her mutter on several occasions, "What do I need?" She said, "I was always taught that it was selfish to think of myself, [that I should be] selfless for the good of the family. But, I'm getting over it—slowly but surely!"

The enmeshed relationships in Families #1, 2, and 6 were characterized by an extreme emotional closeness, an emotional fusion—like two candles melting together. Loyalty was demanded, high involvement and participation were expected, and separateness was generally not tolerated. In these relationships there was a general lack of boundaries or extremely permeable boundaries, in which togetherness dominated and joint activities were mandated.

Boundary management research (Cloud & Townsend, 2002; Petronio, 2000) suggests that establishing boundaries in a parent–child relationship is central to the process of individuation. Nonetheless, among those in enmeshed relationships, boundaries remained unclear through mid- and later life. Katrina (Family #2) indicated an intergenerational perpetuation of this enmeshment when she remarked that her mother "always kept us close and very obligated to her and each other. It's a way of keeping us connected even as we got older. I guess I have my resentment and so forth, but I'm too old to fight it out." Interestingly, Kelly indicated that her mother created a similar climate in their relationship and that she intended to perpetuate this with her own daughters. She said, "[My mother] and I have our differences, that's for sure. But it's important to her and to me that we keep family together. That is probably my number one goal in life. If I could manipulate it, then I would. If I could, I'd use guilt, I'd probably use anything to keep my kids close."

According to Diane (Family #1), "I could not go away anywhere without [my mother] calling me back. It's still like that. Whenever I had a chance to go away for a rest something would happen, she'd get sick and need me ... *some-*

thing to make me come running back to her." Her daughter, Sam, related similar experiences with her own daughter:

> [My daughter] wants it to be just her and me. She's never made any qualms about that is what she wants. If there's anything she could change, it's that I never married again, never had any more kids, it's just the two of us. To this day, I mean, as of last year she told this to her therapist. She never even thought it sounded wrong, or selfish. She just wants to wish everything out of existence and just keep the two of us. (Family #1)

> I always took [my daughter's] suicide attempts seriously and I was always upset, but this is the reaction she wanted. She wanted to get at me through them. When do you get to the point when you stop letting it manipulate you? I've never gotten to that point, but I'm not manipulated as frequently. (Sam, Family #1)

Sam admitted that she also contributed to keeping her relationship with her daughter enmeshed. In a conversation one day among Sam, her sister, and me, we sipped hot cocoa and discussed this issue of maternal domination. Sam issued the following proclamation:

> [My daughter's] and my relationship is good now, but we went through a lot. I never really did want to hear what she has to say. But, with her it's like, yeah, now I do. 'Cause I think of what we've gone through together, [this] has made me decide that I can either stop the pattern of [maternal] control that happens in our family, wanting her to do what I want, and be how I want her to be, have her be around home. You know, this *is* what I would like. But, now I want her to do whatever she wants to do, her choice. Nope, I don't care any more. (Sam, Family #1)

With this kind of enmeshment, relational identities overwhelmed and sometimes subsumed individual identities. These enmeshed relationships heightened the emphasis on the "two of me" phenomenon in which the two identities were linked together with few boundaries, each woman unclear about where one person ended and the other began. At times, the relational identity overwhelmed the individual identity, and instead of too much self-concern there was too little. Morgan believed that by emphasizing emotional fusion and loyalty:

> You become focused all the time on keeping everyone else happy. Because we need approval and acceptance from the other [family members], we can manipulate and control external things to keep them happy or whatever. But when it comes to ourselves, what we're doing, we just say it's not important. Losing who we are and not taking care of ourselves, because that is somehow not as important. (Morgan, Family #6)

Sam (Family #1) perceived that her mother's identity was closely tied to her own children's identities. She stated, "My mom never felt she was a good enough parent or did good enough career-wise, she fell short. So, she lives through [her children] and she gets upset if you aren't up to snuff to her standards. God, she gets upset if you aren't her [*chuckle*]." Kelly, in Family #2, seemed resigned to but frustrated by her enmeshment with her mother. She sighed, "It's so annoying. I'm 37 years old and I've never really liked myself. I try to be who she wants me to be, someone that's not me, but usually that's still not good enough for her [Katrina]. It gets tiring."

One day I walked in on Morgan (Family #6) as she was going through Scout's closet and pulling out clothes and matching them. Scout was sitting on the bed and looking sullen. Morgan exclaimed, "I'm matching clothes for her since she doesn't seem to know how to get an outfit that looks decent." She looked up, saw me glancing at Scout, and added, "I want her to be accepted. So I'm just helping out." I asked her later if she thought that Scout was irritated at her offer of help and she replied, "Maybe. You know, maybe her friends should have helped her, and not me. You know, that's what I think. Maybe it might not have been my job. Oh well." When chatting about this later with Scout, she indeed did not believe it was her mother's "place" to be matching her outfits for her at the age of 18. She complained that her mother had a tendency to "make my business hers."

Neimeyer and Neimeyer (1985) argued that scholars have not systematically examined all the forms of too much "we-ness." Since the time of their study, there still has not been much research attention to this relational area. Identity researchers come closest to exploring this relational phenomenon. Interactionists argue that personal identities are formed within relationships and cannot be extricated from the dynamic relational interactions that serve to construct self. Thus, when enmeshment occurs, the lines between self and other are blurred and relational interactions emerge as vital to the development of self. In Elkwood, the messages exchanged in the enmeshed relationships heavily influenced members' personal identities. In these enmeshed relationships, criticism—even mild criticism, such as "She doesn't seem to know how to get an outfit that looks decent"—issued a particularly nasty bite that was more apt to be integrated into self than in the nonenmeshed relationships. Women in nonenmeshed relationships tended to toss off maternal criticism with a "She's having a bad day" look or comment, whereas women in the enmeshed relationships would absorb the comment and personalize it.

Identity management was also particularly important among the women in enmeshed relationships. Self-presentation of identity is important to all individuals but became especially essential in the maintenance of these enmeshed relationships. Because the line between "we" and "me" was so fragile in these dyads, members would often perceive their partner's behavior as directly threatening to their own face.

On a Sunday afternoon, while walking in a shopping mall, Scout whispered to me that her mother did not want her pushing the stroller in which my infant son rode while we were walking. Morgan apparently believed other people at the mall would suspect the infant was Scout's. Scout walked back to her mother and challenged, "Who cares? I don't know any of these people." Her mother replied, "But, I do! They know me because I'm on the radio" (a Christian radio talk show). Scout responded, "But they don't know *me*." She then proceeded to take the stroller from me and push it down the hall and her mother refused to speak to her for at least 3 hours. Consequences occurred when there were negative evaluations of performances of self. Consequences were most likely to be administered by the older woman in the relationship (e.g., mother or grandmother); however, there were instances when the younger women meted out consequences to their mothers or grandmothers. In an interesting comparison across relational type (enmeshed/connected), Linda, Scout, and I were seated in a restaurant when their mothers—Becky and Morgan—entered the establishment to join us for lunch. The scene played out in the following fashion:

> Both mothers wore short skirts with tailored blouses and entered the room giggling about something. Upon seeing her mother, Scout placed her face in her hands groaning, "Oh man."
>
> Linda asked, "What?"
>
> Scout proceeded to shake her head and whispered, "My mother thinks she's 16. She is so embarrassing."
>
> Linda looked at her own mother, who was dressed and was behaving in the same way as Morgan. She smiled, shrugged her shoulders, and laughed, "Whatever. I think it makes them feel young to dress like that. But it doesn't really embarrass me, you know."
>
> When Morgan sat down, Scout shot her mother a look of disgust, shook her head, and sighed her disapproval with an exasperated, "Oh mother."

Women in the enmeshed maternal relationships often "performed" to garner the approval of their maternal relational partners, whereas women in connected relationships did not necessarily view partners' performances as reflecting on them personally. Consequences also tended to be harshest when there were negative evaluations of the younger women's performances. Whether a woman was a young adult or middle aged, if she chose to express disapproval of her mother or grandmother, she typically did so in fashion that reduced the intensity of her critique (e.g., using disclaimers such as "It's not that important, but ..."). Older women, on occasion, went for broke when meting out consequences. I witnessed several incidents in which a mother would verbally assault her adult daughter or granddaughter, issuing phrases that included, "You ignorant bitch," "You are a loser you know," and "I don't know you, I don't care to know you right now."

Noller and Fitzpatrick (1993) argued that true intimacy is spontaneous, in which one moves out of performance mode (performing for, enacting a role) and into intimate mode where a person feels comfortable enough to be him- or her-self. In these enmeshed relationships, women were frequently in performance mode. Moreover, that performance, as Kelly pointed out, "better be a good one and one she approves of or you're gonna pay."

Grandmothers and Granddaughters in Connection. Grandmothers and granddaughters in Families #1 and 6 developed grandmother–granddaughter relationships interpreted as enmeshed. Generally, the older woman perceived the enmeshed nature of the relationship as comforting and took pride in the idea that she and her granddaughter were extremely close. The younger woman would then find comfort and security in the love of her grandmother and seemed to perceive the grandmother–granddaughter relationship as protecting her from the overwhelming nature of her relationship with her mother. Never-theless, at times, women such as Sam, Kendra, and Scout expressed their desire for their grandmother to be a little less controlling over their lives and respect them more as an individual.

As indicated earlier in this chapter, cohesion levels affected the grand-mother–granddaughter relationship depending on how daughters viewed *their mother's* management of enmeshment with their grandmother. For those women whose mothers were in enmeshed relationships with their grandmoth-ers (i.e., Sam, Kendra, & Scout), they perceived themselves to be somehow dis-loyal to their grandmothers if they attempted to establish relational boundaries in the grandmother–granddaughter relationship. Sam (Family #1) argued that "[Establishing boundaries between me and my grandmother] is just not done. She would feel rejected." She added, "I see how it is with my mom and her. Every time my mother tries to separate away from her just a little bit, my grandma makes a huge deal about it." Scout (Family #6) admitted that her grandmother was "controlling," yet she attributed this to her grandmother being "concerned" for her grandchildren. Scout did wish, however, that her grandmother would "mind her own business" more often. Morgan's understanding of this differed a bit, and she expressed this in the following interview excerpt: "[Meredith] is try-ing to control [her grandchildren's] life. She's trying to fix their lives. It's like she knows there's not a whole lot she can do for her adult children, even though she still wants to manipulate. She's going to that next generation, she feels a pur-pose in life. She messed up the first time, now she's got a second chance" (Mor-gan, Family #6).

In this kind of research, negative cases are of interest because they do not fit the observed patterns. I considered Katrina and Kendra's grandmother–grand-daughter relationship to be a negative case. In contrast to Families #1 and #6, in which enmeshed relationships crossed generational boundaries, the en-meshed relationship between Katrina and Kelly did *not* characterize the grand-mother–granddaughter relationship. In fact, Katrina expressed great pride in Kendra as a woman and encouraged moderate emotional distance and re-spected generational boundaries. Katrina pointed out that, "I had my time mothering her and now it's Kelly's turn. I like being the grandmother. I have the fun but not the worry. I'm on to other things."

Differentiation as a Connection-Separation Management Process

A relational framework indicates that mothers and daughters develop individual identities within the context of their relationship rather than in spite of the relationship. However, this framework does not really account for *how* women move toward an autonomous self while remaining connected to their maternal relational partner. Analysis of these data points toward *differentiation* as a key process by which women move toward this autonomous self, while remaining emotionally connected to the women in their lives. Moreover, these results suggest that the ways in which separation and connection are interpreted in their relational context is central to understanding this process.

Much theory makes the mistake of conceptualizing differentiation as the opposite force of emotional connection (e.g., a connection-differentiation dichotomy). However, I contend that differentiation is not the opposite force of connection, but instead is a higher-order process that serves to manage the inherent tension of the connection-separation dialectic.

Differentiation is a term derived from the field of biology and refers to the ways cells develop. At the onset of life, cells come from same material, but as they divide they begin to differentiate and take on unique properties—the greater the differentiation, the more adaptive the life form. Schnarch (1997) provided a cogent argument based on his years in clinical practice and building on the work of Bowen (1978) that suggested human differentiation results from how well one's parents and grandparents succeeded in becoming well-developed individuals in the context of emotional connection with their family.[19] In his work, he found that differentiation is a person's ability to manage the dynamic tensions between connection and separation by developing and maintaining a sense of self even when that person is emotionally or physically close to others—*especially* when the others are important to him or her. Differentiation is different from *individualism*, a term that emphasizes the self outside of one's connection to others. Differentiation is not a movement away from connection with others, but instead is the process of developing and maintaining yourself in the presence of persons important to you. In his clinical work, Schnarch found that differentiated persons possessed strong emotional bonds with others, but their connection was voluntary, not a connection maintained out of obligation or emotional fusion. Moreover, he argued that humans emerge from their family of origin at the level of differentiation their parents achieved, and that poorly differenti-

---

[19]As I was writing this section, I came upon a text written by Schnarch (1997) that echoed some of what I discovered during my time in Elkwood. Serendipity! This text addressed romantic relationships. However, Schnarch's arguments are parallel to mine and based on his years in clinical practice with couples. For those of you interested in the concept of relational differentiation, I encourage you to refer to that helpful text.

ated parents force their offspring into enmeshed relationships that inhibit their offspring from developing the ability to think, feel, and act for themselves. The women of Elkwood illustrated the intergenerational transmission of differentiation competence described by Schnarch (1997). Enmeshed maternal relationships were manifest across three generations in three poorly differentiated families (Families #1, 2, & 6). These women reported perceiving differentiation as threatening to the maternal relationship. In contrast, clinicians and scholars argue that enmeshed, poorly differentiated relationships are not a threat to the relationship, but instead are a threat to members' personal identity development. Much more information is needed to understand how enmeshed relationships affect healthy identity development of individual members.

Although an unexpected finding, how women in enmeshed and connected relationships uniquely experienced the process of differentiation led to a potentially new area of study. This next section discusses in more detail the complex ways women in both enmeshed and not-enmeshed maternal relationships experienced differentiation.

Differentiation as Experienced in Enmeshed Relationships. In the enmeshed maternal relationships, women's personal identities seemed constructed primarily out of a reflected sense of self, with each woman needing continual validation from the other woman to feel worthwhile. This was the case across the life span. Relational partners—typically the older women—would situate themselves as the mainline to the younger women's self-image. Daughters expressed dependency on their mothers (and sometimes grandmothers) for their affirmation, keeping daughters addicted to maternal approval.

Sam (Family #1) was aware of her dependence on her mother's approval and said that she was "trying to break out of the habit." Yet, in the following excerpts drawn from two separate interviews Sam illustrated dependence on maternal validation for a sense of self-worth:

> I'm like working out and she walks in. The first thing she says is, "Are you crying?" I'm like no, this is what I look like without a shower and makeup. This is a crying kind of look. This is what [my husband] sees every morning. "Oh," she says, "I wondered if you were trying a new makeup or something." It's like I don't like your hair like that, or I don't like your eyes like that. It's like even, it's either you're too heavy or you're too thin. It's not in between. (Sam, Family #1)

> Sam sat at the kitchen table. The children were at school and the dog was at the groomer. I had my tape recorder on and was playing with my son on the rug next to the table when Sam said to me, "I hate, I hate that stuff, ya know even though I try to keep myself up. I hate how I look 'cause I'm never, I'm never, you know, my hair's not ever thick enough, the right color, um, done right, you know, I'm never thin enough, pretty enough, you know, it just affects you."

> I looked at her and asked, "Enough according to your idea of what is enough or someone else's?"

Taking a sip of her cocoa, she replied, "My mom's, my grandmother's too." Looking at my son and me, she added, "But, it becomes mine, don't you see?" She added, "When I was experimenting with makeup, probably in junior high, and I put on blue mascara and went up to Grandma's, this was something I didn't really expect. But she called me a whore. It killed me. She said I looked like a whore, I acted like a whore, and to get home and scrub that makeup off my face. I remember coming down, um, to the house and crying to my mom, and she said, 'You know how your grandma is.' You know, she made excuses for her instead of saying to me, 'You don't look like a whore.' " (Sam, Family #1)

Sam realized the extent of her mother's influence on her own self-image. In her maternal relationships, she actively tried to establish more distinct boundaries. However, she distanced herself from her mother and her grandmother with varied success. One day she admitted to me:

From age 2 up through an adult I've been so dependent on [my mother's] opinion of me. I can't seem to work my way out of that. Now I have to learn to like myself and that's what I have been working on. I can't be around my mom, sisters, or even my grandmother while I'm going through this process. I just can't be around them. I can't be around mom until I can get it together, because I go back then to being that child she always wants me to be. (Sam, Family #1)

Not all women felt they wanted to distance themselves from maternal influences. Some took comfort in their enmeshment. One day Kendra would complain that her mother was controlling, but the next day would stress how close she and her mother had become:

When we finally got to know one another when I was younger, she had a big influence on me. Who I was with or what friends she liked. She didn't like some of my friends and I never got close to some of them because she didn't like them. I always thought what she says is generally right. That she's God, she's all-knowing, you know, like, she was power. I thought it's very important to please her. Maybe it's because she wasn't around before, but I sometimes see me through her. I usually like what I see. (Kendra, Family #2)

Meredith (Family #6) offered a grandmother's perspective, explaining that she felt dependent on others to make her feel good about herself, and she was most comfortable when she received frequent reassurance from her daughters and granddaughters. She provided the following insight on a day when she was feeling rejected by her daughter: "To get me feeling good about myself I need external [approval], like people must think I'm wonderful, so I must be. And when that person doesn't think I'm not a good person anymore, then I must not be a good person. I couldn't bear it if my family didn't love me" (Meredith, Family #6).

In Family #5, Becky believed she had successfully struggled against this need for maternal approval, and offered the following theory on why she believed she had fallen into that trap in the first place: "I think that is how she disciplined me, that I was a bad person. Not that what I did was bad, but I was a bad person because I engaged in [whatever the bad behavior was]."

Interestingly, all the women in enmeshed relationships reported a fear of "not being good enough" and attributed this fear to their mother and sometimes also to their grandmother. Morgan (Family #6) believed that her mother listened to others and not to her. She claimed that her mother listened to me because of my educational background, and to her sister because of her counseling background, but was adamant in her belief that to her mother she was "nothing." Diane (Family #1) also expressed the belief that her mother would "trust anybody but me." As she stretched out on her recliner one day, Sam yawned and quite clearly articulated thoughts I heard from several young adult and mid-life daughters; she said, "All I want [my mother] to do is to accept me for who I am. And that's all I want to be able to do for my kids, is accept them for who they are, no more, no less."

Although many women in the United States struggle with their self-esteem (Anderson & Hayes, 1996), for these women in enmeshed maternal relationships, receiving anything less than their mother's total approval sent their self-esteem plummeting. They wanted to remain emotionally close, but many did not seem to know how to love and support without overwhelming the other or allowing herself to become overwhelmed. This scenario leads to an age-old question, one asked by the protagonist in the novel *The Good Mother* (Miller, 1994): "How could I love her without damaging her, I wondered. Not too much, not too little. Is there such a love?" (p. 43).

Each woman would insist that the other woman in the maternal relationship not change, thus protecting *her own* identity. In this construction of reality, the other's "difference" was interpreted negatively, and difference was considered "a challenge." When there was tension in a relationship, partners frequently attributed it to being "two different people," issuing descriptions of the different other as a "challenge," "too independent," or "a real contrast to me." These women frowned on differentiation, viewing it as "unnecessary" and making the partners feel "disconnected." These women also suggested that creating relational distance might actually have harmed members' happiness and self-worth.

Despite these differences, women reported feeling emotionally close to their maternal relationship partners. What distinguished the enmeshed relationships from the merely connected, however, was the symbiotic nature of how these women perceived their relational identity. Scout (Family #6) admitted, "[My mother and I], we've shared everything with each other. She knows everything about me, I know everything about her, you know, what we think and whatever." The metaphors women use to describe their (enmeshed) relationships included mirror image of each other, two peas in a pod, and the daughter as the missing puzzle piece of a mother's life.

If a woman envisioned herself as closely linked in identity with her maternal partner, then to avoid dissonance she believed that that partner should remain unchanged. Any alteration to the script was typically perceived as directly reflecting on the partner. Sam (Family #1) indicated that her mother "judges you by your accomplishments, by who you are. You make her look bad if you don't [accomplish]." Morgan indicated that her mother held a similar expectation. One morning she pointed out a key rhetorical difference between what I interpreted as an enmeshed expectation and a (more healthy) connected expectation. She said, "My mom was like, 'I don't care what you do, as long as you do it good and make me proud.' I mean that's what she said, and I think that's what every mother wants. Except now I say to my kids, 'I don't care what you do, as long as *you're* happy' " (Morgan, Family #6).

These women resisted feeling responsible for their mothers' sense of self or their happiness. For Sam (Family #1), there were many attempts to establish distance in her relationship with her mother. During an interview several months into my fieldwork, she decided to tell me a story of how one of these attempts was enacted. She said:

> I told her that I'm not responsible for her feelings. She was speechless. "Well, you make me feel ..." she said. I said, "No, I didn't. You've chosen to feel this way." She told me that I made this huge mistake and made her feel sad, I said, "I didn't and I won't take responsibility. You chose to feel this way." And then, you know, there was this big silence.

> I said, "I don't know what kind of relationship we're in now, it's not as close as it used to be, but this is what I expect. This is what I'm going to do. And if you do not abide by my rules, then, I will be distancing myself. I am choosing, I am taking full responsibility. If you have to react this way, that's fine, that's the way you have to react. But the consequence then is [I have to distance myself from you]. It's not gonna be some big surprise. If you're going to react this way, then I'm pulling away."

> She said to me, "Well, it looks like I'm giving up everything." I said, "No, this is just the first time in 38 years I've called you on it. I'm an adult now and my responsibility is to my kids and my family and I'm sorry but your kids are grown and have lives of their own. Your responsibility is to you and your husband. That's all you have to be responsible for." (Family #1)

This account is informative on many levels. First, this interaction was apparently one of the first times that Sam actually voiced to her mother the changes in their relationship. From Sam's point of view, she was following the lead of her therapist and taking a necessary step to distance herself from her mother. Note, however, the consequences tied to the action. Like her own mother and her grandmother, Sam relied on a comfortable pattern of using the threat of rejection to gain compliance—a direct negative consequence. She chose to protect herself and ran away from rather than deal, through negotiation or other means, with the issue in the context of the relationship. Sam believed that her history of interactions with her mother proved that she could not negotiate this boundary and that the only option was to "throw down the gauntlet." When Diane exclaimed, "Well, it looks like I'm giving up everything," I suspect she felt powerless because she had felt powerful for so long in her daughter's life. Sam, however, was quick to reassure her mother that she really was not giving up anything, but that her mother needed to acknowledge they were separate individuals. Sam argued that she had merely reconfigured the boundaries in the relationship so that "I could still be her daughter but have my own life too."

Beyond threats to self, women in enmeshed maternal relationships also had a tendency to view the process of differentiation as undermining relational stability. Many women attributed their difficulty in differentiating to a fear of alienating the other woman. This fear seemed to be well founded. Women in enmeshed relationships were easily affronted when partners established boundaries or increased distance in their maternal relationships. Once when Diane (Family #1) felt excluded from her daughters' lives, she complained, "[My daughters] went every place together, they did everything together, and they still do. Sometimes they include me but after awhile it gets to you. Enough's enough. It's time that I get included in this." Similarly, one day when I was preparing to go shopping with Morgan and Scout (Family #6), Meredith telephoned Morgan, assuming that she would also be included in the shopping trip. Morgan asked me, "How do you say, 'No, we don't want you with us?'" I replied that we might tell Meredith that today the plan was only for the three of us to go shopping and that we would make alternative arrangements for the following week for all of us, including Meredith, to go shopping. This proposal did not fly. Both Morgan and Scout were chagrined at the thought of telling Meredith that she wasn't to be included on this shopping trip, and argued that Meredith would have "pouted" at the suggestion. Soon thereafter, Morgan telephoned her mother and said, "Mom, we'll pick you up in 30 minutes." We picked up Meredith and Morgan subsequently behaved in a disgruntled manner throughout most of the shopping trip.

Beyond mere annoyance, the women frequently cited differentiation as the culprit behind relational instability. Daughters disconnecting and making life choices separate from mothers proved threatening to many mothers enmeshed in their daughter's lives. A daughter's marriage was at times perceived as a negative event that "caused" the mother "to lose" her daughter. In fact, three mothers expressed similar feelings of abandonment when a daughter chose a marital partner "over" her mother. Sylvia (Family #1) sadly recalled, "The night [Diane and her husband] left on their honeymoon, I cried my eyes out. I went up to the bedroom, locked the door and cried because I had lost her." Diane also felt the same sense of loss when her eldest daughter was married. She shared, "When she got married, I tried to stay detached to a certain extent that was very hard to really stay totally away. Gradually, [I] had to let her go and that wasn't easy, that really was not easy." One day Meredith was talking with me when Morgan entered the room and joined us. We had been talking about sons-in-law and grandchildren when Meredith directed the following statement to Morgan:

I had a real problem after your marriage, we discussed this a little bit the other day. Because it was such a sharp breaking off I actually went through, you died for me, that daughter, and I went through all the stages of bereavement. It was a real severing because our relationship just totally changed because he took you from me. (Meredith, Family #6)

Later, when I spoke with Morgan, she indicated that she was surprised at her mother's sense of loss: "It's not like I met him one week and eloped the next." Apparently she and her husband had dated for well over a year before marriage and her mother had "plenty of time to get used to him." Nonetheless, Meredith experienced Morgan's marriage as a significant threat and turning point in their relationship.

At times, perhaps a marital partner *is* a threat. Sam's first husband was abusive, and although Diane was not aware of the extent of the abuse, she and her husband were not happy with how he treated Sam. This situation is not easy in any mother–daughter relationship, but I suspect that it was particularly painful for Diane given her enmeshment with Sam:

My husband and I were really infuriated with Sam's first husband. We went over to their house and were trying to talk to him. But, Sam said that she didn't think that she would see *us* anymore because she did have a husband and she was married to him and she was staying with him. If we couldn't get along with him, she was going to choose him. That really hurt. It just kind of leaves you out in the cold and there's not much you could do about until she decided to come back to us. (Diane, Family #1)

It is not always another person that threatens to come between mothers and daughters. When both Kelly and Morgan "found religion," their beliefs differed from their mothers' and this caused dissension and relational disease. Katrina complained, "First drugs and then this crap to dull her mind. At least with her girls I am the voice of reason." She was not alone. Meredith indicated, "There was about 10 years in there after she really got deeply into religion, that I just let her go. This wasn't something that she invited me into. It just was what she needed to do. It was very hurting."

Differentiation as Experienced in Connected Relationships. In this type of research, often things *not* said ring more loudly than what is actually said. Among the women in the nonenmeshed but connected maternal relationships, there were very few if any references to self-image being inextricably tied to the other. These adult women did not seek continued validation from their grandmothers/mothers/daughters as they moved through their adult life. In the connected relationships women were emotionally connected, frequently involved interpersonally, and togetherness was emphasized. However, in these relationships *personal distance and generational boundaries were respected* rather than perceived as threatening. These women experienced mutuality in their maternal relationships. (By *mutuality* I mean these women were able to balance the competing pulls of autonomy and connectedness.)

Women in enmeshed relationships would frame their mothers' or daughters' "difference" as a challenge, whereas women in connected relationships would frame differentiation as an expected event, and often an event that is fulfilling to observe. Some of the older women indicated that watching younger women differentiate was akin to watching them "bloom," "flower," or "develop." Lois (Family #4) indicated, "It gets to a certain point and they are gonna live their own life." Gina (Family #3) echoed this, pointing out, "I can give them my morals and my values and who I am, but ultimately, they are who they are." As Barb (Family #4) wrestled with her groceries, placing frozen foods in one pile and canned foods in another, she issued the following statement that I believe illustrates a comfortable mother–daughter engagement: "I'm the one who checked out colleges and applied. My mom or dad didn't have much to do with it. I always knew what I wanted to be." Compare this experience with Sam's earlier account of approaching her mother about becoming a licensed practical nurse only to be told that if she was going to attend college it would have to be in the area that met with her mother's approval. Both Sam and Barb were near the same age and came from loving families, but their experiences were very different.

Differentiation in nonenmeshed relationships did not appear to be interpreted as a threat, but instead as a normal process that has very little to do the dynamics of the maternal relationship. In fact, most women in the connected maternal relationships expressed pride in the unique qualities of their grandmothers/mothers/daughters. One day, when overhearing her daughter on the phone with a friend, Barb (Family #4) smiled and said to me, "That Tabby is her own girl, she is unique." Gina (Family #3), too, did not feel threatened by Georgie's active attempt to differentiate from her mother in the following exchange: "Well last year she was like 'I don't want to be nice, and I'm tired of trying to be nice to everybody. I'm not you. You're nice to everybody, I can't stand it.' I said, 'Well, that is okay.' I want her to be patient with people and tolerant. But she is who she is."

Rowena (Family #3) pointed out that, "My mother encouraged me to speak my mind. My girls did too. They had minds of their own and I liked that." This kind of support—not just tolerance—of differentiating partners seemed to be a key factor enabling women to maintain emotional connectedness in their adult maternal relationships. Georgie indicated that her mother and grandmother "have always been very supportive. I can't remember times when they have never been supportive of something I've done or have wanted to do. Even if it is something they didn't agree with." In the following excerpt, Becky tried to explain the differences she saw in the way she interacted with her mother and her own daughter:

> My mother did not support me if it had something to do with what she thought
> was selfishness or self-centeredness. She taught me that it was self-centered to

look in the mirror or be concerned about your body. But I try and support my girls to do things for themselves their own healthy bodies. Like the "Y" for Linda, I would never have done that or been encouraged to do that. (Family #5)

Some women in connected relationships envisioned themselves as cheerleaders for the women in their life. Barb (Family #4) stated, "It goes back to being a cheerleader. There are so many diverse interests that I try and support. I'm behind them—both Mom and Tabby—being their cheerleader!" When I inquired how she functioned as cheerleader for her mother she recalled when her mother was taking a belly dancing class. She said, "Can you imagine! I would never in a million years try something like that. But, you know, she wanted to try it and she's having a blast. I drive her there when I can and I've watched a few times. I even took her to a Middle Eastern restaurant where they have belly dancers who dance during dinner. It was great fun."

Becky (Family #5) also used the cheerleader metaphor when she explained her support of her daughters:

I try to guide my girls, but I'm more on the sidelines or when they need me. Like a cheerleader, applauding their choices and giving them the means to make their choices happen. I get more involved in helping them make things happen than, well, I don't get involved in what they are doing. They do their own thing, I don't do it for them.

Katrina (Family #2) resolutely tolerated differentiation with her granddaughters, whereas she did not afford the same to her daughter. She indicated that Kendra "is pursuing other dreams. I am so proud of her," whereas her support of Kelly was limited. Kelly believed that whenever she attempted to pursue dreams that deviated from her mother's expectations, her mother "was not supportive. Hell, she went out of her way to undermine me. She just doesn't respect me."

On the other hand, Families #3 and 4 indicated that intergenerational respect was a key ingredient to their relational connection. On one afternoon, Georgie, Gina, and I were walking to the park, pushing my son in his stroller. We were talking about their "special" relationship and Georgie said, "It's about a lot of respect for each other. Pride and respect." Gina added, "It is so much more than just loving each other. It's a special bond between us, all of us. We like and respect each other."

Lois (Family #4) also emphasized respect as a central ingredient in her maternal relationships. She said, "We just genuinely like each other and we give respect to each other. Nobody really has had to earn that respect. It has just always been there." Her granddaughter Tabitha added, "It's really encouraging to have so many people in your life who respect you and your choices. I feel that they are totally supportive. They, my mom in particular, may not like the way I see things. But, she's always respected my opinion to think different."

Differentiation is a higher-order process of managing the connection-separation dialectic, facilitating movement of the relational members toward autonomous selves *while remaining* emotionally connected. Women in enmeshed maternal relationships framed differentiation as a threat to both self and their relationships, whereas women in connected maternal relationships framed this process as normal and inevitable in adult relationships. Connected grandmothers, mothers, and daughters tended to feel comfortable in their emotional connection while simultaneously functioning as an interested observer in the other's life, accepting differences and offering support.

Modeling as Connection-Separation Management

Differentiation seemed to be a higher-order process of managing the dialectical tensions of separation and connection, enabling daughters to remain emotionally connected with mothers while writing their own unique stories. Modeling, on the other hand, also appeared to be a higher-order process of managing separation and connection, facilitating connections between two sets of values and behaviors without any one partner hijacking the other's agency to write her own narrative. As women in the nonenmeshed connected relationships moved into adulthood and mid-life, they more readily embraced their identification with their maternal relatives than did those in enmeshed relationships. The following excerpts illustrate how modeling the other may be a means of maintaining connection with the other woman throughout the adult life course, even as partners separately pursue their own unique identities.

Rowena (Family #3) expressed pride in her daughters and granddaughters. She said, "They are real ladies, real ladies each one. I tried my best to show them, to be that [lady]. Yes, it may be prideful to say, but I see myself in them. It warms my heart." Gina embodied the character description of *being a lady* while simultaneously authoring an expanded description of a lady as providing leadership. She said, "[My mother] was always a lady, she always presented a nice picture. She would always show me her picture in the paper for something or her name being in the paper, and I would always think wow, that's my *mom*. Kind of neat." This expanded character development also emerged in Georgie's discourse. She told the following story:

> I grew up in a lifestyle like to always be a lady, always act, look, and present yourself, you know, like a nice, classy lady in front of other people. So that's definitely something that was stressed from my grandmother down to my mom and now down to me, ever since I was young. Since my mom and I have always been very, very close, I've always looked up to my mom. You know, she's been a good role model to me and everything, and I think that's a lot of the reason why we've been so close—cause I've always watched her and seen what she's done and been proud of her for things that she's done.... A lot of people respected her name. It really wasn't until I went to college, though, that I really began to try and be like her in

that way. Like she was president in everything she has ever been on and served on various boards, I think my grandmother was too, so I've kinda followed in their footsteps. I tend to hold offices in my clubs and stuff and like to provide leadership. (Georgie, Family #3)

These women said that both older and younger women learned from one another. For example, Barb (Family #4) said that Tabitha "is real enterprising, extremely business minded and always has been, and [a] very hard worker and organized. She's got skills that I definitely don't have and am working toward developing by watching her!" Lois, too, indicated that she continuously adapts her story to include things learned from her daughter's example. One Sunday afternoon, following church, I sat in the breakfast nook in Barb's home with Lois. We watched Barb interact with her youngest son and Lois said:

Watching my daughter as mother has taught me a lot about myself. I've always been a caretaker. Now, Barb, she lets her kids be independent. If they need something or have a problem she helps them get it or helps them solve it rather than doing it for them. That's one thing that I really felt that God showed me through [my daughter's] life and I try and do that more as a grandmother now. (Family #4)

In the enmeshed maternal relationships, a daughter's deviation from her mother's style of mothering might have been interpreted as a criticism of her mother. In this case, however, Lois interpreted the difference as a blessing and an opportunity for self-development.

Diane (Family #1) was repelled by the thought of modeling her own mother's behavior and sought to model her own grandmother instead. This character development is intriguing in its own right, considering Diane's own daughters' insistence that her character is, in practice, *just like* that of Sylvia. Diane, however, felt that her relationship with her maternal grandmother was not enmeshed, but connected in many ways. She said, "My grandmother was always there for me. I could do no wrong in her eyes. If I did, I never knew about it. When my first grandchild was born it was like I had this role to live up to because I had such a good model to go by."

Grandmothers and Granddaughters Connecting and Separating.   The dance of connection-separation for grandmothers and granddaughters was more like a jitterbug and less like a tango. This analogy resonates for me because of the images. In the jitterbug, partners are connected, often by one hand, sometimes lifted and supported by the partner, but each dancer does his or her "own thing" in time with the music in his or her life. In a tango, partners are often cheek to cheek, bodies flush against each other, peeling away from the other when separation is necessary. At times, in tango, partners rapidly rip their bodies away from each other, and at other times, the peeling is a slow and deliberate movement. Tango partners must step to the music in a common rhythm lest one partner trip and stumble. Finally, any changes in music must be met with a combined adjustment rather than individual change. Although many mother–daughter relationships could be metaphorically described as "tangoing," most grandmother–granddaughter relationships jitterbugged along across the life course.

Granddaughters perceived their grandmother–granddaughter relationships as offering security, providing the balance rather than the directing the entire dance. For grandmothers, it did not appear that personal identity was as strongly mitigated by the grandmother–granddaughter relationship as it was by playing the role of mother. Most grandmothers in this study could step back, hold onto their granddaughters' hands, and watch them dance. Kornhaber (1996) articulated this best when he characterized grandmother–grandchild interaction as possessing a quality similar to a smooth, nonperformance-oriented in interaction; one that's about merely finding joy in each other.

In this section, I illustrated the dynamic nature of identity in negotiating tensions of separation and connection in grandmother–mother–daughter relationships. Because dialectics are ongoing relational processes, the tensions inherent in the separation-connection dialectic appeared "unresolved"; that is, not wholly resolved in adolescence as some developmental literature suggests. These relationships navigated pulls toward separation and connection across the life span in many different ways. Some women privileged connection across the life span with little tolerance for separation, whereas others framed each pole as a companion to the other, encouraging individual members' differentiation and autonomy while retaining emotional connection.

OPEN-CLOSED

Her blonde hair fell in ringlets to her shoulders. Four years old and dressed in a pink flowered sundress with matching socks and bracelet, she bounded into the room to tell me something. As she approached me, I witnessed her face tighten, creases formed in her brow, and she stopped in her tracks. She walked over to her mother, Sam (Family #1), and whispered in her ear. I sat patiently while Sam whispered audibly to her daughter, "It's okay, you can tell." Permission granted, Sam's youngest returned to me with her smile back in place and shared the following information: "My sister is sick today. She has the flu."

I thought to myself, "Why would she feel uncomfortable disclosing that information to me? Why the need to get permission for the disclosure?" Naturally, there is information that you just don't share with people outside the family. However, Madison was literally stopped in her tracks when she considered (what I suspect was) the potential disapproval of her mother if she were to disclose the private information about her sister's illness.

Families have rules regulating information flow internally and externally, with each family system working together to manage the dialectics of expression and privacy. Yet, what struck me about Madison's small display of self-censorship was the look of concern and apprehension that crossed her little face when she stopped herself from disclosing possibly (threatening? embarrassing? damaging?) inappropriate information. Although her mother and her grandmother were very forthcoming with me in formal and informal interviews, it was Madison who made me stop to consider the early socialization that family members receive surrounding the disclosure of personal information. Madison clearly believed she needed her mother's permission to share this bit of information. This is understandable from the perspective of a 4-year-old still struggling to discern which information is considered public and which is private. Yet what about the adult women?

Dialectical theory argues that all relationships negotiate levels of privacy and disclosure of information in a relationship (Montgomery & Baxter, 1998). Moreover, according to boundary management theory (Petronio, 2000), boundaries are erected between relational members (internal boundaries) and between the relational dyad and others (external boundaries) that serve to establish rules governing expression and privacy. The dialectical contradiction internal to the relationship is typically labeled *openness-closedness*. This refers to linked desires to share feelings, ideas, and information with open access between relational partners, and to keep information restricted, private, and concealed with closed access between relational partners. *Revelation-concealment* dialectic is the external contradiction, referring to boundaries around the relational dyad regulating access to information, and how much to share or not share with those outside the relationship.

Openness/Revelation–Closedness/Concealment. "Let me tell you about one time when she ...." This introduction often prefaced revelations of private information. Women who opened their homes to a stranger, agreeing to months of being interviewed and observed, may not be the most closed or private of people. Yet, there was a period of time during which I had to practice patience if I wanted to be included in private information. The older women in the families were the ones to most tightly control disclosures. As an example, the following interaction illustrates Rowena's (Family #3) reaction to my requests to share private information:

> During the first weeks of my fieldwork, Rowena sat on her ornately patterned couch, the gold and mauve threads swirling elegantly throughout the fabric, with her hands in her lap and her eyes on those hands. "I don't feel comfortable talking about myself either," she said. Earlier in the day, she had indicated that she didn't feel comfortable bragging about her family. I perceived her "bragging" as merely

informative, whereas she felt uncomfortable with the idea she was being immodest and self-important when discussing her daughter's accomplishments. I interpreted her reticence to share information more as a concern for her own self-presentation than as an issue of not wanting me to have the information. Would talking about herself make her look self-centered? Conceited? Would bragging about her family convey an attitude of arrogance?

I sat quietly and waited for her to continue. She finally said, "Oh … dear. [*Pause*] I really don't have much to say about myself. I don't have much experience with it. I have a great family though."

This apprehension about keeping oneself closed off to outsiders was common across three of the four grandmothers during the first month of my stay in Elkwood. Sylvia, Rowena, and Charlotte were relatively closed with information during the initial period of my fieldwork, and I discovered that concealment of information from outsiders was due more to age and generational norms rather than to rigid boundaries regulating access of personal information. The older women were simply not used to be asked about their thoughts and their lives, and were certainly not used to talking about themselves. However, after about 1 month, private information became less restricted and I learned much—sometimes more than I bargained for—about these women.

An interesting observation is that the women in connected relationships were more apt to be private and less disclosive with me than the women in enmeshed relationships. Those in the enmeshed relationships demonstrated highly permeable external boundaries, making private information public, while at the same time engineering awe-inspiring amounts of secretiveness within their maternal relationships.

Keeping Secrets and Concealing Information.   Secrets, by definition, are composed of information that is intentionally withheld or differentially shared between or among people (Karpel, 1980; Vangelisti, 1994). This secret keeping may be conceptualized as located at the closed end of the self-disclosure continuum, whereas secrets themselves might be viewed as information that would be disclosed under usual conditions yet are concealed due to their threatening or shameful nature (Derlega, Metts, Petronio, & Margulis, 1993). Secrets are often kept when the risks associated with disclosure are too great and the tolerance for vulnerability is low (Derlega et al., 1993). At other times, information may be concealed merely to reinforce boundaries of personal space between partners. Linda, for example, reported that when she was younger her grandmother's inquiries about her life "didn't bother me too much. They were always about my life because she was just interested." Yet, as she got older, she professed an increased annoyance at her grandmother's questions. She said, "The inquiries began to feel more invasive."

The women in the enmeshed relationships most actively tended a variety of secrets and revealed personal, relational, and family secrets to me. The processes of maintaining secrets, disclosing secrets, and baring the wounds of secrets were intimately tied to relational communication in these enmeshed relationships.

At first thought, one might think that it is counterintuitive for enmeshed relationships, which by definition are extremely connected with few or highly permeable boundaries, to harbor secretive behavior. Yet, these transparent borders may actually have led to more closely guarding information from relational members and challenging external boundaries by sharing secretive information with others outside the relationship. This seemed to be the case when examining the secret-keeping behavior in Elkwood.

Vangelisti (1994) provided a typology of family secrets that is useful for understanding the concealment occurring in Elkwood. She identified three important characteristics of secrets as they affect relationships in families: the form of the secret (from whom is the secret being kept?); the topic of the secret, or the type of information withheld; and the function of the secret (why are family members keeping the secret?). The different forms of secrets consist of "individual" secrets, which are those concealed by one family member from the rest of the family; "intra" secrets, which are those held by some family members and kept from other family members; and "whole" secrets, which consist of information that is held by all members of a family, but concealed from nonfamily members (Vangelisti, 1994). These categories assisted me in labeling and coding the secrets held within each family. However, it was interesting that the categories didn't fully capture the dynamic nature of secrets—how rapidly following disclosure that secrets can move from individually held to whole-family secrets.

In the enmeshed maternal relationships, intrafamily secrets prevailed, although personal and family-level secrets were in vigorous abundance. The following episode illustrates not only secret keeping in Family #1, but also the struggle within this family to negotiate the tensions of managing openness and closedness:

One day, I was wandering in a wooded area that separated Sylvia and Diane's houses. I came upon Sam sitting on a log. She looked up at me and I smiled. Her face looked weary and the stunning smile that so often brightened my day had vanished. After assuring me that she was fine and "just thinking," I proceeded on my walk, kicking rocks and enjoying the smell of the trees, air, and grass. I probably should have known that something was wrong, but I didn't.

The next day I received a phone call from one of Sam's sisters (Julie),[20] telling me that Sam was in crisis. Her voice cracked as she breathlessly gave me the rundown on "what was going on." Apparently Renee (a friend of Sam's who happened to be a therapist) discovered that Sam was taking steps to end her own life. Sam had acquired a supply of prescription medication and was storing it for her suicide.

[20]All names of the participants are pseudonyms, in an attempt to protect the identities of the interactants.

Renee had called Julie and planned an intervention, in which they planned to "out" Sam with their evidence, confront her, and get her to seek help. Julie called me because she wanted me to participate in the intervention.

I remember sitting on the phone, inhaling sharply, and considering the repercussions of my presence during such an event. I asked Julie, "Who all will be there?" She replied, "Just you, me, and Renee." I felt comforted that Renee would be there. She was a counselor, after all, and—frankly—I didn't want to be placed in the position of having to confront a suicidal woman without the presence of a trained therapist. I agreed to participate because a therapist would be there, but I also suggested Sam's mother be invited. *That* was a mistake.

Julie literally screamed in my ear, "Not in a million years!" She then explained that telling her mother would suggest a "betrayal of trust" between sisters. She emphatically pointed out that Sam's peers should handle this situation. She hurriedly explained that I was to arrive at Sam's house later in the afternoon, after the others, so Sam would not feel "ganged up on."

Therefore, I arrived a bit later, carrying a single flower as a harbinger of goodwill. My heart was pounding when I rang the doorbell. I wasn't certain what I was going to encounter when I arrived, but I was very concerned for Sam. Sam opened the door. She received the flower with a shy smile and said, "I feel really stupid." I offered to leave but she assured me it was okay for me to stay and invited me inside. She said, "This is not really a big deal. I guess the secret is out now. But, as you can see, I'm okay."

Before I had arrived, the other two women confronted Sam with their concerns. Sam admitted to stashing the contraband of pills and planning the suicide. But, she argued, the crisis had been five days earlier and she was "over it" now. Sam ushered me into the family room where Renee and Julie stood, with each looking less than happy at Sam's attempt to blow off the seriousness of the event. I entered the room, Sam still playing the hostess and offering me a drink. I declined and we all sat. Sam sat in a large overstuffed chair that dwarfed her, making her look smaller and somehow world-weary. Renee sat on the floor by Sam, Julie sat on the couch across the room, and I sank into my chair off to the side, just listening. Sam's eyes focused on the floor under her feet for what seemed like 10 minutes (perhaps it was only 2, but I could clearly hear everyone's breathing and the tic, tic, tic of the grandfather clock in the room beside us). She asked, "You didn't tell any of this to mom, did you?" Her sister assured her that, "No, no one told mom." Sam continued to look at the ground and apparently decided to close the subject, saying, "You guys, this is my business and if I want to discuss it then I will. But, it's my business." Julie immediately jumped on this statement and encouraged her sister to look her directly in the eyes. She said, "Sweetie, the more secrets you keep, the worse everything gets." Sam placed her face in her hands and shook her head side to side. I thought she would burst into tears, but instead she thrust her hands from her face and balled them into fists. Her face contorted with a pain I had never seen before. She was anguished. She began to talk in fits and starts, retracing her words and then beginning again. We all sat rapt while she explained about the tremendous guilt she had lived with for the past 20 years.

Sam told the following story in a relative monotone. The torment and rage evidenced on her face moments previously quickly settled into a mask of surrender. Her story began with Sam's first marriage to a man who had been involved in a satanic cult that participated in ritualistic ceremonies. "There were animals sacrificed and everything. He gave my children over to Satan." She spat out the last sentence. She wanted us to know that her own involvement was eating her alive. She explained, "I didn't want to be directly involved so I was in charge of watching the little children as their parents participated in the satanic worship ceremonies." Apparently, her role was to keep the children quiet. She indicated that she was told by one of the leaders that "If any child cries or disrupts the ceremony, that child would be sacrificed." While telling us this information, Sam was visibly shaking. Her legs and arms trembled, yet her face held a look of defeat. She said, "During that time when I was the babysitter some children were taken away one ... by ... one. And a few were reported as missing."[21] She offered, "I don't know, but I think these babies were sacrificed." She whimpered, "If I had just kept them quiet then everything would be okay." She talked for about an hour about her feelings of guilt and responsibility associated with failing to keep those children safe.

After that hour, Sam shared with us some additional reasons why she had been feeling suicidal. She said, "I was told to forget it and not say anything. I tried. I have tried for years and years." However, Sam's eldest daughter, Madison, recently began having flashbacks to that period of time in her early youth. She was experiencing recurrent nightmares. Sam told us that she had never spoken about these ceremonies with her daughter, who had been a toddler at the time, because she feared for her daughter's safety. Nevertheless, within the past 3 months Madison's dreams and flashbacks offered glimpses of what had occurred nearly 23 years before.

Madison had approached her mother in an attempt to find out "what the hell went on back then." Her flashbacks/nightmares revealed one particular event when the ex-husband held Sam down on the ground while another member of the cult held down Madison with a gun to the 3-year-old's temple. There was a struggle and the gun went off. Sam remembered looking over and seeing a dog had been shot next to her daughter. This episode, Sam said, "was just to scare us."

I realized that I had been holding my breath during her narrative and when she finally finished telling her story I exhaled softly. Renee broke the silence: "So, if I hear what you have been telling me ... despite the fact that you have been dealing with this for 23 years and that you were suicidal 5 days ago, today it's all okay and you're fine."

I think *not*.

Her secrets lead to other secrets; all were concealed because they were too threatening, shameful, or risky to reveal. The poisonous and insidious nature of this particular personal secret deeply affected Sam's life and threatened to affect her relationship with her daughter. Once she had shared this information with her sis-

---

[21] I want to make clear at this point that these reported incidents are Sam's perceptions of what occurred. The others is the room did not seem to feel that there were actually missing children. They were concerned, however, that Sam *believed* that there were and that she, somehow, was responsible.

ter and others outside the family, alliances were formed and Sam's mother was excluded by the erection of boundaries. Those in the alliances still maintain this secret to this day.

Across most of the enmeshed relationships is a pattern in which the secret began as an individual secret (e.g., cult involvement, planned suicide) that, once revealed to a family member, became an intrafamily secret with alliances within the family system to keep the information from getting shared with others—specifically maternal figures. I heard, "Don't tell mom" on a multitude of occasions in the enmeshed relationships. Several women kept individual secrets of unwanted pregnancies and abortions. They painstakingly kept this kind of information to themselves, shielding mothers from the knowledge of it.

Morgan's pregnancy at the age of 17 was her secret until it became necessary for her parents to know. During the era of the early 1970s, the societal shame attached to illegitimate pregnancies dictated that these pregnancies be secreted away. For two of the women in enmeshed maternal relationships, the individual secret of their teenage pregnancies became intra-family secrets—only known to the mother, daughter, and perhaps father, never being revealed as a whole family secret to siblings or grandparents. In Morgan's case, she kept her pregnancy secret from her younger siblings by going away to a "home for unwed mothers." She was to carry the baby full term, give it up for adoption, and then return back home, never to reveal her shame. Her younger siblings were told she was away at a special college on scholarship. One day, however, this particular secret unraveled when a child taunted her little sister about her "slut of an older sister who was away having a bastard." The younger sister recalled running "straight home from the playground" crying and asking her mother if it was true. It was not until directly confronted that Meredith shared the truth with her youngest daughter.

Truths were often kept from others "for their own good." Women frequently framed secretiveness as merely withholding potentially harmful information. Doing this, they maintained their emphasis on relational cohesion, protecting their maternal relational partner. One example of this occurred when Sylvia became ill during the sixth month of my visit. Her health was failing quickly, and she was 82 years old. Diane told me Sylvia was diagnosed with intestinal cancer, but "the family had decided not to tell her she had cancer." Even Sylvia's doctor was involved in this deception.

Many women in the enmeshed families perceived secrets as protecting either themselves or their maternal partner. This depended, of course, on the type of information contained in the secret. Types of secretive information can be categorized as taboo topics, rule violations, and conventional (Vangelisti, 1994). For these women, substance abuse, sexual abuse, death, and extramarital affairs were examples of taboo topics. Identified rule violations included sexual promiscuity, cohabitation, and lying. Finally, conventional information withheld from certain partners included religious beliefs, sharing information about romantic partners, and positive family secrets such as family recipes, traditions, and jargon shared only with insiders. Gina in Family #3 would not give up her famous "cheesecake" recipe to me until well into my seventh month in Elkwood. She "only shares that information with family" so I felt honored on the day she presented me with the recipe written on a gift-wrapped index card.

Although limited to the enmeshed maternal relationships, an association emerged between secret form and secret type. Rule violations were most often maintained at the individual or personal level. A rule violation such as an unplanned pregnancy would be kept at the personal level until the point when the information needed to be shared out of necessity. At times this disclosure was voluntary, and at others it was involuntary (e.g., the woman was physically showing evidence of the pregnancy).

In enmeshed relationships, taboo topics were maintained at the intrafamily level. Information about members' cult involvement, sexual abuse, abortion, and suicide attempts was shared with only a select few, alliances were formed, and some secrets were withheld from certain family members. Siblings shared disclosures, as sometimes did mothers. However, rarely did mothers or grandmothers disclose this kind of information to their daughters or granddaughters. Siblings might erect a border around taboo secrets, concealing these from mothers and grandmothers. For example, one of the men in Family #6, Jack, had a "drinking problem." His daughter laughed at that euphemism and added, "Yeah, when he drinks he gets drunk." His children were concerned about him, they expressed concern to me and to each other; however, no one would confront Jack or their mother about the problem. Jack was not an abusive man, nor was he a threat to his family; but he was apparently a threat to others on the road. He insisted, "I drive better when I'm drunk!" His daughters were secretly embarrassed and feared for their father and for others riding in cars with him.

Function of Secrets. You may wonder why the younger women did not merely talk with their (grand)mother or (grand)father about their concerns. Yet, the functions of withholding information like this are many. Vangelisti (1994) identified several functions of secret keeping that answer the question "Who is being protected from what by keeping this secret?" Of the secrets maintained in Elkwood, one identifiable function of secret keeping was *bonding*—keeping the family/relationship together. Sylvia's point of view was "That which doesn't kill us, makes us stronger." When I questioned her about the various suicide attempts in her family, she responded, "I think we keep our business to ourselves. There isn't a need to get outside help because we are more aware of each other and what we need than others outside the family can be." Many women saw concealing family-level secrets from others outside the family as a means of keeping the family members closely bonded. When all members of a family knew a secret, and they all knew that they all knew, the secret strength-ened the boundary between the family and the outside world. In this way, se-crets define boundaries and tell us who is "in" and who is "out" (Sieburg, 1985). This addresses the following complaint issued by Morgan's youngest sister: "It was embarrassing. Everyone else knew [about my sister's pregnancy] but me. Even strangers knew!" Indeed, shared secrets may strengthen alliances be-tween relational members, prohibiting partners from revealing the secret to others. When Sam disclosed her fears and guilt to Julie, this strengthened their bond as sisters. However, by mandating that no one tell Sam's mother; they fur-ther reinforced the sister alliance, separating the sister–sister relationship from the mother–daughter relationship.

Secrets also served a stability *maintenance* function. To avoid "upsetting" re-lational partners or other family members, members would withhold informa-tion. Although Sylvia's family members kept the cancer diagnosis away from her to protect her from having to deal with the "hopelessness," by withholding this information, her daughter and granddaughters did not have to deal with her re-action to the news either, providing stability and protecting their family from the potential for this news to "rock the boat." Additionally, not confronting Jack about his driving while drunk served to maintain family harmony and protect Jack from embarrassment.

Withholding information may also move beyond maintaining relational sta-bility. Information may be withheld to serve a *protective function*, out of fear that the information could harm the relationship or be used against the relational members. This was illustrated in Elkwood when individual secrets, such as abor-tions, were often maintained to protect certain relationships. Barb explained, "What [my mother] doesn't know won't hurt her or what she thinks of me." Similarly, intrafamily and whole-family secrets were kept to protect members from harm or embarrassment. To this day, Sam lives in fear because she dis-closed her involvement in the satanic cult to me, her sister, and her friend. She daily fears repercussions to herself and her family.

Balancing secrecy and disclosure is difficult for many of us, because sharing information entails numerous benefits but also numerous risks. This study sug-gests that grandmothers, daughters, and granddaughters are often "protected" from information, whereas daughters frequently intentionally exclude mothers from information.

In connected maternal relationships, there was an open flow of information willingly shared among grandmothers, mothers, and daughters with few de-mands for disclosure; however, among those in enmeshed relationships, the flow of information often was burdened by secrecy. Intrafamily secrets rein-forced boundaries between mothers and daughters and grandmothers and granddaughters, whereas whole-family secrets served to further enmesh the women in each other's lives.

I would like to end this section with the lyrics from a song written for the stage play *Two of Me*, to be sung by a mother and her daughter:

Mother and Daughter: When will the time come?
                         When I can talk to you?
                         When will the time come?
                         When I can tell you how I feel?

Daughter: We go around day by day
                         never managing to say ...
                         anything.
                         Vacant eyes and telling lies,
                         hoping ... somehow to get by.
                         Coexisting in a house where
                         no one looks, no one talks, secrets kept, and
                         no one listens.
                         Today is the day I want to feel
                         Today is the day I want to be heard.
                         Please listen.

Mother: Daughter, can't you see
                         that it's sometimes rough?
                         You can't see that it's sometimes tough
                         You give your time, you give your life,
                         you give it all—yet it's not enough ...
                         [*In a round*]

Daughter: When will the time come?

Mother: When will the time come?

Daughter.   When can I talk to you?

Mother: When can I talk to you?

Daughter: When will the time come?

Mother: When will the time come?

Daughter: When ...

Mother & Daughter: ... can I tell you how I feel?

REAL-IDEAL

According to authors such as Coll et al. (1998) and Rich and Williams (1998), in women's stories good mothers are often passive martyrs who sacrifice themselves for their families, and active mothers are portrayed as intrusive and meddlesome, with daughters struggling to write their mothers out of their own lives' plot. In a popular novel later adapted into a film, *The Divine Secrets of the Ya-Ya Sisterhood* (Wells, 1997), the main character rebelled against her mother by pining for a mother who would fit her ideal image of who a mother *should* be.

The task of balancing an image of a supposed "ideal" relationship with a "real" relationship managed on a day-to-day basis is basic across most personal relationships. When I close my eyes I may envision an "ideal" romantic partner who, like Tom Hanks in *Sleepless in Seattle*, would jump on a plane and fly across the country just to be with me in our united passion. Then I open my eyes and see my husband in front of me.

My wonderful husband would go to the corner drugstore to by tampons for me, but he would not purchase any foolish e-ticket to fly across the country without first examining our bank account. Does my husband pale in comparison to Mr. Hanks? Not really (honestly honey, honest!), but these images do sometimes make me stop and think, "Well, if he really loved me he would [fill in the blank]."

Unfortunately, very little scholarship examines the influence of sociocultural messages about ideal relationships on how people like you and me manage our real ones. There has been a plethora of research focusing on women's body images, what is considered a media "ideal," and offering comparisons that reflect the reality of most women's bodies. Yet, we know little about how idealized images of relational partners affect daily management and satisfaction of our own personal relationships.

Media sources and generalized others are certainly not the only outlets for conveying idealized images of grandmothers, mothers, daughters, and granddaughters. Religious leaders, educators, and politicians send explicit as well as subtler messages to their congregations, students, and constituents about who a woman "should be" in her various roles and how she "should" perform. I always tell me students, "Do not should all over yourself!" Yet, it is human nature to do so. Thus, it would be negligent to disregard the pervasive nature of perceived "ideals" on the experience of maternal relationships.

Close your eyes and picture your image of a "granny." Now that you have opened your eyes, was your image close to that of one of your own grandmothers? If I had asked you to picture an image of any grandmother, would your own grandmother, have come to mind? What is the difference between who is a "granny" and who is a "grandmother"? Isn't a grandmother expected to wear an apron, have permed blue hair, and sit in a rocker? Perhaps she should be in the kitchen making cookies, looking like Grandma Walton or Aunt Bea?

Our ideals, of course, are not shaped by socio-cultural messages alone; they are also affected by personal experiences with others who have grannies, moms, and daughters. When I was growing up, my best friend had a grandmother who I thought was *da bomb*. She roller skated, swam, and took my friend and me to movies where characters actually cursed! This woman dispelled any notions that I had about grannies in a rocker; moreover, she provided me with an ideal against which I could compare my own grandmothers. Of course, I loved my grandmothers dearly, but I doubt if either one even watched roller skating on television. The point is that there are hosts of socio-personal-cultural influences in our lives shaping our perceptions of how "my grandmother/mother/daughter" *should* be.

Whereas before the 1940s messages may have been relatively consistent about women's role functions and role relationships, LaSorsa and Fodor (1990) indicated that the women born in the period 1940–1970 were in the vanguard of change for women in this country. With the development of the women's movement, roles have been altered, and messages about who we are and "should be" in relation to the women in our lives may be conflicting. Nonetheless, in many people's minds they hold images of ideal maternal relationships that may or may not shape their actual maternal ties.

Research does find that some women resist mothering in the same ways their own mothers mothered, but most women *aspire* to mother in the same way, constructing a personal, idealized version of their mother (Golombisky, 2001). Feminist literature refers to this version as the "June Cleaver complex." Women may overgeneralize their mothers' good and bad qualities and then try to pattern their parenting styles on those generalizations.

For the women of Elkwood, idealized versions of grandmothers/mothers/daughters do indeed shape how women perceive and interact with their real grandmothers, mothers, daughters, and granddaughters. An undercurrent of idealized maternal images emerged in their talk; Sam, for example, stated the following:

It's kind of like—hmmm—have you ever seen that commercial where the grandma has her grandkids over and they have a pillow fight and feathers get everywhere? Well, I want to be that kind of grandmother. I've seen what it's like. I don't want to be the kind of grandmother my grandma is and my mom is. When it's convenient, and if you don't make too much noise or too much mess, then I'll have you over.

Diane (Family #1) echoed this ideal when she said that her "grandma was mom. She gave me unconditional love. I never had a *real* mother. She was always too busy with her problems with her husband to pay attention to me. I was more like a possession."

Women's ideas of what their maternal relationships should be like are shaped within a complex web of social influences such as other family members, friends, cultural ideals, and media. The following excerpt offers a glimpse at Becky's frustration in trying to manage the dialectical pulls of real and ideal. She said:

> In movies and stuff it is always the daughter who takes care of the ailing mother. I want to be a dutiful daughter. Do the right thing. I do. Yeah, I am still the dutiful daughter. I'm the only caregiver in my family and, well, I'm really disturbed. I mean it's horrible. It makes me very angry. I'm very angry at my brothers. They're taking no responsibility. I love my mother, but I hate being the one responsible. They are very far away.

Becky also believed that her mother's ideal image for what a daughter "should be" distorted their actual relationship. She lamented, "I get the message [from my mother] that other daughters do this or that for their mothers, why don't I do the same. She says this to me and to others too. She has this idea of what I should do that gets in the way of who we can be together."

Gender ideals were also held in esteem by many women, with clear ideas of what it meant to "be a lady." The following exchange illustrated Tabitha's perception of the transmission of gender ideals. Tabitha revealed, "When [my grandmother] says to act like a lady, you know what that means." I asked, "How did you know what that means?" "To act like she does," she replied.

Mothers and grandmothers were overheard telling (grand)daughters, "Girls should know how to hold babies," "Girls should be kind and helpful to others," "Women should go to church and insist their children do too," and "Women should be put together nicely, you know, hair, makeup, neatly dressed, always attractive." However, daughters did not express their ideals regarding gender to their mothers or grandmothers directly, but instead shared these ideals with me privately. Even when the real satisfactorily matched with the ideal, (grand)daughters were not observed commenting about their ideals with their elders. Articulation of ideals and expectations was a mother's duty.

Real, Ideal, and Identity Frames. Both media and interpersonal rhetoric shape expectations and understandings of who a grandmother/mother/daughter should be and how women view their identities. Hecht et al. (1993) argued that this issue of how we see ourselves—our identity—is most likely linked to *multiple* frames of identity; lenses through which we see ourselves in relation to the world around us. These scholars suggested that a personal frame is how we see ourselves, an enactment frame provides insight into our own self based on our interactions with others, a relationship frame provides insight into who we are in relationship to others in our lives, and a communal frame provides a view of our "self" as linked to different familial, social, cultural, or ethnic groups. From this perspective, grandmothers, mothers, and daughters must constantly balance the tensions among who they are as individuals (personal frame), how they manage interactions with the others (enactment frame), and what it means to be a grandmother, mother, daughter, and/or granddaughter (relational frame) in the same culture (communal frame).

Just as speculated by Hecht et al. (1993), in practice these frames overlapped substantially for the women of Elkwood. I interpreted the multiple identities of these women as nested—frames one inside the other, like a Russian doll. Personal identities (who I am separate from my grandmother/mother/daughter) were embedded within relational identities (e.g., mother–daughter, grandmother–granddaughter), and these nested within communal identities—referring to how I see my relationship and myself through the lens of sociocultural norms and images, and all of these frames in combination affected how identities were enacted on a daily basis.

Grandmothers and Granddaughters Balancing Real and Ideal.   T h e r e have been so many extraordinary changes for women in the past century. These changes have shifted cultural and individual ideals of whom one should be as a woman, grandmother, mother, daughter, or granddaughter. Women's changing roles in this past century have required women to adapt to these changing ideals, but for some of the Elkwood women this adjustment was difficult to embrace on a more personal level. Granddaughters may expect their grandmothers to be nurturing, baking cookies and providing unconditional acceptance; however, when women like Sylvia (Family #1) choose instead to be "social butterflies" and assume the attitude that "I did my job as a mother, now it my daughter's turn because I have my own things to do," her granddaughter felt cheated. Sam remarked that her grandmother was more like a "rich old aunt" and she really didn't "feel" like a grandmother until she was old and sickly. "Now [that she is dependent]," Sam said, "she's my grandmother."

Grandmothers have the vantage point of witnessing decades of ever-changing cultural ideals for women. At times, these changing ideals were embraced: "I want my granddaughters to go to college. I didn't have that opportunity and I want them to. They should." Yet, at other times these changing ideals were met with resistance: "A woman needs a man to take care of her. It is just not right [to be a single mother.]"

The influence of cultural ideals crossed generational boundaries and also affected decision making in families. The following discussion occurred one day after Lois (Family #4) fell and fractured a rib. She was resting in her bedroom and her daughter, granddaughter, and I were sitting in the kitchen having a snack:

Barb rubbed her temples with her forefingers and said, "She's going to start to need a different kind of care soon."

Tabitha offered, "We need to talk with her about what she eventually wants. To be in a nursing home, maybe? What do you think—I mean, I mean, eventually."

Barb hesitated, then said, "I'm thinking that it's scary. You know. Makes you think. It's … it's …."

"What?" I asked.

"It's a throw-away society," Barb responded.

"Um um," I muttered.

Barb was suddenly very emphatic. She said, "You know, throw our parents away. Look at the Waltons, they all live together. We could be really happy. I think it's sad."

Tabitha defended herself and remarked, "Well, I didn't mean we should throw her away. Just ask her what she wants."

Decisions related to caregiving, extent of involvement in each other's lives, what role to play in the drama of each other's lives were sometimes guided by media examples. Despite the sociocultural influences suggesting who one "should" be as a grandmother or granddaughter, most of the grandmothers echoed the following sentiment articulated by Katrina. She said, "Being a grandmother is much different than being a mother. You just go with the flow." These women gloried in the role of grandmother and their ideal images of that role. Although the role itself might have made grandmothers, especially younger grandmothers, feel old, they still embraced that role with its associated ideals. Barb said, "My mother's role in life is to be a grandmother," and Lois responded, "Yes, but I'm not ready to be called 'Grandma.' The kids call me 'Non.' 'Grandma' just doesn't feel right!"

For the women of Elkwood, managing the dialectical tensions of real and ideal was comprised of a dynamic interplay of influences pertaining to expectations about both people in relationship (internal) and the relationship in cultural context (external). These role and gender expectations affected not only how women perceived one another, but also set the stage for the enactment of the next dialectical tension to be discussed in this chapter—the contradictory pulls of powerful and powerless.

POWERFUL-POWERLESS

My grandmother was not mean or evil in any way, in fact, her concerns were always made clear out of love for us. She was always focused on our happiness and our health and nothing got her more involved than worrying about some latest family problem. She was incredibly giving and benevolent with us all, although in return I think she did expect total capitulation to her will. (Edelman, 2000, p. 154)

My daughter has a power over me that no other being on earth has. The power to stop my world with her need and start it up again with her smile. (Barb, Family #5)

Sitting in the dark and eating salty popcorn, Morgan, Scout, Meredith, and I watched home videos on their 27" color television. On the screen, a buoyant 5-year-old Scout donned an apron across her chest, under her armpits, and tied across her upper back. She walked out of the kitchen; the apron was swallowing her as she held out a plate of freshly baked cookies to her father for a taste. Her off-camera father asked, "Mmmmm. Did you make these yourself?" She replied, "Yep," and offered a cookie to her sister. Her father then asked, "Let's go into the other room and show Mommy your cookies." At this comment, little Scout's eyes widened, she looked into the camera, visibly distressed, and said, "No, they're no good. Mommy won't like them." Fade to black.

This fear of maternal disapproval was the root of much of the distress in the enmeshed maternal relationships. Daughters and granddaughters claiming that mothers and grandmothers could make them feel "inadequate," "not good enough," and "like my whole life is a failure," ascribing almost mythical proportions of power to their mothers and grandmothers. Later in the evening, Morgan confided, "I had no idea how much she needed my approval. What incredible power mothers have over their daughters!"

The contradictory pull between powerful and powerless was evident in all Elkwood maternal relationships. Yet, women in the enmeshed relationships reported experiencing the centrifugal and centripetal forces much more intensely. As indicated earlier in this chapter, it is often difficult to capture the complex centripetal (dominant) and centrifugal (countervailing) forces at play in a given relationship. However, in the enmeshed maternal relationships, the dominant anchor dialectic of powerful-powerless was strongly woven among countervailing forces associated with power such as powerful—submission, powerful—victim, powerless—dominance, powerless—victimizer. To understand how this dialectic functioned in Elkwood relationships, I first discuss some terminology related to power and then focus specifically on comparing differences in how enmeshed and connected relationships experienced this dialectical tension.

Powerfulness and Powerlessness

Certain terms resonate when discussing issues of power in the family. Thus, it seems important to clarify the following key terms: *resources, power, status,* and *dominance.* The term *resource* refers to all knowledge, skills, emotions, words, actions, and materials that are at the disposal of a person or group. Resources provide the potential for the exercise of power in maternal relationships. Additionally, *power* is a person's ability to control valuable resources, and may be tied to a person's *status*—his or her place in the social hierarchy of the family (Patterson, 1982). Certain kinds of resources and power accrue as members age within the family, whereas other kinds of resources and power will likely be lost (Klein & White, 1996).

Given the distribution of resources within any specific family hierarchy, power might be evaluated by its outcome, which is dominance. *Dominance* refers to the degree to which a person can influence and impose their will on the other; its counterterm, *submission*, refers to the degree to which a person gives up influence or yields to the wishes of the other. I think it is important to keep in mind that dominance itself is determined by the submissive response of others. Moreover, as Burgoon, Johnson, and Koch (1998) pointed out, "While power enables the display of dominance, and dominant behavior may solidify power—though correlated—dominance and power are not interchangeable concepts" (p. 310).

For adult women, life course events have implications for patterns of power in adult daughter–mother–grandmother relationships. As a younger woman ages, occupying many roles, gathering her own resources, and perhaps mothering her own children, she has less time and energy to be deferent to her elder's will or to submit to her power. She is coming into her own at the same time the older woman may feel she is losing power over certain resources. As daughters age, mothers are invested in their daughters as extensions of self, but they are also invested in maintaining their position as kin keepers and retaining power over resources relative to that position. In Elkwood, how tightly women grasped their resources and how much value women placed on certain resources determined how the contradictory pulls of powerfulness and powerlessness were enacted in their relationships.

Powerfulness and powerlessness are contradictory concepts; yet, as with other dialectics, they exist simultaneously at different levels and across time. Women manage exchange of resources on a daily basis, but normative expectations within the relational culture also dictate resource importance and allocation, affecting maternal relationships across the life span.

For all the Elkwood women, broader cultural norms addressing hierarchy defined the basic power structure in their families—a hierarchy in which the parent was inherently more powerful than the child. Although some developmental researchers argue that this might be a curvilinear relationship as woman moves through her life stages. But, for these women, as a woman aged and assumed new roles of mother and grandmother, her power in the family hierarchy did not as much lessen as it did shift in emphasis. Although certain resources were still within her domain to control (e.g., emotional resources), her power over other resources waned (e.g., material resources). In almost all of the maternal relationships, emotional resources were those that were most valued across the life span and there was acknowledgment and respect for the legitimate power held by any woman (defined by her place in the family hierarchy).

Control of Resources

The adult women of Elkwood gave, received, withheld, and denied themselves a number of resources during my stay. These resources fell into three domains:

support (instrumental, material, emotional), *regard* (respect, approval, affection, attention), and *inclusion* (acceptance). Resources were typically noncontingent—exchanged without strings attached—but this didn't mean that daily power struggles didn't occur. Generally, however, annoyance rather than hostility characterized minor power skirmishes.

Support. Day-to-day support was provided or refused across three domains: instrumental support, material support, and emotional support. *Instrumental support* refers to assisting with tasks, and this was an everyday phenomenon. All women would freely assist other women in their family if it were within their ability. For example, (grand)daughters would pick up groceries for mothers and grandmothers, take them to the hair salon, fix their hair, assist them with computer work, perform home maintenance, and take them on errands and to appointments. Mothers would also do grocery shopping, take their daughters shopping, babysit, provide a variety of instruction, and assist with recipes. Grandmothers would assist their granddaughters with fewer tasks that required mobility (e.g., grocery shopping), but more with tasks that allowed them to assist in their homes or the homes of their granddaughters, such as childcare, cleaning, laundry, and decorating.

Material support was less of an everyday phenomenon, but nonetheless constituted a good deal of the support exchanged among grandmothers, mothers, and daughters. Material goods, money, and time were among the most frequently proffered resources. Women in all roles consistently exchanged goods such as kitchen utensils, clothing, jewelry, use of vehicles, and free access to possessions. Lending or giving money was a significant resource that was highly valued, providing the person who controlled the resource with inordinate power. Two of the grandmothers in this study possessed ample financial resources, and gave financial support to their daughters and granddaughters as needed. Time was also viewed as a resource or commodity that one could give or withhold. Withholding one's personal time from another and demanding another's time were apt to engender conflict.

Emotional support was the most valued of all the different kinds of support exchanged among the women in these families. Listening to others, providing encouragement and hugs, offering advice, and nurturing a positive climate were among the most readily observable forms of emotional support. In adult grandmother–mother–daughter relationships, this support flowed upward as well as downward, with granddaughters offering advice and encouragement to mothers and grandmothers as well as grandmothers offering these to daughters and granddaughters. The metaphor of cheerleader once again emerged when discussing the notion of providing emotional support in maternal relationships—being on the sidelines, cheering for the partner's success. Not surprisingly, the act of giving advice in maternal relationships was more fraught with power issues than was the act of providing encouragement. The act of giving advice itself suggested a unidirectional flow of power in which one relational partner had the "right" information and counseled the other. As adult women, some resented the advice, especially when unsolicited, but others—especially adult granddaughters and daughters—expressed appreciation for advice offered by mothers and grandmothers. Georgie (Family #3) shared her perspective on maternal advice: "I never resented [their advice] at all. I was always taking it, you know, as a helpful pointer. Wow, good, I never knew that before and now I do." As discussed later in this chapter, welcoming maternal advice is not always the case.

As in all personal relationships, the Elkwood dyads all exercised power dynamics. Typically, power was exerted through provision of support (e.g., resources), yet there were also instances of wielding power through withholding support. The importance of a partner's interpretation of the motivation behind provision or withdrawal of support was also significant in these women's interactions. For example, one day Sam (Family #1) was annoyed that her mother was not available to babysit because she had a conflicting appointment. Sam grumbled about it, but "understood" and found alterative care for her child. Consider this in contrast to this episode with Katrina and Kelly (Family #2). Katrina said that when Kendra was younger, "I wanted to help Kelly with the baby. But, when I went over to help she burst into tears! 'You don't think I'm a good mother!' she'd yell. I've learned to hold back. But some grandmas don't." Kendra's interpretation of her mother's offer of support and Sam's interpretation of her mother's lack of support differed greatly. Layered within control and power issues were the provision, withholding, accepting, or denial of support.

Inclusion. A woman could control whether she included or excluded the other women in her life by virtue of what she said, did, or did not say or do. Women included others—made them feel a part of a unique relationship—by sharing their lives, filling others in on their comings and goings; sharing their thoughts, ideas, and dreams. These women possessed the power to embrace the other woman, include her into her life, acknowledge her, and accept her for who she was without judgment. These women also possessed the power exclude the other woman, offering disapproval and negative judgment redolent of rejection. For the women of Elkwood, inclusion of grandmothers, mothers, daughters, and granddaughters in lives was an essential part of every week if not every day, and an act that constituted the relationship itself. Among the acts of inclusion were mothers and daughters lunching together every day, "touching base" with one another multiple times during the week, visiting with each other, accepting each other in success as well as failure, feeling safe in the relationship to "talk about anything." Inclusion was a valuable resource that each individual had the power to manage.

Regard. The attention and acknowledgment associated with inclusion were also tightly linked to managing levels of *regard* in the relationship. Carl Rogers (1951, 1980) brought the phrase *unconditional positive regard* into common usage. Rogers, a clinical therapist, argued in his person-centered therapy that to help clients effectively they first have to feel totally accepted for who they are without any labels or conditions. He further indicated this unconditional positive regard is a basic human need in all relationships and is central to the development of respect. Regard is also referred to in interpersonal literature as *affiliation*, and Dillard, Solomon, and Palmer (1999) indicated that affiliation/regard reflects the fundamental phenomenological content of all relationships.

Most children seek to be accepted by their parents, to please them, and meet their expectations, and thus receive positive reinforcement in return. However, we don't often consider how adult children continue to seek parental (in this case maternal) approval and regard across the life span; nor do we consider the possibility that grandmothers and mothers seek their granddaughters' or daughters' approval. Despite age or social role, the Elkwood women sought to a greater or lesser degree to please those in their maternal relationships, looking for approval and ultimately desiring unconditional positive regard. Linda (Family #5), for example, gave her mother an incredible gift when she expressed regard for her mother in her college application essay. Becky said she will "always remember" that essay and the regard that Linda demonstrated for her mother. Sam (Family #1) persistently attempted to be the "best mom on the block" so that her daughters "will be proud of" her. Georgie indicated the she didn't "try to please my mom. I guess if I thought something would make her happy or please her I would go for it, but it just happens naturally I guess. I treasure our relationship and we just kind of naturally respect each other." Nonetheless, Linda added, "I know that she loves me no matter what—no matter what I do or don't do." Tabitha admitted that she would "feel guilty" if her mother disapproved of something she did or "if I lost her respect." "Respect," she added, "is something you earn and could easily lose."

Guilt and Interpersonal Power

Losing maternal respect was closely aligned with guilt for many of these women. Some thoughts on guilt:

> True guilt is guilt at the obligation one owes to oneself to be oneself. False guilt is guilt felt at not being what other people feel one ought to be or assume that one is. (Laing, 1961, chap. 10)

> Inflected forms: guilt-•tripped, guilt-•trip•ping, guilt-•trips
> *Informal* To make or try to make [someone] feel guilty. (*American Heritage*® *Dictionary of the English Language*, 2000)

> Hey, hey, hey. Come on! I know what guilt is. It's one of those touchy-feely words that people throw around that don't really mean anything … You know, like "maternal" or "addiction." (*Will & Grace*, quoted by Stipko Media, 1998)

Guilt and maternal relationships are somehow almost synonymous. Baumeister (1998) argued that guilt induction may be a normal process of socialization in family relationships. She said that mothers use guilt induction for the purposes of guiding children's day-to-day behavior. References to guilt induction unfortunately are typically confined to studies of parent–child relationships and abandoned on the steps of adolescence. Rarely do studies examine guilt induction within adult child–parent relationships. This study suggests that guilt induction not only crosses the life span of mother–daughter relationships but crosses generational boundaries into grandmother–granddaughter relationships as well.

Guilt is an interpersonally driven emotion, based on the need to maintain attachments to others (Baumeister, Stillwell, & Heatherton, 1994). The closer the emotional bond is between the parties, then the greater concern there will be for the other and for preserving the relationship; subsequently, the greater the potential that guilt will arise. When a sense of self is conceived primarily within the context of the relationship, then guilt is a strong motivator. In enmeshed relationships, particularly, guilt may be a particularly potent emotion. Generating guilt feelings in another—or guilt induction—was another form of power observed in the Elkwood maternal relationships. "Minor" yet insidious attempts at making the other feel guilty as well as more significant efforts to manipulate guilt were observed across many mother–daughter interactions. Fairly innocuous attempts were reported or observed in some relationships. For example, Georgie (Family #3) reported that her mother would, "just do little things. Like, we'll see a cute little girl or little boy somewhere and she'll be like, 'Oh Georgie, just think, some day.' I say, I know mom, give me a few years." Becky admits that she would use the "guilt card" at times although she tried not to. She shared, "I'll catch myself saying things like, 'Even though I've worked all day and I'm exhausted and all you've done is go to classes. *I'll* run to the store.' My God, I sound like my mother when I say things like that." Although these guilt attempts originated from the older women, there were also attempts by younger women to induce guilt. For example Kendra persecuted Kelly (Family #2) for "giving her up" as a baby and Morgan shunned Meredith (Family #6) for 5 days after telling her, "You're not there when I need you to help me with things, like the day I had my open house. So, why should I be there every time you want me for something?"

Many women suspect that power struggles in parent–offspring relationships decrease across adulthood, with most middle-aged offspring reporting fewer struggles than tensions than do younger offspring. In the case of the women in Elkwood, those who demonstrated fewer adult daughter–mother struggles were those in the connected relationships. These women learned or were learning to view their mothers as women instead of as their social role. Most felt secure in their mother–daughter relationship and focused their resources on maintaining positive regard.

Certainly, as young children, daughters are expected to obey their elders, to learn from them, to be managed by them. As the Elkwood women moved through the life course, the ones in connected maternal relationships moved toward a more reciprocal exchange of power—mutually respecting (if not obeying), learning from each other, and managing the relationship from the standpoint of women rather than their social roles as grandmother, mother, daughter, or granddaughter. However, for the younger women in enmeshed relationships, they professed regret at the lack of opportunity to know their mothers as persons—the mother's personality roles; instead, they only knew the older women in their performance roles as mothers who at once were loving and dominating, able to wield both behavioral and psychological control in the relationships.

POWERFULNESS AND POWERLESSNESS
IN ENMESHED AND CONNECTED RELATIONSHIPS

People in successful interpersonal relationships *share* control over their lives. However, the older women in the enmeshed relationships, typically mothers and sometimes grandmothers, constructed images of their (grand)daughters as extensions of themselves and as their (grand)daughter's protector. This perception seemed tied to the mothers' felt *responsibility* to influence their daughters' lives. Because, as Meredith insisted, "As a mother I am responsible for her successes and to blame for her failures." As an extension of self and as a protector, mothers and some grandmothers in enmeshed relationships felt duty bound to exert power over their (grand)daughters, both behaviorally and psychologically, in attempts to control outcomes. In reaction and resistance to these control attempts, powerless daughters perpetuated the "adolescent" struggle for behavioral, value, and emotional autonomy into adulthood; in some cases, across the entire life course.

Recall that within the enmeshed relationships in Families #1, 2, and 6, there tended to be a high degree of connectedness with demands for consensus and loyalty, and members are expected to think and act alike. The following discussion focuses specifically on these relationships, bringing in examples from the other relationships for contrast.

Behavioral Dominance

In enmeshed relationships, women often viewed their adult daughter/ mother/grandmother as a resource at their disposal, and they not only had the right, but the responsibility, to control that valuable resource. I refer to *behavioral dominance* as the degree to which one person influenced and imposed her will on the other to perform specific conduct. Its counter term, then, is *behavioral submission*, referring to the degree to which a person gave up influence or yielded to the wishes of the other to perform the specific conduct. Low levels of dominance may have involved monitoring behavior or setting limits, whereas high levels of dominance often dictated scripted behavior.

Because I lived with Family #1 during most of my stay in Elkwood, I have the most vivid examples from that family. The patterns across all 10 enmeshed relationships were nonetheless striking. In these relationships, mothers and sometimes grandmothers asserted behavioral dominance by closely monitoring adult offsprings' behavior, censoring and criticizing unacceptable performances, and dictating performance expectations. One woman would "pull" the other toward the dominant force of *powerful*, casting this other woman into the centrifugal force that carried her in a whirlpool—sometimes helplessly—toward the force of *powerless*.

Behavioral dominance frequently was accomplished through close monitoring of the other's behavior and expressing criticism both directly and indirectly. Drawing on work by Conger & Ge (1999), criticism is operationalized here as critical remarks, negative verbal comments, negative evaluative feedback, and negative affect. Most of the daughters across the three families referred to this, however, as the "constant comment." Diane (Family #1), for example, would tend to make indirect requests such as, "Do you have a problem with putting things in garbage? Do you need my help?" rather than merely asking someone to place an item in the garbage. She often used "you" statements and "shoulds"—"You should have put more salt in this," "Should have turned on the camera sooner," "Should have helped sooner." Her requests were polite but regularly laced with an element of sarcasm or implied judgment. One day, she approached Sam and me as we were in the car, ready to go to a restaurant for lunch. She avoided looking at me, but instead looked directly at Sam and asked, "If it's not too much *trouble* I wonder if I can't join you this afternoon." Sam later complained to me that her mother often placed her in the position of complying with maternal demands (requests?) or she would "face the consequences." Diane's daughters and granddaughters repeatedly expressed annoyance over Diane's direct and indirect criticism. Sam complained, "If you would go out and you would eat with her or grandma they would make comments. It's like, 'Of course she's not losing weight, look at what she's eating.' Or, um, 'You and [husband] shouldn't go out to lunch.' You know, I am almost 41 years old. Don't go out to lunch! Eat at home and you could lose some weight. Who needs it?"

One evening I joined Sam, her sisters, Diane, and Diane's husband for a quiet evening of playing games. We were settling in our chairs, people joking and laughing, and Sam picked up a magazine and read to us a short article about movie theater concessions. Out loud she read, "And there is no oil in the popcorn." Diane swooped in from the kitchen, strode over to where Sam sat, looked at the article and corrected, "You're wrong. It says no oil *on* the popcorn." The air stood still for a second and a half, and then Sam rolled her eyes and exhaled the word "Whatever."

Diane looked around at the uncomfortable and frankly puzzled expressions of those of us in the room and, in a bid to unravel the tension, admitted, "It's no big deal" (joking, joking) and asked, "Would anyone like some coffee?" Interestingly, Diane did not see herself as being critical or excessively monitoring her daughters' behavior. In fact, she argued that *her* mother (Sylvia, Family #1) was the critical and judgmental one in this grandmother–mother–daughter triad. Diane had vowed to herself that she would never become critical with her children because "I know how it feels." Sylvia, indeed, shared her daughter's penchant for proffering backhanded criticism. One day, Sam and I were helping Sylvia with her housework. While I was making a salad, Sam was cutting up potatoes to be boiled and mashed. Her grandmother looked over Sam's shoulder and said, "You know, you're cutting those up wrong. You don't *ever* cut them up any smaller than fourths." Sam looked at her grandmother with a look of defiance that conveyed to me, "Too bad, I'm going to cut them any way I want to cut them." Later, when I was talking with Sam, she told me, "You know, I'm helping her out, and I'm making them, so I'll do it my way. As if the only way to make perfect potatoes is to cube them into fourths!"

Morgan (Family #6) also complained that Meredith constantly commented on her daughters' behavior. Meredith's approach was even less direct than Diane's, yet still critical. The following episode occurred in Morgan's home after dinner one evening. Morgan was loading the dishwasher and Meredith started muttering something under her breath. I continued to wipe the counters during the following exchange:

Morgan asked, "What's the matter?"

"Nothing," Meredith replied. Clearly it was *something*.

"What did I do now?"

"If I were you I wouldn't put the plastic on the bottom."

"What plastic?"

"That Rubbermaid bowl."

"Oh. Okay." Morgan moved the bowl to the top shelf of the dishwasher.

Later that evening, I chatted with Morgan and asked her about the exchange. She told me that she had washed that particular bowl using the bottom shelf in her dishwasher for several years. I asked her why she moved it to the top shelf, considering it was her bowl and her dishwasher. She replied, "Oh, according to her I never load the dishwasher right. I just have to accept that. I don't say anything, don't get an attitude or anything, and she feels like she's contributed her 2 cents." Yet, Morgan *did* alter her behavior.

Kelly, as a 37-year-old adult, would also complain about her mother's controlling behavior. (Not incidentally, Kendra would make the same complaint about her mother—Kelly.) The night before Kelly was leaving to go on a short trip, she and I were sitting in Katrina's family room chatting when Katrina stormed down the stairs, pointed her finger at Kelly, and issued the following command in a fairly loud voice with an authoritative tone: "Pick up those shirts at the laundry before 9:00. And don't forget to take your dog to get sheared. I don't want any more dog hairs on this couch. And take your feet off that coffee table." I don't know about Kelly, but I felt like I was 6 years old and her comments were not even directed at me!

Katrina's image of herself did not include the persona of a "controlling" mother. One Friday evening after work, Katrina and I were kicking back and relaxing. She was making herself a Bloody Mary while I was nursing my son. The mood was relaxed enough for me to ask her about her own perceptions regarding her maternal dominance. She said:

> Oh my, well, this question's come up before when Kelly and I were in counseling. The counselor brought it up and, I, well, I don't have an answer. We really didn't pursue it because we were [in counseling] for Kelly, not me. But, he thought I needed the control and that's why I was hanging on and everything. I don't see myself as … I mean … I like to have control of my life and I like to have control over a situation, but I don't see myself as controlling with my children, I don't see myself as a controlling person. My theme in my mind when I was bringing my children up was to make them ready for the world and make them independent and shoot them out the door. (Family #6)

Note how she used the phrases "make them ready" and "make them independent" and the agency with which she indicated she would "shoot them out the door." As a parent myself I thought, "Do I assume that I can make my children ready, independent, etc.?" My answer to myself was that I certainly *hope* that my children will be independent and I wish to give them the resources necessary for achieving independence, but I highly doubt that I could *make them* any of these things. Although Katrina did not have an image of herself as controlling, her daughter, others, and at times her granddaughter nevertheless perceived her that way.

Although these brief examples do not do justice to the degree to which mothers and grandmothers in these triads asserted behavioral dominance in their relationships, the examples provide a glimpse into the kinds of interactions that defined the interpersonal exchanges among the women in enmeshed relationships. There was, however, some evidence on the surface level of the interactions that daughters resisted their mothers' dominant behaviors; for example, Sam forged away for the moment and diced the potatoes in the manner that she chose. However, what recurrently happened was that the persistent criticism drew energy from the woman being criticized, leaving her feel drained; as the old science fiction saying goes, she believed that "Resistance is futile." In order to regain the lost energy, she then deferred to the criticizer, capitulated, and sometimes adopted her mother's view of the world. Becky admitted, "Sometimes it is just too exhausting to question [the criticism], you just accept it, do what she wants, and move on." The interesting outcome of this, however, is that by deferring to the critical person's view of the world this empowered the criticizer, reinforced the behavior, and the critical pattern of interaction.

Psychological Dominance

It was truly striking how mothers in the enmeshed relationships situated them-selves as the mainline to their daughters' self-images, shaping both the mothers' and the daughters' personal identities, authoring the story of their maternal rela-tionships. Because provision of emotional resources (e.g., affection, affirmation, attention, inclusion, and support) was regularly contingent on a daughter's "ac-ceptable" performance, daughters (whose identities were closely entangled or fused with their mothers) became dependent on their mothers for their sense of security and personal affirmation. This dependence was similar to an addiction. The powerlessness that resulted from being denied emotional resources created a demand for those resources; that is, keeping daughters addicted to winning ma-ternal approval and affirmation to feel good about themselves. Truthfully, how-ever, these adult daughters recurrently confessed their desire to *stop* seeking the support, attention, and approval of their mothers.

Psychological control refers to the relative degree of emotional autonomy that parents allow (Gray & Steinberg, 1999). Psychological control promises a with-drawal of approval if offspring fail to issue an "acceptable" performance. It pro-motes concern with the approval of external others as the arbiters of accomplishment, rather than reliance on self-satisfaction. The outcome of this is what I am terming *conditional positive regard*, referring to provision of emo-tional resources and inclusion only when *a priori* conditions are met, tying power to manipulating, obtaining, giving emotional capital. Brewin, Andrews, and Furnham (1996) argued that much of what offspring learn about parental conditions for reward—parental expectations—might be learned implicitly rather than by explicit statements from a parent. Subsequently, Miller and Lee (2001) provided some evidence that messages of disappointment from parents conveyed intermittent and strategic rejection of offspring at low levels of negativity that ultimately asserted psychological control over their offspring.

In the late winter of my stay in Elkwood, there was excessive snowfall for the region, causing closings of schools and government offices, and consigning most of us to the indoors, cocooning in the warmth. The talks I shared with the women during these months were some of the most heartfelt and some of the most insightful. Like moths to the light, women who protested most vocifer-ously against their enmeshment with mothers were drawn to them daily.

Most of us were stranded in homes with little opportunity to venture out. My infant son reacted at first with calmness at the change in motion, the stillness, and the lack of activity in the air. Then, after several weeks, he began to be irritable, fussy, wanting to get out and about. Yet, despite the restrictions on movement in the town, these women managed to forge their way across lawns, streets, and

10-foot snowdrifts to visit with grandmothers and mothers; however, rarely did grandmothers and mothers venture to their (grand)daughters' homes.

One afternoon during this winter, Diane's daughters (Family #1) and husband gathered for her birthday party. Her mother, although living right next door, did not attend due to the weather. The mood was festive and cozy, a fire in the fireplace, eggnog simmering on the stove, and candles wafting a scent of vanilla into the air. As Diane sat to open her cards and gifts, Sam pointed out that her sister, Julie, was the one who planned this get-together—Sam was making perfectly clear who was to "get credit" for the event. Diane opened the first card and it was from Sam. She read the text, looked at the picture, and—sure enough—turned the card over (just like in the Hallmark advertisements)! She then exclaimed with a satisfied smile, "There is no way Julie can beat this card." Apparently there was an ongoing competition among Diane's offspring over who could give the *best* present, the *most moving* card. I learned that the competition included multiple categories: the "who can make mom cry with the most sentimental card" category and "the most underlines on the card" category. Lo and behold, Julie's card proved to evoke tears. Thus, Julie won for presenting the card with the most "heartfelt sentiment," whereas Sam won for the most underlines. Although Sylvia wasn't physically present at this party, her words from earlier in the week echoed in my mind; she had said, "Diane always feels like she has to prove herself to me to get my attention." I marveled at the transmission of this pattern across generations, the feeling of being in competition, having to prove oneself to feel included in the mother–daughter relationship. Later in the day, Sam, Julie, and I talked a bit more about the concept of maternal approval. I asked them if they perceived this as a pattern across generation, and their thoughts concerning this pattern. Sam shook her head sadly from side to side, gnawed on her thumb, and replied:

> I think my Grandma [Sylvia] always wanted acceptance from her mother. I know mom always wanted acceptance from her parents; I know we all want acceptance from our parents. It's a pattern, but really until this year, I'm like in a lot of therapy and stuff, It's like, why? I don't need acceptance. If I can't accept myself first, nobody else is going to accept me. I don't even look for my acceptance. I realize for the first time in my life, that I'm 41 … that I've never liked myself, I never liked who I was, I always tried to be somebody that wasn't me, just to please her, and that's like why I've done a lot of things in my life.

Julie added:

> Back in May I had just got done telling her that my posters were chosen to go to the state convention. I was only one of hundreds who submitted artwork for this display. I showed her the posters and do you know what she said? Not "Good job," … but "You really should take an art class. These show real promise!" Promise?! These were already chosen; they weren't works in progress! I knew what she meant. I just wish she could say "Good job" and leave it at that. I just couldn't

shake it, but I just wasn't very excited about the showing after that. It took a lot of joy out of it.

I asked them why they elected to "buy into" this need for their mother's approval even as adults, and they looked at one another and broke out laughing. I wasn't quite sure why this was funny, but they assured me they weren't really laughing at the question. Julie said, "It's just that if you don't laugh, well …." Sam interrupted, "Well, then you cry!" Julie overlapped, "We've wondered about that question for years." Although seeking the answer in therapy and through spirituality, these adult women in their 40s had not yet achieved a satisfactory understanding of why their desire for maternal approval affected their lives.

Later that week, Diane was dusting her living room. She had numerous crystal and porcelain collectibles to clean, and as she dusted, she wondered aloud, "Why the housekeeper can't seem to dust under items rather than just around them." I turned on my recorder, assisted her with the dusting, and we talked about the weather and her collectibles. Finally, the topic moved to Diane's mother, Sylvia. Diane said, "With you asking all these questions I've been thinking about this a lot lately." She stopped and continued to clean. "Well," I said, "what have you decided from all this thinking?" She stopped dusting and directed me to the sofa, where she and I sat. She replied:

All [my mother's] tries at suicide were just attempts to manipulate us. I can remember when I was 6 years old my mother threatening suicide. She was going to cut her wrists, and having the bathroom door locked and my dad beating on the door yelling for her and all this kind of thing, so that's the first memory I have of the suicide thing, although it has gone on all my life, for at least 10, 15, 20 times; I don't know how many times. Some of them have been very serious. There have been several times when we didn't know whether she would pull through or not. … I always took the suicide attempts seriously and I was always upset, but this was always the reaction she wanted. I don't think I've ever gotten to the point where I have not been manipulated. I'm just not being manipulated as frequently. But my Dad … well he spoiled her rotten, and what she gets is what she wants. All these were attention getters for him, but when he wouldn't give [her] the attention, then she demanded [it] from others, and I was the giver. I was always a giver, I felt I was always the giver in practically all situations, not just with her but I felt I was a giving person. I always felt I had a lot of love to give, and I gave it freely and easily. It wasn't a hardship and that's what I felt. (Family #1)

Diane learned at an early age that "attention" was a resource given and withheld. From her perspective, her value as a daughter came from giving attention and (as I learned later) "earning" the attention of her parents. For Diane, the normal way of interacting with offspring was to demand, manipulate, withdraw, and offer attention, inclusion, and regard in exchange for another resource. She frequently solicited her daughters for emotional support (this was not surprising, given the enmeshed nature of the relationships), and she indicated that they "should" provide it for her because "that's what daughters do." Indeed, that is what she was required to do as a daughter—to be the emotional support, to "drop everything in her life to attend to her mother's needs." Tragically (or not—depending on your perspective), her daughters were learning to resist her demands for emotional support and inclusion in their lives. During the time I was in Elkwood, Sam said she was "actively fighting against the pull of her mother's needs." Because Diane had continuously—even to her current age of 64—provided this support to her own mother, she felt cheated by daughters who were erecting boundaries and "ignoring her needs."

Although moving, this relational dynamic was not unique to Family #1. Kendra (Family #2) suggested that her mother (Kelly) is "a God … [thus] it is very important to please her." Yet, Kelly argued that she was always seeking the approval of *her* mother "to make up for the 2 years [during my youth] where I screwed up." Kelly was a self-proclaimed perfectionist. She admitted, "If I'm not the best then I quit. I need to get As, at grades, everything. I laugh at myself now. I get down on myself if I don't succeed. My friends say, 'Kick yourself some more.' I'm superwoman. I'm a workaholic."

Morgan (Family #6) also indicated that she was "tired of always needing [my mother's] approval." She didn't, however, believe she could escape this. She said, "I think everyone [in the family] is just trying to please everyone and it's so stupid, we just have to accept people the way they are, each person, individually, that's what they are, you know. I know that everyone is insecure. I don't know, I'm very insecure with myself so I don't know if I can do it though." Morgan's daughter, Scout, believed that her grandmother intimidated her mother. She seemed very sure of her belief that:

> Mom fears Grandma's reaction. She even says, "I'm afraid she'll get all upset and there will be a problem." Just last week I came home from my trip to Jersey and my Mom says, "Did you return the call to Grandma? You don't want her to get nervous." She reminded me twice. Boy, did I feel like a child having to be told what to do and how to conduct my behavior. Of course, I didn't say anything and I called Grandma right away cause I didn't want either one of them to get upset.

Getting "upset" typically entailed withholding affection, ignoring the other, withholding support, or expressing "disappointment in" the offspring. The use of disappointment as a strategy to induce guilt recurred frequently in the enmeshed relationships. Becky (Family #5) said that she "feels invisible when not pleasing my mother, when she is disappointed in me." Both disappointment strategies and guilt were linked to psychological control within the enmeshed relationships in Elkwood.

Disappointment.   Schafer (1999) and Miller and Lee (2001) argued that the affective experience of *disappointment* has not received the analytic attention it deserves. Feelings of disappointment are typically tied to feelings of regret. If we have high investment in something, that investment is linked with hope, desire, and promise; when the investment doesn't pay off, then disappointment ensues. Vvan Dijk, Wilco, van der Pligt, and Zeelenberg (1999) argued that disappointment has a greater association with the absence of a positive outcome than presence of a negative outcome. However, these examinations of disappointment do not address the transactional nature of expressing disappointment "in" another person.

Research by de Waal (1993), Jordan (1993), Mann (1998), and Miller and Lee (2001) revealed that the interpersonal strategy of conveying disappointment in a person (as opposed to expressing feeling disappointment *for* a person) might be a form of exerting psychological dominance. Disappointment in another conveys to that other that he or she is responsible for both your shattered hopes and the fact that your investment in him or her did not pay off. Williams and Bybee (1994), in their research on schoolchildren, discovered that nearly 60% of parents expressed their disappointment in their child to provoke the child's guilty feelings. Of course, intermittent expressions of disappointment do not necessarily contribute to psychological dominance. We pointed out in Miller and Lee (2001) that two kinds of disappointment are salient to understanding disappointment as a psychological dominance strategy: state disappointment and trait disappointment. *State disappointment* refers to present feelings of being let down based on failure of another to meet a current expectation, and *trait disappointment* refers to ongoing or frequent feelings of being let down by others (Miller & Lee, 2001). State disappointment may be most common in relationships, and repeated state disappointment may lead to trait disappointment. This process served as a tool for achieving psychological dominance among the maternal relationships in Elkwood.

A Model of Maternal Dominance

An intriguing pattern of interaction emerged as I spent more time in the homes of these women. This pattern suggested a process by which mothers in the enmeshed relationships, along with grandmothers such as Sylvia, Diane, and Meredith, achieved dominance in their relationships with daughters and granddaughters. Although I will present some evidence to suggest that this pattern was reciprocal (e.g., daughters achieving dominance through a similar pattern with aging mothers), among the relationships observed in this study the older women were most likely to achieve dominance—most significantly, psychological dominance—over younger women. Fig. 4.1 illustrates this model.

Unconditional Love With Conditions. As mentioned earlier, scholars don't often consider how adult daughters continue to seek maternal approval across the life span. As I saw in Elkwood, this was not a highly salient issue for the women in connected, healthy relationships. However, it emerged as being immensely important in the enmeshed relationships. In these enmeshed maternal relationships, a (grand)daughter's continued acceptance by a mother or

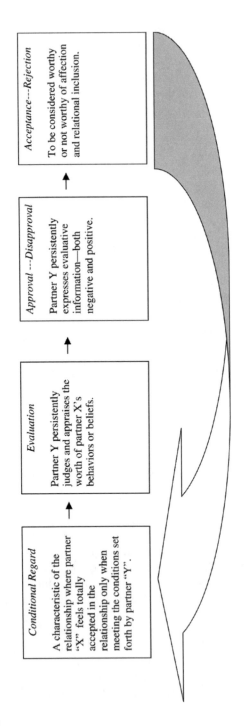

Conditional Regard

A characteristic of the relationship where partner "X" feels totally accepted in the relationship only when meeting the conditions set forth by partner "Y".

Evaluation

Partner Y persistently judges and appraises the worth of partner X's behaviors or beliefs.

Approval --Disapproval

Partner Y persistently expresses evaluative information—both negative and positive.

Acceptance---Rejection

To be considered worthy or not worthy of affection and relational inclusion.

FIG 4.1.   Model of maternal dominance in enmeshed relationships.

grandmother was conditional on the daughter or granddaughter meeting maternal expectations. Positive regard was conditional on receiving a favorable evaluation of behavior, thus receiving approval. Consistent negative evaluation, most often in the form of criticism and profession of disappointment, led to persistent low levels of rejection. Thus, as the model in Fig. 4.1 illustrates, in enmeshed maternal relationships with perceived conditional regard, lower-status women experienced an intense need to elicit positive evaluations and approval from the higher-status woman to assure relational acceptance. In this model, approval and relational acceptance were manipulated emotional capital.

Dowling (1988) stated, "Most girls growing up learn that mother has particular expectations of them. Daughter is the alter-ego after all. The one who is most like mommy. It's important that she be wonderful in whatever ways society, at that moment in time, deems women to be wonderful" (p. 12). This quote illustrates the importance of maternal expectations in defining the mother–daughter relational identity. For some of the women in Elkwood, the measure of a good mother was her daughter's or granddaughter's performance; the measure of a good daughter was maternal approval.

We are vulnerable to what our mothers think of us, whether we like it or not. The differences between the enmeshed and merely connected maternal relationships was that in the connected relationships, pleasing (grand)mother was important *but not necessary.*

Sylvia and Sam (Family #1), Kelly (Family #2), Becky (Family #5), and Meredith and Scout (Family #6) argued in a unified voice, a pain-filled chorus, that she (mother or grandmother) *judges me constantly and is constantly disappointed in me.* Sam, in Family #1, said that she constantly felt "like a failure, a disappointment, because I could never could live up to [my mother's or grandmother's] expectations." She believed that her mother always wanted her to "go to college, get good grades, be wealthy, and beautiful." Unfortunately, things did not turn out that way in Sam's frame of reference. She pointed out that she "married a man who was abusive, I really don't have a career she approves of, I'm not pretty." Sam indicated that her mother would only provide positive evaluations for accomplishments of some sort, "for looking good or doing good." She was frustrated by her desire for her mother's approval. She indicated, "Yes, I need her approval. All the time. Goddamnit, it is annoying!" She claimed that this constant competition for her mother's approval is why she dislikes Christmas. She pointed out:

I hate Christmas here. Cause we always have to dress up and look nice here. Christmastime and Thanksgiving ... Easter over at my mom's is the biggest anxiety. Because I know I'm going to have a bad hair day, I need to find something new to make me look nice, look good, so that I get a positive not a negative comment. At home [just with my husband and children] I can concentrate on what the holiday means. Here at my mom's it is "What are you wearing?"

Sam's daughter indicated that she, too, found her mother to be the "ruler by which she measures" herself; her mother's approval "defines my self-worth" and that if her mother is disappointed in her "it is very hard."

Sam's mother, Diane, also felt "like a failure" in the eyes of her parents: "I was never acknowledged .... I'm still not." She tried to be "the best person she could be" but she perceived that in her mother's eyes "that was never enough." One insight she did share with me was that she also encourages her children to be "the best they can be and live up to their potential" because of an experience she had in college. She did not perceive this to have anything to do with her relationship with her mother, however. She related the following:

> When I graduated from nursing training, the supervisor would call you into the office and give you your pin and talk to you for a little bit, and I went in and her first words to me were "Miss Turner, I must tell you that I have been very disappointed in you." I was so upset. I didn't know why. I had good grades, I didn't excel in any one area, but I had more than passable grades. Then she showed me. We had taken aptitude tests, 16 hours of testing over 2 days and I had the highest scores ever to come across in the whole school—ever. Every one of my grades was almost at the very top of that chart. Then I felt terrible that I hadn't put forth more effort.

> Maybe that's why I try my best and encourage my kids to do their best. I had no high expectations of myself. Had I known that I was capable of doing this, I had no idea, no idea. But had I known, I would have tried to live up to it. I had finally found I was a worthy person.

This last sentence very informative. Diane consistently indicated that she did not perceive herself to be worthy in her mother's eyes. She was consistently "judged" and "blamed" and did not feel important to her mother "no matter what she did." In her experience, recognition of her abilities *by others* determined her sense of worth. If her mother could not author Diane's identity, then she would let others determine what that identity was to be. For Diane, to be successful and "be your best" became the means by which she then began to judge herself. "Unfortunately," Sam added, one day as we were discussing her mother, "since she has little opportunity to feel successful in her life. Her worth is now based on how much [her children and grandchildren] accomplish." According to her daughter's perception, Diane's measure of her worth as a person was inextricably tied to the performances of her children. Sam, for one, was tired of trying to provide a stellar performance.

For Meredith, Morgan, and Scout in Family #6, a similar pattern unfolded. Scout, as one of the youngest in the family, shared with me the following perception of the women in her family:

> Everybody is so critical and judgmental. Very. I think that's what has built the insecurity in everyone. I think the women just try to please everyone and it's so stupid. We just have to accept people the way they are, each person, individually, that's what they are, you know. I know that everyone is insecure. I'm very insecure with myself and I know my sisters are definitely, which is obvious.

From Meredith down to Scout and her siblings, insecurity was manifest. This insecurity led to perfectionism that, in my opinion, often got in the way of their day-to-day happiness. One day into the sixth month of my stay in Elkwood, I was on my way to Morgan's house, where Scout was cooking dinner for her family and me:

The weather was fair and dry and the sky was a watercolor of navy and powder blues, along with the burnt orange of sunset. As I struggled into Morgan's front door with my stroller and the 500 lbs. of requisite baby paraphernalia, I heard Scout in the kitchen exclaim, "God almighty what am I doing!"

After dumping all unnecessary materials into the corner and scooping up my son and my tape recorder I went into the kitchen to see what was up. There was Scout with pasta dough sticking to her fingers, plastered on her cheek, and spotting her silk blouse. A pot of liquid was boiling on the stovetop and dishes were stacked on the table waiting to be placed for dinner.

"Gosh darn it!" She wrinkled her brow and pulled semi-crisp croissant rolls from the oven. They still looked good to me. Morgan walked in and took my son from my arms and I offered to help set the table.

"It is all messed up," complained Scout.

"What is?" I asked.

"The dinner. I had this great menu planned and now it's going to suck."

"I think it looks great."

"Oh yeah, well, this homemade tortellini looks more like apple dumplings, burnt croissants, I couldn't find Boston lettuce for the salad and so we're stuck with red leaf ... anyway, it doesn't matter. I just wanted this to be nice and now it sucks."

Morgan interrupted, "Say it stinks or this is awful, not 'It sucks.' "

Scout scowled, "Why?"

Morgan said, "It doesn't sound right, it sounds coarse."

Scout turned to me. "Whatever. Anyway, um, I'm sorry this didn't turn out better."

I repeated, "It smells and looks great to me."

After dinner, we all retired to the family room to digest the meal and chat. Morgan turned to Scout and offered, "Honey, that was a good meal."

Scout hook her head. "Thanks, but it could have been better."

Morgan shook her head and said to me, "You see? I see her constantly set herself up, and I tell her all the time ...," turning to Scout, "don't I ...?" then back to me, "She sets herself up with such high expectations that she will definitely fail." Then back to Scout, "You then berate yourself because you did fail. That's where you're comfortable, I think."

Scout replied, "Well ... you know that because you're like that."

Morgan sat for a minute, looking at her daughter, then at me, and answered, "Yeah. I see it because I understand it, because it's me."

This day-in-the-life scenario provides a glimpse into the world of most of the women involved in enmeshed maternal relationships—a need to please and an almost palpable aversion to failure. Becky (Family #5) admitted, "Even today it is hard to fail. That's something that is new for me to learn. I mean it's *okay to fail*. I've instilled that in my children and they're okay not getting perfection tests or not real competitive in sports. It's okay to fail, you're an okay person, you're still loved. I have to learn that myself."

Sam's daughter (Family #1) perceived that her mother was "always below" her aunt in her grandmother Diane's eyes, because this aunt "went out and succeeded." She admitted that because she was taking some time off from college that she "felt like a failure and that's the worst thing—being a failure." She further admitted that she "hate[s] failing herself, but what's worse is failing others … especially my grandmother."

Scout indicated that her "Mom is trying to break the cycle of how her grandmother treated her mother and how grandma [Meredith] treats her." Her perception is that with her grandmother she "doesn't live up to the expectations, like I am constantly disappointing her. I know that my mom feels that too."

Morgan admitted that "one note of criticism from my mother and it's enough to ruin my self-confidence for a month!" I had the opportunity to discuss this issue with Morgan on many occasions, and we talked about her daughter and her perception of how she had perpetuated this cycle of maternal dominance. Morgan was astute enough to observe it, but was honestly dumbfounded that her daughter "feels the same rejection that I did [when I was growing up]." She offered, "When Scout was growing up I corrected her to make her better. But, she didn't see it as a correction but as failure. That she was bad as a person, not that her behavior was bad. In her mind there was no room to be different."

Meredith was equally confused by her own daughter's insecurity. One morning, as we were sitting and talking on her front porch swing, she shrugged her shoulders and said, "[Morgan] perceived herself as not being accepted and not being loved and, you know, I just couldn't see this because of the way I felt about her. I never saw that, which was really difficult when I hear her say these things, because I still can't see her in that light."

These mothers and grandmothers in enmeshed maternal relationships rarely saw themselves as rejecting or contributing to their (grand)daughters' insecurity, although Becky (Family #5) pointed out that when her mother punished her she conveyed that Becky was a bad person, "not that my behavior was bad, but that I was a bad person." Charlotte, on the other hand, had no recollection of these messages in rearing her daughter. Yet, even at the age of 63, on more than one occasion she mentioned "If Becky was a good daughter …" then somehow her life would be different.

Somehow (grand)mothers' happiness, their identities, were entangled in their (grand)daughter's positively or negatively evaluated performances. The requirement for appropriate performance sometimes extended to external evaluation of performances by others outside the family circle. Diane indicated, "[My mother] would share my sister's accomplishments with others—not to highlight my sister—but to somehow prove she was a good mother." Morgan reported that she "would never have the money, the career, and the externals that her mother needs [to fulfill her conditions]." She added, "And those are the things that make her happy."

Kelly (Family #2), Morgan and Scout (Family #6), Becky (Family #5), and Diane and Sam (Family #1) consistently indicated they had to "prove themselves" as worthy to their mother or grandmother. Scout pointed out that she knows her grandmother "loves her and her expectations are because she wants me to be happy. But, I'm tired of trying to make her happy. I want to do what makes me happy." Sadly, Sam pronounced that she wanted to change this pattern in her family. She said, "I just want my kids to be happy. You know, I don't know if my mom would accept me if I was a garbage collector. There would be certain things that, I think my mom does have unconditional love with conditions. You know, and maybe, maybe not when it came right down to it, I don't know, but I wouldn't want to test it."

The younger partner became highly dependent on her maternal partner's positive evaluation and approval in order to feel accepted in the relationship. These women professed love for each other in many, many ways; they shared resources and provided support. Yet, the women who felt powerless reported an intense dependence on their mothers' approval to define their own identity. Near the end of my time in Elkwood, Sam came to a realization that she shared with me: "I've always tried to be who [my mother] has wanted me to be. But, now I see that I can only be who I am and ask her to accept me for who I am. But, ya know ... I don't know who that is really. I just don't want to do that to my kids. They can be who they are, no more, no less. I can't tell them who they are. They need to figure that out for themselves."

Approval in Connected Relationships. The experience of the women in the connected relationships was in direct contrast to that of the women in the enmeshed relationships. I would hear, "I can't relate to a time when [my daughter] has disappointed me" or "No, I never felt like I disappointed [my mother] by something I did or didn't do. No, she was good at making me feel good about myself. If I was disappointed in myself or something she would just make me forget about it." Linda (Family #5) said that her mother was her supporter rather than her critic:

I'm going to college and I expect to get a Master's in social work, to work with the homeless. I think what my mom wants for me is to be well rounded. She's good about it. Actually, I think I'm a lot harder on myself than she is ever hard on me. She's good about it, encouraging me in what I do. I've never heard her say, "Oh, you should have, why didn't you do that better." I've never heard her say anything like that.

Gina (Family #3) pointed out that her mother never really "said a whole lot about my successes. I didn't get rewarded or complimented … or punished. It was something that made me proud and that was my motivation." This approach seemed to be transmitted intergenerationally. Georgie indicated that "never, never in her life were my mother or grandmother more loving or affectionate if I did well or less if I didn't do good." Tabitha added her voice to the chorus: "Nuh, uh. I've never really felt any pressure from my mother. She's not like that. I kinda motivate myself."

In these connected relationships, success and failure were framed as personal issues, not as relational issues. Disappointments were framed as being "disappointed *for*" rather "disappointment *in*" the partner. Barb said, "Of course, I still wanted to please my mother and I think that Tabby wants to please me, but it is because we respect each other." These women demonstrated unconditional positive regard for one another with noncontingent rewards. Moreover, respect and personal motivation were what guided behavior, rather than a motivation to please others in order to avoid rejection.

Rejection in Enmeshed Relationships.   Approval is the state of favorable regard and satisfactory evaluation. The women in the enmeshed maternal relationships reported that it was paramount to achieve maternal approval in order to receive acceptance from their mother or grandmother. Acceptance as expressed by these women was the state of being acceptable or worthy.

During an emotional afternoon of talking and crying with Sam and her sister approximately 10 days after Sam's disclosure that she was feeling suicidal, Sam reiterated, "I have got to work on me. I know we all want acceptance from our parents. But it is a pattern in our family. My mom wanted acceptance from her mother; I want it from mine. But, if I can't accept myself first, then nobody else is going to accept me."

Remember, these families were emotionally close. It was not as if grandmothers or mothers emotionally rejected their offspring in an explicit manner. Daughters and granddaughters who did not meet the *a priori* conditions were just not *fully* accepted, not given as much attention as others in the family—emotionally manipulated. What occurred were a series of low-level rejections embedded within criticism or manipulation of emotional resources (e.g., withdrawing attention, shaming, and encouraging the other to feel guilty for authoring a disappointment). These low-level forms of rejection were subtle manipulations, but women reported that such manipulations nevertheless made them feel "invisible," "like a failure," "not worthy," "always off-center and insecure," and "uncertain about how to make her happy with me."

When Sam was pregnant with her last child, she was in her mid-30s. When she told her mother of her pregnancy, her mother's reaction was to say, "How can you be so damn selfish?" Sam professed to be hurt and shocked by her mother's reaction. She revealed:

> My mom said that it was not that she didn't want another grandchild, it was just that she thought it was selfish of me to have a child late in life. She said something like, "You'll die and leave your husband as a widower with four other kids, just because you want another baby. All you think about is yourself. How could you do that?" It wasn't like she said, "Oh gee, there are risks you know and I'm concerned about that, we'd miss you." It was like, "You're selfish and not a worthy mother."

This sense of unworthiness pervaded the talk of daughters in the enmeshed relationships.

Summary of the Powerful-Powerless Dialectic

In this discussion of the powerful–powerless dialectic, the term *power* referred to a person's ability to control valuable resources and was linked to a woman's status in the hierarchy in her family. Dominance, on the other hand, referred to the degree to which a woman imposed her power or will on her relational partners.

These data suggested that as daughters aged and struggled toward autonomy, all mothers were invested in maintaining connections with their daughters. Differences began to emerge, however, in how mothers across the enmeshed and connected relationships struggled to adjust their power base in their maternal relationships. As daughters developed into women and mothers in their own right, mothers/grandmothers in the enmeshed relationships struggled to retain control over emotional resources, manipulating these resources in ways that tightly bound (grand)daughters into the web of enmeshment. Thus, this enmeshment discouraged the younger woman from differentiating and seeking emotional and even behavioral autonomy from mother. In some cases, this dominance was transmitted across three generations (e.g., Families #1 & #6), whereas in others this was observed in only one generation (Families #2 & #5).

Much of the literature on mother–daughter relationships mentions the "perfect mother myth," yet in these data I witnessed the "perfect daughter" syndrome. To some extent, daughters did want their mothers to be infallible, to be powerful. Yet, a key distinction is that these women wanted and admired powerful mothers but did not desire these mothers to exert power *over* them as adults. The thing about perfection is that, ultimately, if you expect someone to be perfect sooner or later you will criticize that person for his her faults. High expectations, criticism, and disappointments along with love and concern colored all of the enmeshed maternal relationships, whereas acceptance, support, and respect characterized the connected maternal relationships.

Mothers are typically the emotional caretakers of the family, and the older women in Elkwood tended to feel the burden of responsibility for keeping things "running smoothly" in their relationships with daughters and granddaughters. Yet, as the younger women matured, those in connected relationships appeared to share the responsibility of maintaining their maternal relationship. For women in connected relationships, adjustment to changes were accomplished with relative ease, discussed, and even welcomed. In the enmeshed relationships, many mothers felt "forced" to relinquish control and this was often accompanied by feelings of loss and powerlessness. Manipulating emotional resources became a way for many of the dominant women to retain strong emotional and behavioral connections with their daughters and granddaughters. By establishing high expectations for their offspring, they felt they were doing their jobs as mothers and grandmothers. Unfortunately, in these enmeshed relationships, daughters and granddaughters risked maternal rejection if they did not meet these expectations. Moreover, it was the older women who controlled what were "acceptable" levels of differentiation to be tolerated in the relationship. For women in the enmeshed maternal relationships, there was an overarching need to please others to avoid rejection, often to the *exclusion of pleasing self.*

PERSON-POSITION ORIENTATION

Power and manipulation of resources are related, as well, to the final dialectic identified in these data. The adult women in Elkwood braided their lives around powerful anchors of accountability to one another. They began by anchoring their relationships in a sociological role as granddaughter, daughter, mother, or grandmother, then weaving layers of individuality and uniqueness across, under, and over that anchor. As each woman grew to see the other as a unique person and not in her social role, she still maintained her role status, but learned to respect the other as a woman in her own right. I began to see quite clearly how the balance between interactions with the other woman as a unique person with whom one *wants to* interact met with resistance from the countervailing force of interacting with her as one's family member with whom one *has to* interact.

Although Sam clearly experienced animosity toward her mother, she still maintained that her mother "is family and family is everything," and although Rowena was more than 45 years older than Georgie, she made a point to have frequent interaction with her granddaughter. She explained, "I love her because she is my granddaughter. I like her because she is a good person, a friendly girl." Among the more connected maternal relationships, a person orientation was dominant, whereas among those women in enmeshed relationships, a position orientation was most dominant. Nonetheless, among all the women in Elkwood, there was a conspicuous desire to be seen as a unique person and not interact purely at the level of one's social position (e.g., daughter, mother, grandmother). At the same time, there was a desire to learn about and see the other woman as a person, rather than just as her social position. Interestingly, the women in the connected relationships seemed to have satisfied these desires more capably than did the women in enmeshed maternal relationships.

Person-Position Dialectic and Relational Theory

The dialectical tension that existed within the person-position duality perfectly illustrates the strength of relational theory to explain maternal relational experience. Human development and psychological theories to date have suggested that young women must move away from family—from mothers and grandmothers—to become autonomous mature women, independent from maternal ties. An alternative that makes much more sense is the suggestion in *relational theory* that healthy adult maternal relationships emphasize interdependence, balancing competing pulls of person and position with one's relational partner as well as one's relational self. Fishbane (2001) pointed out that we are "relational selves," simultaneously a unique person and one who is embedded in a relationship with the other. The autonomous self "does not come at the expense of the relationship; rather, it occurs in the context of relationship," and being mature is seeing self within the context of your roles and relational positions (Fishbane, 2001, p. 275). Women in the healthier, connected relationships in Elkwood maintained their own personal history but also acknowledged their "relational embeddedness"; they were able to ground their own identity in their existing relationships. In the enmeshed relationships, women were not as successful in accomplishing interdependence of personal identity and role position. The pull toward position or social role (e.g., as a mother) almost always served as a dominant force pulling these women away from acknowledging the unique person who was their daughter, mother, granddaughter, or grandmother.

Position and Role Responsibilities

Providing protection and care for maternal kin were key responsibilities tied to maternal roles. The need to protect one's kin did not automatically stop once a woman reached adulthood. Indeed, as Morgan (Family #6) said, "You just need to protect them from different things." Her daughter Scout also felt protective of her mother. Scout shared, "I feel like I've spent my life protecting her, to do anything to make sure she's protected. I won't tell her things that could hurt her. I want to protect her; I'm her daughter." Some women professed that it was a function of the maternal role to protect kin and expressed hurt when they didn't receive that expected protection.

When Sam (Family #1) discussed the incident in which her friend's father "felt her up," she interpreted this event as a time when her mother did not protect her. The father of her friend would coerce 12-year-old Sam and another young girl into sitting on his lap in order to place his hands under their shirts or between their legs. She recalled that this man would have each girl sit, in turn, on his lap while he drove his car out on country lanes; have them sit on his lap as they watched a favorite television show; sit on his lap before they could go to bed during sleepovers. Sam reported that after a few instances of this "inappropriate behavior" she elected to tell her mother what was happening. Her mother's response was to say, "Well, then you can't go back." Sam confided to me that she didn't think her mother did "anything about it." Yet, what really hurt Sam was that 1 month later her mother invited this man to a dinner party at their home. Sam was astonished Diane would betray her like that, and revealed that she expected her mother to protect her, but regrettably felt that "in the end, she didn't [protect me]."

Although Gina and Georgie had maintained a dominant person orientation in their relationship, Georgie acknowledged that she appreciated the times when her mother "mothered" her and provided protection. She confessed that during college she dated one young man for several years but had been unhappy. Her mother was "very direct. She doesn't have a problem with being the mom when she has to be. She said, 'You shouldn't be unhappy and crying all the time. If you love him and he loves you and this is a relationship worth having, then it would make you happy and not miserable.' " Georgie believed her mother "was right to intervene. She just wanted to protect me from being hurt any more."

Grandmothers in the connected relationships almost all expressed an awareness that they could do very little to protect their daughters and granddaughters. Many tried to influence their daughters, but most insisted that is was "the mother's job to protect and give advice .... I just have to be there to support my granddaughter." Lois said that the role of a grandmother is to merely "be present." Grandmothers would assist and provide such care as with homework, childcare, gifts, and activity coordination. It was up to daughters and granddaughters to provide care once mothers and grandmothers became more dependent or infirm during their elder years.

Two thirds of the elderly receive some level of care from their children, with daughters functioning as the most common caregiver (Cantor, 1992). The women in Elkwood were not an exception to this pattern, but those in connected relationships experienced this role function a bit differently than did those in enmeshed relationships. The connected women tended to view caregiving as an activity that was merely another dimension of the relationship, and expressed desire to provide care for the person in need. Lois indicated that when her elderly mother was declining in health, "We got together every week, and my sisters and I cared for her the last year, took turns going in and staying with her. It was difficult, but I enjoyed that time with her and when it got too hard we had another lady stay with her for spells." The women in the enmeshed relationships, however, felt more duty bound to provide care. For example, Becky envisioned herself as the dutiful daughter who was the only one responsible for her ailing mother, and resented that she has "to take care of her [mother]." Note how the sense of community in Lois's family contributed toward a relatively enjoyable caregiving experience, in contrast to the burden interpreted by Becky for being obligated to take care of her mother.

The history of Becky's relationship with her mother certainly contributed to her caregiving experience, but not to whether or not she actually provided care. Becky said that she does everything in her power to make sure her mother has "what she needs." Research by Parrott and Bengston (1999) discovered that a history of conflict in parent–adult child relationships did not interfere with exchanges of help and support in the parent's elderly years. This research commented on the actual exchange of support and assistance, but did not truly address the qualitative experience of providing care in the context of a relationship that has been riddled with a history of conflict or nonreciprocal support. Katrina recalled that her mother "was very ineffective [as a mother] and didn't take care of us, and then when she needed us to take care of her, I think that's when it hit me. *I don't want to take care of you. You weren't there for me.*" Katrina, however, admitted that ultimately she, along with her siblings, cared for their mother in her remaining years. She argued that her mother "kept us very close and made us feel very obligated. It's a way of getting people there, like don't forget me ..."

Some women, like Diane (Family #1), were so invested in their role as caretaker that it inhibited their ability to view maternal kin as individuals outside of their role positions as people who needed care. Diane provided some insight when she shared with me that she "babysat a lot" for her younger brother. "He had asthma and several times I would have to call [my parents] home because he would have asthmatic attacks, but even with that, now, I am thinking, I was supposed to take care of that too." Moreover, when her mother would make a suicide attempt, Diane was the one who was contacted. She shared, "I was always called before anybody else was called, and then I would have to take over and take care of everything, get the doctor, and all that kind of thing. It happened in my 20s, 30s, 40s, and onward." Even later in life, when her daughter Sam tried to release her from the responsibility of being the only caregiver, Diane didn't seem to want to relinquish the power that the role afforded her. Recall that, as an adult, Sam told her mother, "Your responsibility is to you and your husband. That's all you have to be responsible for [now that your children are grown]." Diane indicated that she did not see this offer as one to release her from a burdensome responsibility (responsible for others' care), but instead viewed it as a rejection of that care.

During the latter period of my stay in Elkwood, I was able to witness a family drama unfold that centered on some of the difficulties involved with managing person-position tensions related to caregiving. This event pointed out the importance of acknowledging the *person* who often is performing the role of daughter, mother, or grandmother.

In Family #6, Meredith's mother Bonnie, age 83, and her father Frank, age 87, were getting on in years and their health was deteriorating. Meredith had recently located a home health agency and had employed a woman to assist her parents with errands, household chores, and basic health care, including handling medications and assisting them in trips to the restroom. The following events occurred about 1 month after this woman was employed to work in Bonnie and Frank's home:

The setting was Scout's 18th birthday party. Meredith, Meredith's mother and father, Morgan, and Morgan's husband and daughters were gathered in Morgan's home for the party. A Diana Krall CD was playing in the background, and wonderful aromas of garlic and onions wafted in from the kitchen. We were all sitting in the family room, drinking after-dinner liqueurs and coffee. Bonnie remarked that she was not very happy with the home health nurse and did not believe the "arrangement was going to work out." Meredith shot her mother a look brimming with defensiveness. She barked, "Well you have to try. It's just too bad. You need to get along." Meredith then turned on her heels and literally stomped out of the room, rippling the curtains and causing the lampshades to tremble. Bonnie called over to her granddaughter Morgan and said, "Your mom is mad at me, but this is not working out." Morgan attempted to keep the peace and listened to her grandmother explain the situation. Morgan listened quietly, asked a few questions, and as she told me later, she "tried not to take sides." Meredith eventually came back into the room, scowling and ignoring her mother and father. Scout soon drove Bonnie and Frank back to their house to, "just get out of there."

As soon as Bonnie and Frank were out of the driveway, Meredith felt she could talk freely. Although I offered to leave, she insisted I stay and continued to vent to her daughter. "I knew this would happen!" she complained. "She didn't even give it a chance. What *has* to happen is that everyone [grandchildren and children] will have to go up to your grandparents' house all together and present a united front of agreement. If they [the grandchildren and children] don't agree to go up … then tough … they still have to. Tell your grandparents they have *no* choice and they must [keep the home health nurse]!"

Morgan's sister Ali replied, "Maybe, but this is no time to bring all this up. This is Scout's birthday party." It seemed to me that she was felt nervous talking back and challenging her mother. Her gaze quickly averted to figurine on the table and there was a slight quiver in her voice. I also sensed that everybody is the room was noticing this too, but did not address it. There was a *big silence*. Meredith looked stricken. Then, as if someone flicked a switch, almost every single person in the room began nervously chatting with their neighbor. Meredith regained her composure, walked over to Morgan, and pulled her aside to talk privately. Later that evening, Morgan told me, "She wants me to get in middle of this and I won't. She just takes everything so personally."

The next day, they invited me along with children and grandchildren to go to Bonnie and Frank's house to discuss the care arrangements. I did not feel particularly comfortable refusing the "invitation." I felt more or less compelled to participate so as not to offend Meredith. Interestingly, only the females in the family showed up at the grandparents' home. What is more, several female members of the family asked Meredith's permission not to attend; participation was expected and absences excused only with the Meredith's permission.

Morgan had arrived earlier than the rest of us to try and "smooth things over." As she later told me, "Everybody was there to solve a problem, but my mom [was] there to pick a fight. She arrived antagonistic, argumentative, and confrontational. Her attitude [was] you *will* do it my way." This did appear to be the case. During the discussion, Meredith's parents discussed how they felt uncomfortable with the "woman in their house" and Meredith talked about how they did not appreciate her efforts to find them care. There was virtually no discussion about alternative care arrangements. The discourse quickly turned to the fact that Frank was feeling powerless. His tone with his daughter was condescending and aggressive. When Meredith argued that her efforts were selfless and meant to keep her parents in their home instead of in a nursing facility, Frank mocked his daughter and thanked her for "allowing me to stay in my own home."

Meredith responded to her father, saying, "I'm just trying to help you. All I want is for you to say you are sorry for how you have been treating me."

Her father replied in a nasty tone, "I'm soooo sooorrrry."

It was at that moment when Meredith rose to leave the room. As she exited, she lobbed the last shot, "I still love you even though you treat me like shit."

Morgan's eyes followed her mother, then she looked at her grandfather and asked, "Why do you treat her like that? She's your only daughter."

He just smiled.

Later, as we all gathered down downstairs in Meredith's home, she sought agreement from all in attendance when she asked, "They were the ones not being reasonable, right?" She professed she would "never forgive" her father. Then she opened up the floor and invited feedback from others. "Well, what do you all think?" she asked. Morgan responded with, "Mom, ya gotta relax. He smiled after and said everything [was] fine. So, it's fine!"

"*No it's not*," screamed Meredith.

"He smiled, so it's fine, forgotten" Morgan persisted.

"No, no it's not. He can't talk to me like that."

"Oh mother, you need to forgive him. He just needs to feel in control. You can't let him get to you."

This comment from Morgan became an ultimate betrayal for Meredith. She ran out of the room in tears and that's when those of us remaining finally left.

Later that day, Meredith tearfully confided in me that she felt *she* was not receiving the support she required. She said she couldn't "tolerate being told that I am in the wrong—again." She explained that she was just trying to help her parents and all she "[got] for it" was rejection. When Morgan told her she needed to forgive Frank and let it go, what Meredith heard Morgan saying was, "You are wrong." "Once again," she lamented, "I feel like a failure." Moreover, she complained that

Morgan was "always taking her grandparent's side." The idea that Morgan's loyalty skipped a generation was "wounding" to her.

Later that same evening, after I put my son to sleep, I found myself back at Morgan's house. She told me that all she wanted was to keep everyone in the family happy and to figure a way to make a "happy compromise." She admitted that her grandfather "spoke out of turn." Yet, she contended that her mother "pushed it so he got snotty." "Plus," she added, "she asked for my opinion." Morgan also asserted that she received very little respect from her own mother. A few days after this confrontation, Meredith finally decided to talk with her daughter and Morgan said to her, "Look, mom, I've had to forgive too [so you should too]."

Meredith replied, "But you've never been treated as badly as I have. We've never treated you like this."

Morgan merely looked away. She later told me that she was thinking, "Yes, you have!"

Neither woman felt respected or valued in her maternal relationships. Each woman attempted to enact her role as a mother, daughter, or granddaughter, with neither woman really listening to the other. In Meredith's mind, the "caregiver" is the role of a daughter. She wanted to enact this role effectively, so she took it "into her own hands" and made sure her parents were cared for adequately. She was playing her role, but failing the audition in her parent's eyes. Here parents did not acknowledge this performance and resisted it. She, in turn, felt rejected as a daughter and as a person. It seemed, then, that she projected the requirements of the daughter role as caregiver and supporter onto her own daughter, assuming that Morgan would support her in this conflict. When she did not receive the desired (and expected) support, she felt rejected as a person on all sides. Concurrently, Morgan thought that her position as a granddaughter required her to be the peacekeeper and mediate the interactions of her mother and grandparents. She wanted to be able to contribute to the grandparents' care, too, but believed her mother just wanted her to be the "obedient daughter and do whatever she decided was right." She believed her mother only saw her in her role as daughter and failed to see *her* as a person.

Personal identity for these women remained linked to relational acknowledgment. Yet, despite the need for relational connection, neither woman fully took into account the relational consequences of their individual actions. Fishbane (2001) suggested that the mark of a mature and healthy relationship is an embedded autonomy that includes "clarity about one's own needs and desires and ... a willingness to stay connected even through conflict, to hear the other's narrative even while articulating one's own, and to negotiate differences" (p. 276). The women in Family #6 appeared to be mired in the need to have others truly *hear* them, only to shut out the possibility of truly listening.

Fishbane also posited that a dominant person orientation can be achieved while simultaneously respecting the legitimate social role of the other by giving *power to* a relational partner. This suggests a process of holding one's ground while simultaneously being open to listening to a partner's narrative. This is in contrast to having *power over* the other. When the women of Elkwood grasped tightly to the legitimate role power over their maternal kin, this often led to disconnection and withdrawal, viewing conflict as a threat, and damage to the relationship.

Among those maternal relationships interpretable as being relatively healthy, people were able to maintain connectedness while respecting both partners' roles in the family hierarchy and each individual voice—they had achieved mutuality. For example, although Gina shared with Georgie her concern over her unhappy romantic relationship, the conversation did not end there. According to Georgie, Gina's comments merely "opened the door" so that "we could discuss the relationship" and why it was making Georgie so unhappy. In these connected relationships, I observed a reciprocal support and respect of both person and position, integrating both into the management of the relationship, and interactions proceeded out of desire. For most women in the enmeshed relationships, neither support nor respect were reciprocated, and interactions proceeded out of a sense of duty.

SUMMARY

This chapter included many stories—some stories authored by individual women straining to define a self that is distinct from their maternal relationships, and other co-authored stories constructing relational narratives of grandmothers, mothers, and daughters. Dialectical theory was applied to these data in order to interpret the patterns that emerged. These patterns pointed to several relational contradictions experienced by the women in Elkwood—dialectical forces specific to these maternal relationships.

Mothers and daughters as well as grandmothers and granddaughters managed stability and change, and constancy and variation, across their lifetime and on a daily basis. Most relationships were relatively stable, with points of change marked by relational turning points. These required minor adjustments for some and major relational redefinitions for others. Turning points included events such as pregnancy and childbirth, changes in proximity, violating relational expectations, and caregiving experiences.

These maternal relationships were also challenged to navigate the competing pulls of connection and separation, to balance the "me" with the "we." Among the relationships observed in Elkwood, two patterns of connectedness emerged that served to divide the relationships into two distinct groupings:

those that were so extreme in cohesion—*enmeshed*—that the process of differentiation was perceived as being threatening to the relationship, and those that were moderate enough in cohesion—*connected*—that the process of differentiation was perceived as being a normal process that offered no particular threat to the relationship. Within this sample, 9 of the 18 relational dyads were interpreted as being connected, and exhibited spontaneous intimacy, mutuality, and the ability to move out of "performance mode" into an intimate mode in which the woman was comfortable enough to be what she perceived as her true self. Nine of the 18 were interpreted as being enmeshed, and exhibited rehearsed and often competitive intimacy with an observable "performance" of their roles as daughters, granddaughters, mothers, or grandmothers. In these enmeshed relationships, consequences occurred when there were negative evaluations of those performances.

The process and experience of *differentiation* also arose as a key concept that distinguished connected from enmeshed adult maternal relationships. Differentiation is the process by which women move toward this autonomous self while remaining emotionally connected to the women in their lives. For those women in the enmeshed relationships, they tended to perceive differentiation as being threatening to the maternal relationship. Many of these women's personal identities and senses of "self" were heavily influenced by their maternal relational partners, with each woman needing her partner's continual validation. The pattern revealed a tendency for the younger women to become addicted to maternal approval in order to feel whole. The entangled nature of their identities often led one partner to insist that her partner not change, so that her own identity would not be affected. Thus, differentiation was related to relational instability. The women in the connected relationships, however, did not tend to seek continuous validation from their grandmothers/mothers/daughters/granddaughters as they moved through their adult lives. In these relationships, women were emotionally connected, frequently involved interpersonally, and emphasized togetherness. However, personal distance and generational boundaries were respected rather than perceived as being threatening, differentiation of members was inevitable and mutually encouraged, and family members tended to function as each other's "cheerleaders."

The regulation of public and private information was an additional contradiction to address in these relationships. Connected dyads tended to experience healthy boundaries between public and private across personal, dyadic (mother–daughter, grandmother–granddaughter), and triadic (grandmother–mother–daughter) levels; whereas those in enmeshed relationships were more apt to regulate information closely, build alliances on the foundation of information, and exhibit permeable boundaries between ownership of information.

This chapter also discussed how these women managed the contrasting images of who one *should* be in a relationship, and who one actually is on any given day. Idealized versions of maternal relationships were shaped within a multifarious array of social influences. These idealized versions were put on trial every day in Elkwood, as women compared and contrasted their everyday interactions with the "real" versions of their relational partner.

The "real" day-to-day interactions with partners emphasized the importance of being powerful and powerless in maternal relationships. Resources were shared and manipulated. Support, regard, and inclusion were exchanged freely in connected relationships or conditionally in enmeshed relationships. Across a life span, women are required to shift their control of different resources in their family. In the enmeshed relationships, mothers and some grandmothers struggled to retain control over the resources at their disposal, especially emotional resources. Therefore, struggles over power and dominance emerged as being central to defining relationships in the enmeshed pattern. In two cases, these issues affected maternal relationships across all three generations.

Another ongoing struggle was to balance the competing pulls of person and position with one's relational partner. I argued in this chapter that by recognizing the relational embeddedness of self, women can escape and avoid framing this as a struggle; they then can embrace the dialectic and respect the uniqueness of self while simultaneously acknowledging the legitimate power of the other in their family roles.

Much of the emphasis in this chapter focused on mother–adult daughter relationships over different developmental periods, but findings also pertained specifically to grandmother–granddaughter relationships. Things that were consequential to the relationship between mothers and daughters did not often have the same effect on grandmother–granddaughter relationships. In these latter relationships, "Each little thing doesn't become defining." Most grandmothers and granddaughters did not reflect the symbiotic identification that characterized some mother–daughter relationships. Rather, grandmothers' identification with granddaughters was a more loosely tethered connection. For most of these women, grandmothering was more relaxing than mothering, because as grandmothers they did not have the primary responsibility for rearing children on a day-to-day basis. Moreover, the connection between grandmothers and granddaughters seemed to be moderated by the mother. The quality and characteristics of the relationship in the older mother–daughter pair affected and influenced the grandmother–granddaughter relationship. I find this interesting and disturbing, because it points to the importance of grandmothers needing a voice in the grandmother–granddaughter relationship that resonates outside of the walls of the grandmother–mother–daughter relationship. Unfortunately, opportunities for hearing a grandmother's voice may be muted by a cacophony of unresolved tensions between grandmother and mother.

5

Patterns of Interaction:
Best Intentions,
Bitter Regret,
Resentment,
and Love

Most memories of my mother consist of, oh, I don't know, getting bee stings on my foot and her saying, "That's what you get for walking barefoot" or "Clean your room," "Make your bed." And God forbid if I had a question of what I considered importan[t] during her "naptime." I got real good at ducking incoming pillows. It seemed like she was always mad at me. Mad if I spilled my milk, mad if I didn't finish the crust on what seemed like endless peanut butter and jelly sandwiches. And really mad when she found the 3-year supply of bread crusts behind the washing machine. [sigh] I guess I don't understand it .... She never told me I was pretty. Hey mom ... you remember Sheila Woshosky? I went to her house one day to pick her up on the way to a school dance and she was standing in front of her dresser getting ready ... and her mother came into the room, stood in the doorway and said, "Oh, Sheila, You look so beautiful!" ... She had a hook nose and she was fat!! God, how I envied her. [pause] I don't know, what did I do to make you so angry at me? I mean, [mom] even seemed upset when I started my period. Now, I can hardly be blamed for that, can I? I mean, I understand her getting upset when I stopped up the toilet with tampons—well, I couldn't figure out how to get them in right. I guess I just wanted her to like me. I guess I still do.

—Excerpt from *Two of Me* (Miller, 2000, p. 41)

T racy (2002) intimated that talk does identity work, and identities work to shape talk. This assumption is fundamental to the discussion in this chapter. For the grandmothers, mothers, daughters, and granddaughters in Elkwood, discursive practices reflected who these women were as individuals and who they were in relation to the others with whom they interacted. Talk was the instrument through which interactants negotiated their maternal relationships. Different patterns of talk were reflected in the enmeshed relationships when compared with the connected maternal relationships.

Discursive practices are talk activities—the ways in which people communicatively interact—and may include a variety of speech acts, such as giving information, reproaching, or requesting, with differing styles of directness and different interpretive frames to make sense of those activities (Greene & Burleson, 2003; Tracy, 2002). Social interaction scholars and interpersonal scholars point out that a speaker's talk situates his or her partner in a certain identity, serving to "maintain, support, and challenge" that partner's multiple identities (Tracy, 2002, p. 23). How we talk and act toward others casts them in a role and serves to write their story for them. Sometimes this is an explicit process, as when Diane called Sam a "selfish bitch." More often, however, it is a more implicit process. Views of self, other, and us are built from and reflected in discursive practices. In this chapter, I want to describe a few of the discursive practices I observed during my time in Elkwood that—to me—emerged as salient differences across connected and enmeshed maternal relationships. Then I offer my interpretation of how these communicative interactions become scripted in maternal relationships with the potential for intergeneration transmission of patterned communication behaviors.

Communication Is What Creates and Maintains Relationships

According to Montgomery and Baxter (1998), "Communication is an interactive, involving, and situated process that produces multiple meanings that simultaneously both differentiate and connect participants. Communication is the vehicle of social definition; participants develop their senses of self, partners develop their senses of relationship ... through the processes of communication" (p. 161). All verbal and nonverbal behavior (including silence) either directly or indirectly comments on the nature of the relationship between the interactants. The social interactions between relational members are performances that express a unique relational culture. Reciprocally, relational cultures "create, express, and sustain personal relationships and identities of partners" (Wood, 2000, p. 77). A relational culture emphasizes the notion of relational partners collaboratively creating a unique culture in an ongoing fashion, making modifications, and redefining the relational culture over time. As partners change, cultures adjust and transform to reflect those changes.

For the 18 women in Elkwood, across all mother–daughter and grand-mother–granddaughter dyads, maternal relationships were organized by their cohesion (enmeshed, connected), and the rules associated with those levels of cohesion (what was "appropriate" or normative in that particular cohesion structure), affected by the underlying dialectical tensions (e.g., ideal-real), and expressed in symbolic practices. Furthermore, specific patterns of symbolic practices emerged that were *distinctive* to each relational cohesive type.

As may be seen in the illustrations of some of the patterns enacted in these relationships, patterns of symbolic practices may not always be healthy or func-tional. When Wood (2000) said that "unhealthy relational cultures harm or fail to support the well-being of at least one member in the relationship" (p. 82), she was noting that relational cultures can sustain patterns that are unhealthy and unsatisfying. Applying Wood's definition to the maternal relationships ob-served in Elkwood, the enmeshed relationships appeared to be less healthy than were the connected.

Speech Acts

Social meanings associated with short segments of talk may fall into one of sev-eral categories of *speech acts*. These may include giving information, compli-menting, criticizing, requesting, and narrating (Tracy, 2002). In contemporary Western culture, the performance of these speech acts may threaten treasured maternal relationships, placing both personal and relational identities at risk for change. As Tracy (2002) pointed out, one cannot direct, threaten, or criticize just anyone. For example, lower-status people cannot perform authority-related speech acts. Grandmothers and mothers are more apt to perform these acts, but daughters or granddaughters might also be cast in an authoritative role, requir-ing an adjustment to relational culture and an adjustment of norms.

As suggested in chapter 4, one of the key distinguishing features of enmeshed relationships was their resistance to cultural adaptation or adjustment to change. Yet, healthy relationships *do* change over time (Cochran, 1990). They are not fixed, so that discursive practices such as speech acts enable relation-ships to facilitate change and maintain their "health" (Greene & Burleson, 2003). The following specific speech acts served to distinguish the enmeshed from the connected maternal relationships in Elkwood. Although these were not the only speech acts observed, they did emerge as having the most distinction across relational cohesion types.

Reproach.   A *reproach* is a speech act that expresses disapproval, censure, or criticism, and implies intellectual, moral, or positional authority. Reproaches were observed in both levels of cohesion (enmeshed and connected), but were highest in frequency and intensity in those maternal relationships that were en-meshed. For example, consider the following dinnertime exchange at Meredith's (Family #6) home:

Meredith's extended family, daughters, sons-in-law, and grandchildren were gathered in her home for an Easter celebration. A table was set with formal dinnerware, candles, crisp linens, and polished silver. The men and younger children sat at the table, talking and laughing, and Meredith, her daughters, and adult granddaughters carried in dish after dish of fragrant food. Because I was still nursing my infant son I was relieved of kitchen duty. With a blanket thrown over my shoulder to shield the others from the suckling baby, I was able to observe, tape record, and listen as Meredith directed the activities of the others in preparation for the feast.

Scout had made deviled eggs for the dinner and was unwrapping the plastic wrap from the dish to set on the table. Meredith said, "No one is going to eat those, plus they will take up too much room. Just set them on the counter for people to snack on throughout the afternoon."

"But Grandma," complained Scout, "I made these for the dinner!"

Morgan inserted, "Maybe you can put them back in the fridge; they might be a nice snack for later."

Scout began to noticeably tense. "But I made them for dinner," she said to her mother.

Meredith sighed heavily. "All right, then," she continued, "find someplace but [the dish] better not take up too much room."

Scout placed the dish on the table and there was plenty of room, but scowls remained on both Meredith and Scout's faces. Nonetheless, Meredith recommenced with directing the women, telling them what to place where, and when. She was adept at this organization and the presentation of the meal was beautiful. Once the table was set, we all took our seats to eat. My son was placed in his carrier at my feet, the conversation was light, and the food was delicious. Approximately 10 minutes into the meal, Morgan whispered loudly to Scout, "See, the deviled eggs were the first to go!" Then several of the men commented that they "loved" the eggs and wanted her to make more for an upcoming family dinner in May.

"I guess you were right and I was wrong," Meredith mumbled with a defensive edge to her voice. "But I was right about that dish, anyway, it is too big for this table." The others just stopped and looked at the dish, shrugged their shoulders, and resumed eating.

Almost 20 minutes later, we were all sated, content, and loosening our belts when Meredith remarked to Scout's sister, "You only ate the starches. If you do that too much you are going to have a problem!" Then she turned her attention to Morgan: "You need to teach these girls to slow down their eating and what they should and shouldn't be eating or they're gonna regret it. Mark my words." No one responded to this remark, but Scout and her sister stood up and began clearing the dishes. Morgan said, "Great meal, Mom, thanks," and they all left the room. Later, when I was talking with Scout's sister, she confided, "I hate when she makes a comment about what I should or shouldn't do. It's so annoying. Now I'm going to be paranoid about what I eat for the rest of the day!" At the end of the day, even Scout began to question her own judgment; she confided, "Maybe I shouldn't

have even brought the eggs. This is her thing—these dinners—I'll just let her tell
me what to bring or not bring from now on."

There were several acts of reproach during this episode, and each act manifested the underlying dominant dialectical tensions in the respective relationship. For example, Meredith's statement that "No one is going to eat those, plus
they will take up too much room" reproached Scout for her judgment in making
the eggs in the first place and also offered a criticism of her choice of plate. This
speech act implied an authority over all processes and products of this particular
meal. Moreover, the dominant forces that underlied Meredith and Scout's
grandmother–granddaughter relationship were reflected in this interaction. In
this relationship, I could discern numerous characteristics: a conspicuous pull
toward a position orientation, in which Meredith was the grandmother who was
to be respected as the head of the household, the one who had the legitimate position in the family to issue commands and reproach; a tension between
Meredith's power in the domain of food preparation and presentation and
Scout's relative powerlessness in this domain; a dominant deference to stability,
with the eggs threatening the consistency of predictable food items at this celebration; and an attempt by Meredith to sustain control over Scout's behavioral
autonomy by directing her to "Just set them on the counter for people to snack
on throughout the afternoon."

Scout's compliance and obedience to this directive would have reinforced
and respected the dominant forces at play in this relationship. However, she
countered by challenging her grandmother with an assertive, "But Grandma, I
made these for the dinner!" Scout's reproach was in the form of a direct assertive, a confrontation that challenged her grandmother's position, power, and
need for stability. Interestingly, Scout's mother Morgan's first instinct was to
oblige Meredith and ingratiate herself by suggesting that Scout "put them back
in the fridge; they might be a nice snack for later." In this cross-generational interaction, Morgan legitimated her own mother's position as matriarch of the
family and accommodated the pull toward her mother's dominance in their
mother–daughter relationship, simultaneously asserting her own position and
power in her relationship with Scout. Morgan issued an indirect directive, a
proposal prefaced by "Maybe you can put them ..." that suggested a willingness
toward change and reinforced her own role position as Scout's mother, thus possessing legitimate power, and a separate role position as obedient daughter to
Meredith. Meredith's capitulation, expressed in her heavy sigh and her statement "All right then," seemed to be a management strategy to integrate the opposing forces of stability and change. Yet, she immediately asserted her position
orientation and power in the situation by issuing a directive with an implied
threat: "find someplace but [the dish] better not take up too much room."

The metaphor of improvisational jazz music introduced in the previous
chapter seems particularly appropriate when interpreting this dinnertime
exchange. The dominant dialectical force within any given dialectic in a re-

lationship served as the progressive chord guiding the improvisation—the management—of countervailing forces. Morgan's indirect reproach of "See, the deviled eggs were the first to go!" served both as a reproach to her mother and a statement of support, connecting with her daughter. Meredith clearly heard the reproach and responded with a self-deprecating, "I guess you were right and I was wrong." She then struggled to recapture the dominant rhythm of power in her relationships with both her daughter and grand-daughter with a follow-up reproach: "But I was right about that dish, anyway, it is too big for this table."

Perhaps Meredith felt a need to recalibrate the powerful-powerless dialectic when she persisted with her reproaches near the end of the meal. However, in-stead of directing her remarks about eating starches to Scout, she moved her target to include a less resistant subject (Scout's sister, Tonya), and simulta-neously reinforced her position and legitimate power in her relationship with Morgan. Morgan and Tonya both chose to avoid the reproach, however. Over-all, however, in the enmeshed relationships, women are very vocal about how harmful frequent reproaches are in their maternal relationships.

Sam (Family #1) complained that her mother and grandmother "always have to make the *constant comment.*" Many daughters and granddaughters in the enmeshed relationships complained that the older women were constantly reprimanding their adult daughters and granddaughters, saying, "I should have put more salt on this," "should have turned the camera on sooner," "should have helped sooner," "commenting about how I look," "commenting on what I eat, what I don't eat, how I eat," "it's like I don't like your hair like that, or I don't like your eyes like that. It's either you're too heavy or you're too thin. It's not in be-tween" and "how I've disappointed her," and "how I'm a failure." As Sam's eld-est daughter explained to me one day:

> Everybody is so critical and judgmental. I think that's what has built the insecu-rity in everyone. Very judgmental of good and bad and this is success and this is failure, although we do really love each other. It's just that some always think they have the clout to make those judgments because we're close, we're family. Right. I think that.
>
> I think everyone is just trying to please everyone and it's so stupid, we just have to accept people the way they are, each person, individually, that's what they are, you know. I know that everyone, the women [in this family] are so insecure.

Kendra (Family #2) argued that her mother's reproaches, such as "*ruin* the whole pie," negatively affect the relationship. "It's hard," she said. "You know you need like 13 positive comments to outweigh one negative comment." Ac-cording to Becky (Family # 5), it's like a constant voice telling you that you can do better. Morgan (Family #6) said that her mother is "always correcting me." Diane, who often issued reproaches in interaction with her daughters, com-plained about her own mother's use of reproach: "What I do is never good enough. I wasn't a boy, you see. So, no matter what I accomplished she always questioned my judgment, always made some comment."

One day, while watching Morgan and her sister argue over something that had occurred when they were younger, Meredith said to them, "No, you are both wrong." Morgan stopped talking for a moment and then reacted to this reproach by asking, "Is this *your* memory? Were you there?" Meredith replied, "No." "Well," continued Morgan, "then there is no need to comment." Yet, not 5 minutes later, Morgan began to question her own account.

For the women in enmeshed relationships, reproaches were sometimes laced with attitudinal quality that implied the pseudo-seriousness of the rebuke—*I'm just kidding!* The joking quality served to soften the edge of any criticism, but the message was still conveyed. Scout laughed as she kidded her mother about "never listening"; Kendra smiled and told her mother that she was odd and paranoid. When Meredith's reproach of Morgan that the "butter [is] in the popcorn" instead of "butter [is] on the popcorn" was witnessed by an unreceptive audience, she laughed it off and proceeded as if the reproach was humorous. Truthfully, some of the reproachful messages were not threatening, but many were aggressive and served to firmly entrench the speaker as the dominant member of the relationship.

Kelly recalled when she was about 8 years old and had broken her arm. Her mother insisted, "it didn't look broke." To "see if it really hurt," Katrina forced Kelly to carry a 6-pack of Coke with the broken arm. Kelly recalled her mother saying to her during the subsequent doctor's visit, "If [your arm's] not broken then you are in big trouble." Her mother really thought that Kelly was faking so that she wouldn't have to help bring groceries inside. What is interesting is that Sam experienced a similar event with her mother when she was younger. Sam broke three fingers on one hand; Diane did not believe her, and threatened punishment if "when we got to the emergency room I wasn't really hurt."

Threats, commands, name calling, and reprimands were frequently used in the enmeshed maternal relationships, even when the daughters and granddaughters reached adulthood. It appeared, however, that indirect reproaches were also common as an insidious means of asserting authority without being confrontational. Morgan recalled a time during the previous year when she and her mother had been at the home of one of Morgan's friends. Apparently, Morgan went to the refrigerator and took out a drink without asking permission, and Meredith issued the following indirect reproach: "Sally, I can't believe she did that! I didn't raise her like that. I'm so sorry." Morgan said that she was mortified that her mother would feel the need to reproach her and apologize for her behavior at her own friend's house. Morgan told me, "I didn't say anything but I couldn't believe it." Interestingly, Morgan noted that she continued to feel guilty every time she was at this friend's home, even though they both laughed about the incident and established a rule that "each friend was welcome to anything in the other's kitchen."

Diane's granddaughter pointed out that the indirect reproach is often more painful than the direct criticism. She said, "My grandmother, and sometimes my mother, will just not really say the criticism. They'll be displeased or disappointed and not come right out and say anything ... she just pays less attention to you or gives you the cold shoulder. Then you know you've done something she doesn't approve of." There were multiple instances of adult women hinting, implying, and suggesting that the other woman had come up short in some way. Most troubling, and consistent with previous work (Bowker & Klein, 1983; Campbell, 1981), were the interaction patterns within enmeshed relationship pairs that evidenced high levels of negativity and low levels of positivity.

Reproaches were not absent in the connected maternal relationships, but their frequency and intensity were very different. For example, one day when I was at Barb's (Family #4) house, her daughter Tabitha was laying my son on the couch and propping pillows around him for his safety. Barb believed that the pillows were not sufficiently secure to protect the baby and offered the following reproach to her daughter: "I don't think those are in tight enough. Here, let me help" and then walked over and adjusted the pillows. This speech act implied that she knew the appropriate way to arrange the pillows, but it did not belittle her daughter. She took responsibility for her own opinion and did not cast a shroud of guilt over Tabitha for arranging them incorrectly. The interaction was underscored by positivity, rather than negativity. This underlying positivity was common across all of the connected relationships. Georgie (Family #3) reported to me that her mother "was always laughing and joking. So, when she was serious, I knew she meant business. Even now, it's not like she has to be happy all the time, but when she looks stern—eyes halfway open, I always know that look—I know that I did something that she isn't happy about. She'll usually just be pretty direct and tell me what the problem is." Her mother's general positivity may have moderated the effect of the reproach on Georgie's level of self-blame or perceptions of injury. In most of the connected relationships, a person who offered any criticism or negative judgment owned their speech act, stated the reproach in an assertively direct fashion, and the overall climate of interactions in this relationships were positive and confirming. Becky, for example, used a gentle approach whenever I witnessed her reprimand her youngest daughter. She would use direct eye contact without glaring, was even tempered in her delivery, and her nonverbal cues were consistent with her verbal cues. Sheer frequency of reproaches may have also affected the general climate of the relationship. I documented approximately 10 reproach episodes in the enmeshed maternal relationships ($N = 216$) for every one in the connected maternal relationships ($N = 20$).

Some scholars claim that people who issue frequent reproaches such as negative judgments and criticism are prone to low self-esteem and insecure attachments (McCranie & Bass, 1984; Thompson & Zuroff, 1999). A reproach imbues the speaker with a sense of authority and sense of power—a power to induce guilt in the partner.

Clearly, in relational interaction, we affect our partners' emotions; guilt is a fundamental emotion and an interactional phenomenon. According to Vangelisti, Daly, and Rudnick (1991), guilt is something that can be "aroused in a person by others" (p. 6) and *guilt induction* is the act of one actor explicitly or implicitly suggesting that the other actor is responsible for a failure. Vangelisti and her colleagues' research did not identify frequent and intense reproach as a strategy of guilt induction, but they did find that guilt induction was used as a relational maintenance strategy. This finding seems to be supported in my results as well. I believe that many of the Elkwood women in enmeshed relationships used reproach as a guilt-inducing strategy in order to assert dominance and assuage personal feelings of inadequacy. This is supported by other research that indicates that parents who express limited warmth are also more likely to be self-critical (Holahan, Moos, & Bonin, 1999). Adult self-critics often recall parents who placed a heavy emphasis on high levels of performance; this has been associated with women's perfectionism (Kerpelman & Smith, 1999; McCranie & Bass, 1984). Indeed, this was the case among the women in the enmeshed relationships in Elkwood.

Directives.   In addition to reproaches, the act of getting a partner to do something or not do something—*directives*—seemed to take different forms in connected and enmeshed maternal relationships. In the enmeshed relationships, the women with greater status in the dyad tended to use *commands*, directing the other adult women with authority, typically when the directive was for instrumental assistance. For example, older women were often heard issuing direct commands in an authoritative tone to their adult daughters or granddaughters, such as "Put the dishes over there" or "Get those shoes off the floor!" Additionally, *hints* were frequently used when the directive was related to emotional or social support. Many lower-status women admitted annoyance with these hints. Sam complained, "It's so annoying! She just pussyfoots around when she needs something. She expects me to read her mind." One day, I was with Katrina as she spoke with Kelly on the phone and said, "I'm exhausted, but I have to go to the grocery still and pick up the dry cleaning" and ended the statement with an elongated sigh. They talked a bit more on the phone and then hung up. Katrina was furious within minutes of hanging up the phone. She said to me, "She should have at least offered to go to the grocery or pick up the laundry for me!" Wading into dark waters, I asked, "Oh, I didn't hear you ask her to do that for you." She looked at me as if I had asked the most obtuse question of the century and replied, "Oh, I asked, she just didn't take the time to hear me." This may have been so, because indirect hinting was a common form of directive in these relationships, with lower-status women being very adept at interpreting nonverbal cues.

In these enmeshed dyads, the women with less status would typically issue query directives, direct requests, or hints. *Query directives* are posed in the form of a question, asking the partner to do or not do something, leaving the door open for compliance or noncompliance. An example of this can be seen in the following interaction between Scout and Morgan. Morgan had borrowed a dress from her daughter to wear to a recent event and had returned the dress unlaundered. Scout approached her mother and said in a respectful tone, "Mom, I don't care if you borrow my stuff, but next time you wear something of mine could you make sure you wash it before you send it back to me?" Direct requests are directly asking the partner without disclaimers or queries to soften the directive. For example, one Saturday Kendra asked Kelly to "Please watch the kids for me while they're napping so that I can go to the grocery."

In addition to the cohesiveness of the dyad (connected/enmeshed), the dialectical pulls between position and person also seemed to be closely tied to these different approaches to directives. Bernstein (1975) argued that families typically manifest a *preferred* way of engaging in speech acts, using specific codes, based on if the family is position or person oriented. As illustrated throughout this book, the enmeshed adult maternal relationships tended toward position orientation, with a reliance on the formalized and entrenched status of persons when making decisions or communicating with one another. The connected adult relationships tended toward a person orientation, with a reliance on individual level or psychological qualities of the interactants when making decisions or communicating. Position-oriented maternal relationships tended to have a closed communication system, in which challenges to the personal and relational identities and novel meanings were discouraged. Conversely, person-oriented maternal relationships tended to have a more open system, which welcomed new meanings and as flexible in adapting to and shaping new identities.

Although all of the maternal relationships shared, to some extent, unique nonverbal codes (e.g., when I see "the look" I know she is angry), I observed a disproportionate amount of restricted codes in the position-oriented dyads. *Restricted codes* refer to the exchange of information in an interaction that relies heavily on nonverbal cues, gestures, and intonation to communicate attitude (Gumperz, 1982). These nonverbal signs were most fully intelligible to the relational partner, and I (as an outsider) often needed to seek clarification of meanings in order to accurately record my observations. Moreover, these women more often made positional appeals than personal appeals to their maternal relational partner. The following scene illustrates both the reliance on positional appeals and restricted codes in another dinnertime scenario. This time I had dinner with Family #1:

Diane had invited her mother, her daughters, and their families to her home for dinner and to watch home movies. The younger children were in her living room putting on a "Star Search/American Idol" show while the older children, parents, and grandparents watched, laughed, and applauded. Soon the adults were joining in on the act, using pretend microphones and belting out show tunes. Sam's sister, Julie, stood to the side of the room. Sam caught a glimpse of her from the corner of her eye, and then stuck out her tongue. I heard an elongated sound that was similar to "ttthhhaaaa." Upon hearing this call, everyone began to laugh and Julie joined her sister and others "on stage" for the performance. Later, when I asked Diane, Sam, and Julie what exactly "ttthhhaaa" was all about, they began to laugh.

Sam informed me that it was a "sister thing."

Diane corrected, "It is a Jones' women thing."

Overlapping this comment, Julie added, "If you are a Jones you know that you come and participate or you are in trouble!"

"So," I asked in confusion, "sticking out your tongue and making that sound means come on?"

"Yes and no," said Sam.

"Sorta," replied Julie.

Diane rolled her eyes to the left and pursed her lips. Seeing this expression, Sam exclaimed, "Okay Mom, you explain it, you're dying to be the one to tell her."

Diane jumped at the invitation and explained, "It means you better come join us—or else. But it's also something that we do, um, have always done, to include others."

"No others!" Julie argued. "Who else besides us do we do that to?"

"Um," Sam thought.

"Well, now that Michelle knows what it means she can join us too!" Diane asserted.

I asked, "Do you use that signal with the guys in the family?"

Sam replied, "Ha, *not*! They're not as fun as us girls."

Julie added, "It wouldn't work. It's a gal thing. We are the *thang* women. And the guys ain't got that thang."

As I sat among the laughing women, I was intrigued not only by the special nonverbal code that these women had developed among themselves, but also by the positional appeals inherent in this code. The essence of a positional appeal is that the receiver is explicitly linked to others in the referent group (e.g., the women in the family) and in that appeal the receiver is reminded of her commonality with the others. When appeals are positional, the "I" becomes subordinate to the "we." Whatever Julie wanted to do at the time of the performance, she knew, just by the nonverbal request of a loud "ttthhhaaa," that if she wanted to enact her role as a "Jones" woman she had better come on up to the stage and perform. This kind of appeal positions the receiver on the basis of group membership or inclusion. Positional appeals were observed across all of the enmeshed dyads, including an abundance of appeals to altruism (e.g., "Don't think of yourself, think of your grandmother"), negative esteem (e.g., "If you can't do this one thing for me, how can I think you are a person I can trust?"), and ingratiation (e.g., "I just stay on her good side and she will typically listen when I ask her for something"). Note the positional orientation of these appeals, maintaining the structure and power relations of the interactants in the appeals themselves and making the stakes much higher if a request were to be refused.

Restricted codes such as the "ttthhhaaa" were observed more frequently in the enmeshed relationships than in the connected. They suggested a unified frame of interpretation and a sense of undifferentiated partners. In these enmeshed and positional relationships, a slight shift of pitch or a gesture contained meaning that—at first glance—I did not pick up. It was only after spending months with these women that I learned how to interpret the lexicon of these relationships. In fact, a large number of requests in the enmeshed relationships were expressed *indirectly*. The meaning of hints and nonverbal expressions and gestures were assumed to be collectively understood and thus emphasized group membership, because only those with insider status knew the meaning of the code.

Even as positional appeals characterized most of the requests made in enmeshed relationships, I observed that personal appeals and direct codes were more characteristic of the connected relationships. By their very nature, personal appeals engage the receiver as an individual rather than as a member of the relational culture. The pattern of requests that emerged in the connected relationships were appeals based on personal regard for one another rather than positioning or power in the relationship; fewer guilt-inducing appeals and more appeals based on regard and positive self-feeling. An example of this occurred one morning when Lois was helping Barb shuck corn for a barbeque that was to occur later that afternoon:

> Sitting in Barb's kitchen with a pile of 20–30 unshucked ears of corn at her feet, Lois sat concentrating on her work. Without looking up from the task at hand, she made a direct request of Barb: "Please pass the bucket over here when you get a chance."
>
> Barb, who was busy loading dishes into the dishwasher, responded, "Yep, just a second and I'll be right there." However, the telephone rang and Barb left the room to answer the phone. When she returned 10 minutes later, her mother had already finished loading the dishes and was back to shucking the corn with the requested basket in hand.
>
> Barb murmured, "Thanks," and smiled at her mother. Lois smiled back and proceeded to shuck her corn while Barb moved on to making some coffee.

When I asked Lois and Barb about the request, the noncompliance, and what they were thinking during this episode of request and response, Lois did not articulate displeasure with Barb's not honoring her direct request. In fact, Lois said, "She had her hands full, too. I thought maybe I could just help her out." Barb also did not express any guilt about not honoring her mother's request right away, and did not feel that their relationship was compromised in

any way by her noncompliance with the request. Moreover, although apprecia-
tive of her mother's assistance with the dishes, this too was taken as a common
exchange of assistance and not as a secret test of their relationship. Requests in
these dyads were most likely *direct* and subject to respectful refusal or challenge,
whereas refusal of requests in enmeshed dyads tended to threaten the
equilibrium in the relationship.

Consider the following exchange between Kelly and Kendra. This exchange
is similar to the one between Lois and Barb, but note how the nature of the request is more positional than personal, and how the response is reacted to on
the relational level:

> Kelly was sitting in Kendra's living room, folding cloth diapers. Kendra was in her
> kitchen, sterilizing baby bottles and listening to the radio. Kelly and I were chat-
> ting about a local band that was scheduled to play that weekend, which Kelly
> hoped to go see. Her lap was filled with unfolded diapers and I was nursing my son,
> so she raised her voice and called into Kendra issuing a directive: "Ken, hon, bring
> in two glasses of water."
>
> Kendra replied, "Just a minute, okay, I've gotta go to the bathroom."
>
> Kelly chatted with me a few more minutes, then with a huff of frustration flung the
> unfolded diapers from her lap, knocked over one pile of folded diapers, and hur-
> ried into the kitchen, getting two glasses of water to bring into the living room.
>
> When Kendra emerged from the bathroom about 5 minutes later, she noticed that
> her mother had already gotten the water. She remarked, "I was gonna get those in
> just a few minutes."
>
> Kelly responded, "No, I know. Since I'm the mom, I can come over and help you
> with your laundry but you can't even take the time to get me a glass of water.
> Whatever."
>
> "Sorry," said Kendra. "Can I get you anything now that I'm out? Are you hungry?"

The two scenarios are similar, yet this discourse illustrates identity work. For
Barb and Lois, the use of a personal appeal engaged the other person as an individual who faces unique contingencies. Their identities were connected by mu-
tual respect, allowing the other her personal space and needs. In Kelly and
Kendra's exchange, however, Kelly initially used a personal appeal, but she
quickly adjusted to a positional orientation when her request was not honored
and her status of mother was presumably not respected. Kendra handled this by
ingratiating herself to her mother with the queries "Can I get you anything now
that I'm out? Are you hungry?" In doing so, she accepted her mother's evaluation and attempted to repair the situation by reaffirming her mother's status.
These episodes are moments in time that seemed to capture the positional-per-
sonal dialectic in the relationships.

In this section, I discussed two speech acts—reproach and directives—and
how differences emerged in their use across enmeshed and connected maternal
relationships. Additionally, positional-orientated messages emerged as central,

maintaining the status of interactants in the enmeshed relationships, whereas person-oriented messages were the norm in connected relationships. Finally, these similar patterns were observed in mother–daughter as well as grand-mother–granddaughter relationships. Mother–daughter interaction "scripts" were observed *across three different generations*. When I first began to observe these women I expected to see unique interaction patterns within each of the six family cultures, but what occurred after about 7 weeks into my fieldwork was the emergence of two script types: one enacted in enmeshed maternal relation-ships and one enacted in connected maternal relationships. These scripts were played out on the relational stage in mother–daughter and grandmother grand-daughter relationships across the life span. The remainder of this chapter de-scribes these script types and then addresses the discovery of a grounded theory that came into view while considering these scripts.

Scripted Interaction

Scripts are guides to action that structure our everyday interaction (Guerrero, Anderson, & Afifi, 2001; Wood, 2000). Here I focus on relational scripts—scripts that organize interpersonal knowledge and direct interactions with oth-ers (Duck & Wright, 1993). Based on previous interactions and experiences, re-lational scripts represent what the communicators view as expected or appropriate behavior within a given context, and scripted interactions exem-plify relational work (Tracey, 2002). Over time, family members develop a num-ber of scripts that guide them through different kinds of interactions in their relationships with each other.

All of us have scripts that we use in different settings: The general social script for answering a question in class typically requires a question issued from the teacher, the student raising his or her arm to request acknowledgment, the teacher calling on a student to answer the question, and the selected student providing the answer. Of course, unique scripts may be developed depending on the composition and interaction in any particular classroom climate. Similarly, enmeshed and connected maternal relationships in Elkwood tended to follow general interaction scripts that dictated normative ways of issuing directives and responses. These scripts crossed generational boundaries, served to posi-tion members in a hierarchy of the family structure, regulated the flow of mes-sages, and managed dialectical tensions. Two sets of script types emerged: the *directive-response script* and the *novel-meanings script*. These scripts are outlined in Table 5.1 and discussed in this next section.

SCRIPTS GUIDING ENMESHED RELATIONSHIPS

In enmeshed maternal relationships, higher-status women's power over daugh-ters and/or granddaughters was particularly powerful. As pointed out in chapter

TABLE 5.1
Script Types

Assert-Response Scripts

	Higher-Status Woman Directive— Lower-Status Woman Response		Lower-Status Woman Directive— Higher-Status Woman Response	
	Enmeshed Relationships	Connected Relationships	Enmeshed Relationships	Connected Relationships
Directive assert	*Hint or direct statement directive *Command *Evaluative (positive praise and negative judgments) *Reproach *Certainty language *Superiority	*Direct query or statement directive *Descriptive statement *Provisional language *Orientation toward respect rather than equality	*Query directive *Direct request *Hint *Strategic *Guarded altruism	*Direct query or statement directive *Descriptive statement *Provisional language *Orientation toward respect rather than equality
Response	*Deferring *Obliging *Avoiding *Implicitly endorsing *Embedding challenges in humor *Invalidating assert, conveyed with nonverbal cues *Personalizing	*Discussing *Acknowledging *Negotiating *Compromising *Empathizing *Challenging	*Ignoring *Evaluating (positive praise and negative judgments) *Reinforcing status *Personalizing *Acting defensive *Embedding challenges in humor *Invalidating assert, conveyed through nonverbal cues *Providing or withdrawing resource	*Discussing *Acknowledging *Negotiating *Compromising *Empathizing *Integrating
Novel meanings	*Novel meanings discouraged *Novel meanings reacted to as threatening *Necessary convergence with dominant meaning system	*Novel meanings introduced by both members *Novel meanings discussed *Novel meanings negotiated and integrated into shared meaning system		

4, in enmeshed relationships the normal process of separation was often perceived as a betrayal, and hints of the offspring's autonomy were negatively sanctioned. This control drama was played out in many interactions across generations. The *novel-meaning script* guided how women handled the introduction of novel information—any new information, attitude, or opinion introduced into the relational culture. Enmeshed maternal relationships tended to be closed systems in which novel meanings were discouraged and perceived as threatening, and convergence with the dominant meaning system of the higher-status woman was required in order to maintain harmony in the relationship.

Enmeshed *directive-response scripts* differed significantly from connected directive-response scripts. The purpose of a directive is to get a partner to do something or not do something. The women in all six families made requests of their partners, anything from "Pass the corn" to "Can you babysit for me on Friday night?" The nature of the scripts altered, however, across connected and enmeshed relationships. Moreover, in the enmeshed relationships the status of the women issuing the directive appeared to affect the script.

Higher-Status Woman Directive—Lower-Status Woman Response Pattern. Typically, when a higher-status woman issued a directive and a lower-status woman responded, the script was played out in the following manner:

> The mother issued a direct command or hint directive posed in an evaluative fashion with language that conveyed certainty and/or superiority. The daughter then responded by providing implicit endorsement of the older woman's status, obliging and/or deferring to her. Novel meanings were not resisted for long, and the daughter assimilated the meanings assigned by the higher-status woman.

As an illustration, let me share one particular documented episode. On this morning, Sam and I were sipping lemonade. I was feeling a bit grumpy due to not getting enough sleep the night before, but Sam seemed to be in good cheer. Diane was not in the room with us. I had turned on my tape recorder and Sam and I were talking about her relationship with her mother:

> Sam said to me, "My hair was never the right style for her. To this day I am overly sensitive to how my hair looks in public. Sometimes it would ruin her day if she didn't like how my hair was done."
>
> I observed, "I think it looks nice today—cute hair clip."
>
> She replied, "Thanks, I like it like this, it's cooler in this heat."
>
> "Is the hair thing still an issue between the two of you [as an adult]?" I asked. Then I looked up and Diane had entered the room. She walked over to us and sat down next to me.
>
> Diane looked at Sam, began pouring some lemonade from the pitcher, and promptly said to her daughter with a tone of disapproval, "What have you done to your hair?"

The timing was perfect. Sam just laughed, looked at me with a smile, and said, "Yep."

Within 30 minutes of this conversation, Sam escaped to the bathroom and came out with her hair down falling around her shoulders, not pulled back in its previous style. I asked her why she changed her hair, even though she admittedly liked it pulled back, and she replied, "Oh, it makes her [my mother] happy and I really didn't like it that way anyway … I guess. Besides, I don't want to have to put up with her annoying gazes."

Over and over again I witnessed a deferential or ingratiating response to a critical remark made by a higher-status woman. What is more surprising to me is that these *adult* daughters and granddaughters not only deferred to higher-status women in the family, but repeatedly over-accommodated the elder's perceptions of the world—higher-status women's meanings were privileged. Instead of negotiating or coordinating perceptions, the lower-status women almost inevitably demonstrated this skewed deference. Sam changed her hairstyle in response to her mother's remark, but more interesting to me is that contrary to what she had expressed not a half-hour earlier, her interpretation began to shift toward her mother's interpretation. She said, "I really didn't like it that way anyway … I guess." She was shifting from her own interpretation into an assimilation of her mother's, the "I guess" suggesting that she had not yet fully assimilated the alternative interpretation.

There were many reenactments of the same script during my months of observing these women. When Scout brought her eggs to the holiday feast and Meredith disapproved, not only did Morgan accommodate her mother's directive but, in the end, Scout began to question her own judgment about bringing the eggs. Recall when Julie's artwork was selected from among hundreds for an exhibition. Julie told me:

I showed [my mother] the posters and do you know what she said? Not 'Good job' … but, 'You really should take an art class. These show real promise!' Promise?! These were already chosen; they weren't works in progress! I knew what she meant. I just wish she could say 'Good job' and leave it at that. I just couldn't shake it but I just wasn't very excited about the showing after that. It took a lot of joy out of it.

In fact, Julie reported to me about a month later that she had signed up for an art class. She echoed her mother's interpretation: "I see the need for a lot of improvement. I can't get around seeing all the flaws in my style."

Walsh (1998) pointed out in his research that dysfunctional relationships often exhibit a skewed deference of one partner to another, and that this overaccommodation often leads to resentment. Although these scripts were enacted again and again in the enmeshed dyads, there were clear resentments. Lower-status women in the hierarchy of the family structure would complain, "I don't know how she always gets me to feel bad about myself" and "Of course she is the one always right, never wrong." Although these scripts guided lower-status women to be deferential to the higher-status women, sometimes scripts were changed, with lower-status women issuing resistance or a challenge. Almost inevitably, however, challenges were masked in humor ("Kidding, kidding, she is always pretending to be kidding") or conveyed nonverbally rather than verbally ("I just give her a dirty look"). Women in the enmeshed relationships tended to express their resentment and anger "backstage" when the older-status women were not around. Kelly shared the following insight with me on a day when her mother was not present:

> All of the women in my family are verbally abusive. I would like to look real good on that paper. You know, a good mother .... But I marked down that yes I'm verbally abusive too, to my kids. Not directly to my mother, I'll talk *about* her. My own grandmother, how she was verbally abusive to me growing up, called me every name in the book and said that because of what I done, that I wasn't a granddaughter of hers, I was a slut. And I believed it all. My grandmother talked about my mom behind her back and my mom talked about my granny, now I talk about my mom and, um I suppose my daughters talk about me ....

These women would gladly talk with me—an outsider—about their mothers or grandmothers, but when it came to actual interaction episodes, I witnessed only a few instances of lower-status women "breaking out" and challenging their mothers beyond short-lived resistance or enacting an alternative script (e.g., one posed by Scout, to say "To hell with you, I am going to do, think, act, feel what I want to ... thank you!").

When I questioned lower-status women about why they converged their interpretations to fit with their mothers' or grandmothers' interpretations, they would talk about being aware of this script. Morgan said, "It is sick, especially at my age," and Diane argued that she "hate[d] the way" her mother made her question herself all the time and "I try not to do repeat the same thing with my daughters." But the observational and interview data suggest that these patterns *are being repeated across generations*. The lower-status members (daughters and granddaughters) in these enmeshed relationships pointed out that they deferred to the dominant member in order to receive resources and to maintain the relationship. As I discussed in the previous chapter, higher-status women in these relationships tended to manipulate support, regard, and inclusion. It appears that the lower-status women converged their own meaning system with that of the higher-status woman because the lower-status women perceived that *affection and inclusion in the relationship was contingent on that convergence*.

A daughter, for example, whose continued acceptance in the enmeshed mother–daughter relationship was conditional on meeting maternal expectations would converge her meaning system with her mother's for relational maintenance purposes. Failing to assimilate a mother's interpretive frame into her own meaning system would mean risking her precarious acceptance and approval within the relational culture. Thus, there was a *necessary convergence* of meaning in which the lower-status woman in the family structure exhibited a skewed deference to the higher-status woman's interpretive frame in order to obtain the higher-status woman's approval and avoid rejection, and hence did not risk her membership in this relational culture. Morgan felt loved by her mother and revealed that she too felt emotionally connected to her, but complained that if she resisted her mother's interpretation of the world then her mother would "I don't know, it's hard to explain but she would like not necessarily pay enough attention to you but puts her attention on someone that meets her approval. Someone doing what she expects or seeing the world in the same way she does. She just shuts you out until you come over to her side." Morgan laughed at her use of that phrase and added, "to the dark side."

Author Ayn Rand (1993) referred to this script in her novel *The Fountainhead*. Rand argued that individuals in enmeshed relationships tend to be "second-handers"—people who don't judge for themselves, who just repeat what others close to them say, embrace it, and make it their own. What I witnessed in the data collected over my many months in Elkwood was that, yes, there might be scripts that resist novel meanings and guide lower-status individuals into overaccommodating dominant members in relationships, but beyond these patterned scripts I believe scholars need to gain a more thorough understanding of the interpretations that relational members have of these exchanges, and what these exchanges mean to them in the fuller context of their maternal relationship, in order to fully understand the motivations that members have for following such scripts. Moving on this impulse, I proceeded to expand my inquiry and asked women about their interpretations of these patterns. This led to the development of the grounded theoretical framework to explain the phenomenon of necessary convergence of meaning. This emerged directly from the juxtaposition of observational and interview data, and is covered more thoroughly in the next chapter. Before moving on to this theoretical development, however, I wish to discuss the scripted interaction that tended to occur when lower-status women issued the directive and higher-status women responded in enmeshed relationships.

Lower-Status Woman Directive—Higher-Status Woman Response Pattern. This script took on the following general pattern:

- The lower-status woman in the family hierarchy (e.g., daughter or granddaughter) would issue a directive in a guarded fashion, resulting in a query directive or hinting. Directives tended to be strategic in nature.
- The higher-status woman would respond to this directive in a manner that served to reinforce her family-level status. If a particular directive honored her status, then the response would acknowledge the lower-status woman and resources such as regard and respect would be freely offered. If the directive somehow conveyed disrespect for her sta-

tus, then the response would be evaluative or defensive, tending to in-validate the request, or threaten the withdrawal of resources.

I shared with several of the daughters and granddaughters my perception that lower-status women's directives tended to be strategic. Their reaction was that this strategic use of directives was due, in part, to an underlying agenda. The un-spoken agenda for many of these women was to convey three different messages when each issued directives: (a) to meet personal goals in getting the other to respond to her directive, yet to also (b) respect and defer to her partner's status in the family and relationship, and (c) avoid upsetting the other person with the directive. In an earlier example, I mentioned how Scout wanted to make sure that her mother washed any clothes she borrowed before returning them. In her directive, she was careful to neither offend her mother by this request nor chal-lenge her mother's status. Scout approached her mother with the query: "Mom, I don't care if you borrow my stuff, but next time you wear something of mine could you make sure you wash it before you send it back to me?" With this query, Scout did not erect boundaries; she indicated that she "didn't care" if her mother borrowed her stuff, implying that her mother had every right to her clothing. The soft tonal quality of Scout's voice suggested respect rather than annoyance, yet she made her request for clean clothes clear to her mother. Mor-gan, in turn, responded by delivering the following comment with certainty: "All right, fine, but the same with my clothes. I don't remember you washing my things after you borrow them." Morgan consented to comply with her daugh-ter's request, but was a tad defensive and made a point of reinforcing her status in the family with her "one-up"—making sure that Scout would wash items be-fore returning them, too. A compromise and an implicit agreement to keep bor-rowing clothing from each other were reached, with the provision that any borrowed clothing was to be returned laundered.

These maternal relational scripts served to guide members' behaviors in ways that reinforced the hierarchy of the relational structure across the life span and generations, and also appeared to keep lower-status women dependent on higher-status women for relational inclusion.

Scripts Guiding Connected Relationships

Scripts guide interaction and are typically unconscious; they are a communica-tion sequence "overlearned" through repetition (Sillars, 1995). For women in the enmeshed relationships, scripts were learned and practiced across the life span because development and change were resisted even as younger women entered adulthood and middle age. The women in the connected relationships, however, reported developmental changes in their scripts across the life span. *Development* is concerned with maturational process and—for the connected mothers and daughter, grandmothers and granddaughters—personal matura-tion was intertwined with relational development and renegotiation of relational scripts at different points in the life course. The patterned interactions (scripts) that I witnessed between women in the connected relationships were very similar across generational boundaries despite the status of the woman issuing the directive. The retrospective accounts of these women, however, provided additional information about how interactions in their relationships were "rescripted" during different developmental points in time.

Directive-Response Pattern in Connected Adult Maternal Relationships. Observational data revealed the following scripts across adult grandmother–mother–daughter relationships:

- One woman issues a direct query or statement that is descriptive in nature. Her language is provisional, with an orientation toward person rather than position. Respect rather than equality is conveyed in the directive—respectful acknowledgment of the relational partner's status in the family hierarchy.
- The lower-status woman responds in kind with an acknowledgment of the relational partner's status in the family hierarchy. Novel meanings are discussed, negotiated, and sometimes challenged. Respect is conveyed even when the response is a challenge. Challenges are directly expressed.

I found it intriguing that the scripts were essentially the same whether the older or the younger woman issued the directive. This does not mean that women did not acknowledge the status of partners in the family hierarchy—indeed, each did recognize the status of the other woman—but they respected their relational partners as women with status but also as unique individuals. Both women in these dyads issued statement directives and introduced novel interpretations. The issuance of these directives was provisional in nature, meaning that the directives were open to discussion or alternative points of view. Descriptive rather than evaluative language was used; therefore, defensiveness was minimal and responses were most likely to include direct compliance, discussion, or negotiation. This paints a rosy picture of the responder as being happily compliant, but that kind of response was not always the case. In situations where the responder was resistant to the directive or wanted to challenge a novel meanings, she would do so directly (i.e., front stage) rather than by hinting or by agreeing to her partner's face and then challenging the partner behind her back.

The following episode occurred during one of the many moments I witnessed related to the preparation of Georgie's wedding. I believe this illustrates the relational script enacted in connected adult maternal relationships:

> After dinner one evening, as we sat chatting and drinking coffee, Georgie told her mother that she had picked out the dress that she wanted her bridesmaids to wear

at her wedding. She left the room and brought back a bridal magazine with the page turned to this particular dress.

Gina looked at the picture of the dress, said, "Hmmm," and then handed me the magazine. The dress was beautiful (in my opinion). It was an entirely black off-the-shoulder dress in silk or rayon, with a plunging back and a small train.

As Gina handed me the magazine, she looked at Georgie and said, "I can see why you like the dress, it is very classic and beautiful. But I don't think that a black dress is really appropriate for a wedding. Does it come in any other colors?"

Georgie took the magazine from me and looked at the caption, then looked back at her mother. "Mom, I don't know, but then again I like it because it *is* black. I think I want a totally black-and-white wedding."

"I don't think that is necessarily a good choice. I like to see color in weddings, color signifies happiness. Don't you think that black is depressing for a wedding?" asked Gina.

"Not really, mom," replied Georgie. "Actually, I've seen a few pictures of weddings using the black-and-white theme and it is gorgeous. Stunning, really. White roses and lilies, black dresses, my white dress, his black tux, maybe white flowers in the bridesmaid's hair."

"Hmmm," Gina said again, looking once more at the photo. "It's your wedding, and I do like color. But that sounds different and kind of fits your personality, now doesn't it!" she said with a laugh. "Have you asked Paul [Georgie's fiancé] about what he thinks yet?"

"I'm going to tomorrow. I think he'll love it, but I wanted to show you first and get your impression."

"Well, my impression is that I like color, but I can see this working. You guys need to choose what works for you. Also, remember you need to consider the cost of these dresses and if they might be out of range [financially] for the girls [to purchase]."

During this exchange, Georgie issued the first directive, directly asking her mother to look at the picture of the dress. Gina's response was provisional, acknowledging that she could see why Georgie liked the dress, descriptive in the merits of the dress, but also directly stating and owning her opinion, which differed from her daughter's ("I don't think that a black dress is really appropriate …"). The rest of the interaction involves discussing the idea of using black bridesmaids' dresses, with each woman stating her opinion ("I think I want a totally black-and-white wedding," "I like color"), clarifying her point of view ("color signifies happiness"), issuing direct challenges ("Not really, Mom"), but ultimately acknowledging and respecting the other ("It's your wedding," "I wanted your opinion").

The novel meaning of black in the context of a wedding was discussed, negotiated, and ultimately integrated into the shared meaning system of the relational culture. Gina still preferred colorful dresses in weddings, but over the course of this conversation she and George coconstructed a new meaning of what is appropriate for a wedding; a meaning that, after all, might not cast the color black as depressing in the context of a wedding celebration, but instead would celebrate the uniqueness of the bride and groom. Once this new meaning was negotiated, the women could move on to other topics such as the price of the dresses.

Over the course of the 8 months of my work in Elkwood, this script was repeated numerous times, regardless of mother–daughter or grandmother–granddaughter relationships and at different points across the life span (e.g., young-adult daughters as well as mid-life daughters). However, after prodding the women in these connected relationships for their interpretations of this relational script, I learned that this script became repetitious once lower-status women entered adulthood. They described an alternative script that was more common during a daughter's or granddaughter's adolescence. These women claimed, however, that the alternative script transitioned into the more "adult" script described previously as the women navigated the developmental trajectory of their maternal relationships. In fact, some of the younger women sometimes "reverted" to these alternative scripts, especially with grandmothers, although this was not observed very often ($n = 5$). Based on those few observations, along with the description of the "alternative" script offered by participants, the following is an example and description of this alternative script for nonadult connected maternal relationships. This script was similar in that it emphasized respect for the other, direct requests or statements, descriptive and provisional language, with open discussion, challenges, and the encouragement of novel meanings. However, the alternative nonadult script emphasized status more directly, with assertions and responses reinforcing the status of the members in manifest ways:

> One day, Tabitha—one of the youngest of the participants in this study—wanted to secure her grandmother as an ally in her campaign to adopt a puppy. Because Tabitha still lived in her mother and father's house, she needed to get their consent before adopting the puppy and so sought her grandmother's assistance in obtaining this consent.
>
> Tabitha asked her grandmother, "Nana, I need your help. I want you to convince Mom that this dog is a good idea. I know she will listen to you."
>
> Lois looked amused at this. "And why do you think that?"
>
> "Because you're her mom!" Tabitha laughed, "She has to listen to you." This was said with a smile in her voice, conveying that she was kidding but thought the argument might work.
>
> "I can only tell her that this is what you want. But you'll need to convince her on your own. Honestly, I don't blame her, what will you do with this animal when you go off to school?" Lois responded.

They continued to discuss the matter and Tabitha ended up trying to convince her mother—on her own—that adopting the puppy would be a good idea. In the end, they did not adopt the puppy and life returned to normal.

Developmental researchers have recently extended the time of adolescence upward to the ages of 22 to 24 (Romer, 2003). Many youth do not truly enter adulthood until they move from their parents' home and encounter the unique challenges of adulthood, thus exemplifying this definition. Tabitha (although 18) might be considered a late adolescent rather than an adult. Therefore, it makes sense that in this interaction she appealed to her grandmother's status as her mother's mother. Living at her parents' home, Tabitha was still subject to the permissions and consent of her parents, and the interpersonal scripts that guided her interactions with them at times emphasized the family hierarchy. Yet, because she was 18 she was beginning to see herself—and her mother and grandmother were beginning to see her—as an adult. Interview data from women in connected relationships suggested that once an "adult" grandmother–mother–daughter relationship was negotiated, appeals to status and responses reinforcing status were no longer necessary.

What I find unique is that in connected maternal relationships, relational scripts were reportedly adapted and *rewritten* to account for developmental changes in the relational culture. Scripts tended to adjust over time as the younger women moved into adulthood and different role relationships were established. As adults, status no longer needed to be announced in a directive nor reinforced in a response. Moreover, in contrast with women in enmeshed relationships, the higher-status woman's promise of resource provision or the threat of resource withdrawal was not even present in connected relational scripts.

SUMMARY

I began this chapter with an idea promoted by Tracy (2002) that talk does identity work and identities work to shape talk. The findings described here provide support for this idea. Discursive practices such as use of reproach, directives, and relational scripts differed substantively across the enmeshed and the connected maternal relationships I observed in Elkwood. These practices reflected the individual identities of the partners in interaction, but this talk also was the instrument by which these partners negotiated and managed their relational identities. Dialectical tensions such as autonomy and connectedness were overtly managed during discursive episodes, with different scripts guiding enmeshed and connected maternal relationships. The enmeshed scripts reflected a relational culture that was closed to novel meanings, autonomy, and challenges to the status of women higher in the family hierarchy; the connected scripts reflected a relational culture that was open to novel meanings, and encouraged a person orientation and autonomy within the context of emotional connection, respect, and challenge.

So, what does this entire body of results mean? As described in chapter 2, at this stage of the research a qualitative researcher is compelled to ask how disparate results *fit* together given current theoretical knowledge in the area. Additionally, I was compelled to ask how the findings reported in these last few chapters *contribute* to the body of knowledge that currently exists in the area of maternal family relationships. Chapter 6 addresses existing theory and the emergence of a grounded theory that surfaced after examining the results, and then explains some of the implications of the grounded theory that I am calling the *necessary convergence of meaning.*

III

The Denouement

6

Theoretical
Development

Theoretical work on communication is important for understanding the dynamics of the modern family.
—(Koerner & Fitzpatrick, 2002, p. 70)

But relationships, like life, are complex, and our attempts to categorize, synthesize, and capture them intellectually are, by definition, insufficient.
—(Wilmot, 1995, p. 134)

Although several theoretical frameworks have already served to organize these findings, unfortunately no family communication theories explain many of the results outlined in the previous chapters. I am aware of no theories that adequately address the intergenerational transmission of enmeshed and connected maternal relationship patterns, and certainly none that help us to understand how enmeshed patterns of interaction might have affected the "meaning-making" processes in these relationships or increased the Elkwood women's vulnerability to problem behaviors.

Bowen's (1978) intergenerational family theory posited that functional and dysfunctional family processes are transmitted across generations, only to be repeated in successive generations. However, Bowen's theory does not address the process of transmission. This is unfortunate, because communication is central to the intergenerational transmission process, with family-of-origin communication providing blueprints for the communication patterns of future generations (Burleson, Delia, & Applegate, 1995). Communication scholars need to fill this gap and seek to explain how patterns of interaction shape meanings conveyed across generations; the theory proposed in this chapter begins to fill that gap.

The theoretical framework of *necessary convergence of meaning* is grounded in the data, inductively derived, and offers an explanation of how a unique pattern of enmeshed maternal interaction may become routinized in family culture. Additionally, the framework is extended into an ecological model that describes how this unique interaction pattern might compromise women's health. The purpose of this chapter is to introduce the theoretical framework of necessary convergence. To that end, I briefly review the process of grounded theory and then outline how the theoretical framework of necessary convergence offers a road map to help scholars and practitioners better understand enmeshed maternal relationships.

GROUNDED THEORY

Glaser and Strauss introduced grounded theory in 1967. They argued that theories are naturally induced from data and that "only in this way will theory be closely related to the daily realities (what is actually going on)" (Strauss & Corbin, 1998, p. 164). A grounded theory begins inductively; that is, as data are collected, a theory emerges and begins to take shape. As these data become saturated (i.e., no new information is being revealed over time, even after adding new participants), then the theory can enter a final phase of abstraction. Grounded theory as a theoretical approach has been classified as the "discovery of regularities" and further defined as the process of identifying (and categorizing) elements, and exploring their connections (Tesch, 1990). Essentially, the basic purpose is to enable the researcher to think systematically about data and relate them in complex ways. Charmaz (2000), along with Strauss and Corbin (1998), suggested that grounded theories are "middle-range theories" and can explain collected data in particular contexts. After data are identified and organized (e.g., key dialectical tensions, scripts), their connections are explored and the theory is delimited (Kinach, 1996).

In chapter 2 I talked about how this study began as a heuristic endeavor, hoping to illuminate and increase understanding of multigenerational, Caucasian, middle-class maternal relationships and the role that communication plays in these relationships. I did not set out to develop theory—the theory found me. Approximately 9 weeks into my fieldwork, I could not ignore that the collected data were "taking shape." Within the overall sample of six grandmother–mother–adult daughter triads, three of these triads included (grand)mothers and (grand)daughters who reported participating in negative health behaviors (e.g., disordered eating), and at least one woman in each of these triads had made a serious suicide attempt as an adult. The term *risk behaviors* is used henceforth to denote behaviors that placed the woman at risk for negative health consequences (Gottfredson & Hirschi, 1994; Romer, 2003). Table 2.2 outlined the risk behaviors self-reported by the women in three of the six families. Interestingly, the other three families did not seem to encounter similar challenges; not one of the members in Families #3, #4, or #5 self-reported suicide attempts or any of the other risk behaviors reported in Families #1, #2, and #6.

Additionally, each woman who reported a suicide attempt was in maternal relationships identified as enmeshed. Recall that two different kinds of cohesive maternal relationships emerged in this study—enmeshed and connected— with each of the 18 maternal relationships falling into one of these categories. These enmeshed and connected relational patterns crossed generational boundaries and were evident in mother–adult daughter as well as grand-mother–adult granddaughter relationships. Enmeshed and connected relation-ships were characterized by their own unique patterns of dialectics and interaction. The unexpected emergence of this naturally occurring comparison group provided me with the opportunity to explore the distinctive characteris-tics of each type of cohesive relationship.

Hence, moving from heuristic description and interpretation to abductive theory development,[22] I delimited my inquiry to include theoretical speculation about enmeshed relational patterns because the phenomenon of necessary con-vergence was only observable at this particular level of cohesion in the Elkwood families. In each of the enmeshed relationships at least one woman reported a suicide attempt (and more than one attempt in some cases). Delimiting served to narrow the sphere of applicability for the claims I make to Caucasian, mid-dle-class, suburban women in enmeshed maternal relationships.

NECESSARY CONVERGENCE

The theoretical framework I call *necessary convergence of meaning* offers a road map for understanding the phenomenon of necessary convergence that was de-scribed in chapter 5. *Necessary convergence* refers to a communication phenom-enon that occurred among women in enmeshed maternal relationships. During certain communication transactions, adult daughters and granddaughters would defer to the higher-status woman in the family, overaccommodate the higher-status woman's interpretation of events, and ultimately converge to-ward her interpretive frame for relational maintenance purposes. The remain-der of this chapter reviews necessary convergence, argues that a chronic pattern of necessary convergence might compromise women's health, and finally offers theoretical speculation about how the phenomenon of convergence might be transmitted across generations.

---

[22]*Abductive theory development* refers to the process by which the researcher works back and forth between data and the building blocks of theory, in which negative cases are impor-tant, and the researcher seeks to account for all he or she can and then discuss that for which he or she cannot account. When there is a "surprising" or novel finding, the researcher specu-lates as to the meaning and then moves back to the data to test this speculation.

Building on the firm foundations of relational communication theory (Burleson et al., 2000) and family communication theory (Koerner & Fitzpatrick, 2002), several assumptions guided my theoretical speculation. These theories provided a lens through which I could interpret both observational behavioral data and the interview data when trying to understand the emergent patterns of maternal relational communication.

A Priori Theoretical Assumptions

Communication Enacts Relationships. The state of being in a "relationship" is inherently a communication process and must be understood as a series of transactions in which messages are exchanged. Relationships are formed across repeated transactions, with each new transact adding new information to the one that came before, building a cumulative database of information about the relationship (Burleson et al., 2000; Duck, 1992; Guerrero et al., 2001). Transactions are units of interaction affecting both interactants and carrying commentary on the interactant's relationship. As Watzlawick, Beavin, and Jackson (1967) pointed out, each message (both verbal and nonverbal) carries information at two levels—the content level and the relationship level. The relationship level enacts the current state of the relationship and provides information about how the communicators see each other, themselves, and their relationship.

Communicative Transactions in Close Personal Relationships Have Implications for Personal and Relational Identities. Relational members encode and decode information about the other as information about themselves, and then extrapolate this to the relational unit (Aron & Aron, 1986). The self is conceptualized as inseparable from dynamic interaction, with each transaction contributing to both self- and relational knowledge. Early work by Mead (1934) identified the centrality of message exchange in personal identity management. More recent work in relational communication points out that both personal and relational identities are cocreated communicatively within the context of relationship (Wilmot, 1995). Personal identity development is really the unfolding of the self while retaining relational ties; identities are constituted and managed through relationships, not to their exclusion (Adams & Marshall, 1996).

Communication Is an Emergent, Creative Activity Through Which Meanings are Constantly Coordinated Via Interpretive Schemata. People approach the world through processes of interpretation. As human social animals we are in a constant state of interpreting and managing meanings, and interpreting meanings is an interdependent process.[23] The assumption is that mean-

---

[23]For a more detailed discussion of humans using symbols and interpreting animals, see George Herbert Mead's work *Mind, Self, and Society* (1934), or Herbert Blumer's (1969) discussion of symbolic interaction.

ings are not inherent in objects, but instead arises out of social interaction. During social interaction, meanings are coordinated through interpretive schemata—mental structures consisting of organized knowledge about relationships.[24] Interpretive schemata represent accumulated knowledge—the sum of past experiences—which help an individual interpret, understand, and predict the outcomes of interactions with others (Burleson et al., 2000; Cragan & Shields, 1998; Koerner & Fitzpatrick, 2002). Moreover, interpretive schemata include expectations about what should happen in a given situation and serve to guide behavior.

Interpretive schemata specific to relationships—relationship schemata— influence the "encoding and decoding of information, the inferences and evaluations people make ... and ultimately their interpersonal behavior" in relationships (Koerner & Fitzpatrick, 2002, p. 80). This assumption presumes that the process of "making meaning" activates interpretive frames. Communicators then coordinate their meaning systems filtered through these frames and negotiate agreement. Understanding between the members builds intersubjectivity and hopefully leads to consensus (Crotty, 1998; Solomon, Dillard, & Anderson, 2002). Implicit in this assumption are claims of coordination and negotiation. *Coordination* implies a state of equal rank, equal power, and harmonious order, whereas *negotiation* suggests that communicators confer with one another in order to reach an agreement. Coordination involves collaboration of all communicating partners.

Family Culture Shapes Interpretive/Relational Schemata for Family Relationships. Family cultures consist of shared meaning systems, routinized patterns of interaction, and norms that structure members' roles and behaviors (Wood, 2000). These cultural norms shape family relational schemata (Koerner & Fitzpatrick, 2002), and these schemata are socialized within a family culture. Socialization involves the "social and communicative processes through which cultural knowledge, resources and practices are made available and internalized" by cultural members (Burleson et al., 2000, p. 35). As Entman (1993) demonstrated, culture is the stock of commonly evoked interpretive schemata and [family] culture might be defined as the "empirically demonstrable set of common interpretive frames exhibited in the discourse and thinking of most people in a [family]" (p. 53). Family relational schemata are the mental structures that are socialized within a family culture, organize knowledge about family relationships, and are used to process information relevant to these relationships. Therefore, family cultures will share common schemata about maternal relationships, and these schemata will be reflected in the communication practices of family members.

---

[24]For a more complete discussion of constructivism, interpretive frames, and relational schemata, see Brant Burleson and associates (1989, 1995, 2000); Mark Baldwin (1992); Cragan and Shields (1998); Delia, O'Keefe, and O'Keefe (1982); and Fletcher and Thomas (1996).

Interpersonal Scripts Emerge From Relational Schemata. Scripts are one form of communication practice enacted within family relationships that emerge from relational schemata (Koerner & Fitzpatrick, 2002). As indicated in chapter 5, relational scripts direct interaction, exemplify relational work, dictate normative ways of issuing directives and responses, and may cross generational boundaries. Scripted interactions are often routine, habituated, and overlearned through repetitive practice in the family culture (Sillars, 1995); however, these scripts are useful in directing the "typical" ways in a which an interaction should be handled given the particular relational schema. A "maternal relationship" schema in any particular family culture may honor only certain kinds of relational enactments. When relational members become practiced in these roles and memorize their lines, these enactments become scripted. That is, women may not think about their day-to-day ways of interacting with grandmothers, mothers, and daughters on a conscious level, but they may still tend to communicate in patterned ways with well-defined scripts that enact "appropriate" relational behavior.

Through the lenses of relational and family communication theories, the basic assumptions that guided my grounded theory development were that *multigenerational family culture shaped women's knowledge of maternal relationships; each woman's accumulated knowledge of maternal relationships helped her to coordinate meanings with her maternal relationship partners; patterned or scripted communication behavior emerged from these maternal relationship schemata; and this communication behavior was consequential for maternal relationships.* As I began to place the patterns of these data in juxtaposition (e.g., dialectics, discursive practices, levels of relational cohesion, and problem behavior), a grounded theoretical framework emerged that provides a potential explanation for the phenomenon of necessary convergence in enmeshed maternal relationships.

Necessary Convergence as a Communication Phenomenon

I suggest that *necessary convergence* is a communication phenomenon representing a specific form of relational intersubjectivity. Necessary convergence was a significant patterned occurrence within the enmeshed maternal relationships in Elkwood. This phenomenon occurred during periods of symbolic transaction, privileged the interpretive frame of the higher-status woman in the relationship, impeded meaning coordination, and promoted the lower-status woman's submission to the higher-status woman's symbol interpretation and assignment of meaning in communicative interaction. When the relational schema for the lower-status woman was based on *conditional regard*—that is, she believed that her acceptance in the relationship (her receipt of emotional resources) was contingent on receiving maternal recognition and approval—then she would converge her own interpretations with her partner's for relational maintenance purposes. Not to converge with her (grand)mother's interpretation of symbols in any transaction would risk her precarious acceptance and approval in the relationship. Thus, there was a necessary convergence of meaning that privileged the interpretive frame of the higher-status member in the family hierarchy in order for the lower-status woman to achieve approval and avoid rejection.

An *interpretive frame* is defined here as cognitive structure or system that contains mental representations of meanings, *necessary* infers that convergence was perceived as essential to achieve a certain result, and *convergence* indicates a tendency toward one point. Thus, to obtain maternal approval and avoid rejection, there was a necessary convergence of meaning toward the interpretive frame of the higher-status woman. Within this framework, convergence was relationally adaptive.

As described in chapter 5, the phenomenon of necessary convergence of meaning (NCM) occurred when adult daughters and granddaughters deferred to higher-status women in the family and overaccommodated their perceptions of the world. Instead of negotiating or coordinating perceptions, novel meanings were seen as relationally threatening; thus, lower-status women almost inevitably demonstrated a skewed deference to their relational partners' interpretations. This next section outlines the key identifying characteristics of necessary convergence and discusses some of the conditions that may be necessary for the development of necessary convergence in enmeshed maternal relationships.

I want to revisit an example of necessary convergence I used in chapter 5 to illustrate and discuss this phenomenon. The example is the "hair clip" episode. Recall the following dialogue:

Sam: My hair was never the right style for her. To this day I am overly sensitive to how my hair looks in public. Sometimes it would ruin her day if she didn't like how my hair was done.

Me: I think it looks nice today—cute hair clip.

Sam: Thanks, I like it like this, it's cooler in this heat.

Me: Is the hair thing still an issue between the two of you [as an adult]? I then looked up and Diane had entered the room. She walked over to us and sat down next to me.

Diane [*with a tone of disapproval*]: What have you done to your hair?

Sam [*laughing, then looking at me*]: Yep.

Within 30 minutes of this conversation, Sam had escaped to the bathroom and came out with her hair down falling around her shoulders, not pulled back in its previous style.

Me: Why did you change your hair? You said you like it the other way.

Sam: Oh, it makes her [my mother] happy and I really didn't like it that
        way anyway ... I guess. Besides, I don't want to have to put up with
        her annoying gazes.

Note in this example how Sam's convergence toward her mother's interpretive frame was not observable until Sam changed her hairstyle. Sam perceived that by changing her hairstyle it would secure a valuable resource
(make her mother happy) and avoid a negative sanction (an annoying gaze).
But merely deferring to her mother and changing the hairstyle in and of itself
did not illustrate convergence. Sam's admission that she "really didn't like
[her hair] that way anyway ... I guess" was the key indicator of necessary convergence. She *overaccommodated* her mother's interpretation of the hairstyle,
giving more importance to her mother's meaning system and actually starting
to converge her interpretation with her mother's interpretation to gain resources. She changed her own interpretation of the hairstyle, saying that she
didn't like her hair held up in a clip, even though minutes before she indicated
that she *did* like her hair styled in this way. The "I guess" was likely an indicator
of the cognitive dissonance experienced when full convergence had not yet
occurred and Sam was still holding onto remnants of her own interpretation.
    Convergence with a higher-status partner in the family relationship privi-
leged the interpretive frame of the higher-status woman and impeded meaning
coordination. When NCM occurred, meaning coordination was coercive
rather than cooperative. Although Diane did not insist that Sam change her
hairstyle and Sam suggested that she changed her style because she wanted to
avoid her mother's annoying gazes and make her mother happy, this does not
provide the full context for the interpretation of this interaction. Sam's alteration of her hairstyle and her internalization of her mother's opinion are only
fully understood when contextualizing this interaction in the context of Sam's
overall schema of the mother–daughter relationship.
    Recall that a characteristic of all these enmeshed maternal relationships, in-
cluding Sam and Diane's, was that lower-status women perceived maternal
dominance and *conditional regard* from their mothers and/or grandmothers (see
Fig. 4.1). These lower-status women in the hierarchy of the family perceived
that affection and inclusion in their maternal relationships were contingent on
meeting the maternal conditions of convergence. Thus, the lower-status
women exhibited a skewed deference to higher-status women's construction of
meaning in order to obtain their approval and avoid rejection. When a higher-
status woman manipulated valuable resources such as inclusion, support, or acceptance, convergence tended to be perceived as necessary to secure these resources. Messages that required convergence were not merely more
domineering; they were functionally more complex. They did not merely elicit
the desire to comply, nor did they merely elicit the desire for the relational partner to behave in a certain way, but, in addition, they called on the partner to ac-
tivate relational *scripts* that reaffirmed entrenched maternal relationship

schemas. In these enmeshed relationships, scripts required that the lower-status woman refrain from challenging the higher-status woman, and actually encouraged the lower-status performer to change her own interpretation by assuming the dominant member's assignment of meaning. Women who perceived convergence as necessary would make admissions such as "I am who she tells me I am" and "Her meanings become mine ... don't you see?"

Characteristics of Necessary Convergence

Based on the observational and interview data in this study, NCM seemed to be comprised of three separate characteristics: equilibrium, weighted proportion of meaningfulness, and motivation. These characteristics are illustrated in Fig. 6.1 and can be assessed in terms of their valence and intensity in any given maternal relationship.

Equilibrium. When necessary convergence occurred, there was disequilibrium in the relational coordination of meanings. *Equilibrium* refers to an equality of distribution; however when disequilibrium occurs, there is unequal power to determine meanings in interpersonal interaction. As discussed in chapter 4, power is a person's ability to control valuable resources and is often tied to status. When NCM occurred, the woman who was higher in the social hierarchy of the family would be dominant in *imposing*, rather than cooperatively negotiating, meaning on the lower-status partner. Moreover, as one per-

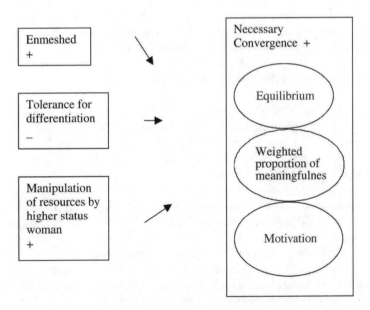

FIG. 6.1. Model of necessary convergence of meaning.

son's power to determine meanings increased, the other person's decreased, which then led to an unstable situation in which the importance of one partner's interpretive frame outweighed her partner's.

Weighted Proportion of Meaningfulness. The second characteristic of necessary convergence occurs when one partner actually submits to the unequal distribution in "meaning-making" power. Dominance requires submission. Consequently, when a lower-status woman submitted, she afforded the dominant partner's meanings more weight—more significance—in the transaction. If the lower-status woman resisted the imposition of meaning and challenged her mother or grandmother's meaning construction, then necessary convergence did not occur. The presence or absence of resistance seemed to be determined by the lower-status woman's motivation for convergence. Therefore, the third characteristic of NCM is motivation.

Motivation. Motivation is a reason for action, an incentive. When the compelling reason for convergence was to avoid undermining the relationship and to secure relational acceptance, there was increased motivation to converge with the higher-status woman. When acceptance in the maternal relationship was perceived to be conditional on that convergence, the event of convergence was perceived as relationally adaptive and the woman was more likely to perceive convergence as necessary. Necessary convergence, then, might be viewed as a form of secondary control. According to Rosenberg (1990), "Secondary control is an attempt to accommodate to objective conditions in order to affect a more satisfying fit with those conditions" (p. 147). Although convergence was not demanded in any explicit sense, the lower-status women *perceived it as a condition for relational acceptance.*

Conditions Antecedent to Necessary Convergence

Certain conditions were antecedent to NCM in maternal relationships. The following conditions were observed in Elkwood, as illustrated in Fig. 6.1, and may possibly predict necessary convergence. These conditions were explained at length in previous chapters, but they are summarized here as components of the NCM theoretical framework.

Enmeshment. The phenomenon of necessary convergence appeared to occur only within enmeshed maternal relationships. Recall that the enmeshed maternal relationships exhibited a high degree of emotional connectedness. The members were expected to conform to relational norms and adhere to scripts, were highly involved in each other's lives, and boundaries between individuals tended to be permeable. In these dyads, relational identities often subsumed the individual member's personal identities, with those identities becoming fused with the partner's. When this fusion occurred, transactions between relational members assumed extreme importance for the development of each member. In these relationships, the lower-status woman's attention typically became focused on pleasing her partner in order to feel good about herself, and a higher-status woman tended to perceive her partner's behavior as directly threatening to her own sense of "face." In these enmeshed maternal relationships, the women's personal identities were highly dependent on a reflected sense of self, with each woman needing continual validation from the other woman in order to feel valuable. Thus, convergence may have served a protective function for both relational identity and one's sense of self.

Impeded Differentiation. NCM occurred in relationships where there was low tolerance for differentiation. Recall that differentiation is conceptualized here as the process by which women move toward an autonomous self, yet remaining emotionally connected to the other women in their lives. In the enmeshed maternal relationships, the process of differentiation was perceived as threatening to the relationship and thus emotional autonomy was discouraged; therefore, for lower-status women, differentiation of self was inhibited. Developmentally, as most young women begin to acquire personal authority they naturally become differentiated from mother even as they remain emotionally connected (Nadien & Denmark, 1999). However, in the enmeshed Elkwood relational cultures, differentiation was perceived as a threat. Novel meanings were interpreted as threatening when there was a low tolerance for differentiation among members.

Manipulation of Resources. NCM occurred when higher-status women in the enmeshed relationships asserted their dominance by manipulating resources of support, regard, and inclusion to assert their dominance. As a form of psychological control, higher-status women would offer and withhold these resources contingent on evaluation of the lower-status women's "performance." Convergence was an expectation and thus was considered the only acceptable performance of the relational script. Nonconvergence would have risked the lower-status women's precarious acceptance, their support, and almost always the regard offered by the higher-status women. Thus, the manipulation of emotional resources to achieve psychological dominance was observed as a condition for necessary convergence. The provision or withdrawal of these resources provided a compelling motive for lower-status women's convergence.

Theoretical Suppositions of Necessary Convergence

Whereas theoretical assumptions are claims already supported in the research literature, *suppositions* are considered true or existing but not yet proved. The rich data set from this study produced several suppositions about the phenomenon of necessary convergence. I believe these suppositions may provide the necessary building blocks for theory development and offer future directions for empirical testing. (The suppositions are illustrated later in this chapter in Fig. 6.3, which depicts a proposed NCM model of risk). The suppositions account for the conditions predicting necessary convergence, the characteristics of necessary convergence, and then extend beyond these to include informed speculation about how necessary convergence may function as a risk factor to compromise women's health.

Supposition #1.   Maternal relationships that possess the characteristics of enmeshed levels of cohesion, low tolerance for differentiation of its members, and high incidence of maternal dominance through manipulation of emotional resources will positively predict necessary convergence.

Supposition #2.   Coordination of meaning involves power and control; meanings can be hijacked. When both partners share moderate levels of power in the relationship, they enjoy equilibrium in the negotiation of meaning during communicative transactions. However, those with more power (higher status) exert more influence in determining meaning in any transaction and those with less power (lower status) exert less influence (see illustration in Fig. 6.2). Although studies exist that explore social stratification and power in terms of race, gender, and larger cultural hierarchies (see, e.g., Altheide, 1995; Lyman, 1994), rarely do scholars explore interpersonal dominance in their attempts to understand meaning construction.

Supposition #3.   Under conditions where there is disequilibrium—unequal power—in determining meanings in relational transactions, both partners afford the dominant (higher-status) partner's meanings more weight—

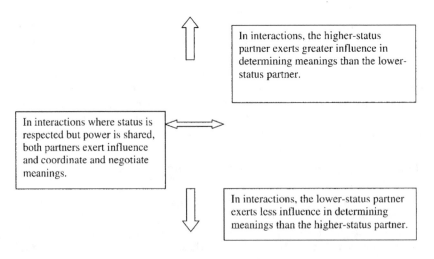

FIG. 6.2.   Status and the power to determine meaning.

more significance, and the compelling reason for convergence is to secure relational acceptance and avoid rejection, a lower-status woman will perceive convergence as expected and required.

Supposition #4. The act of convergence is relationally adaptive. Converging with a higher-status partner's assigned meanings will function to maintain the relational identity. The act of convergence in any given interaction will serve to protect the entangled identity of the interactants and function to maintain the relational status quo.

NECESSARY CONVERGENCE AS A RISK FACTOR

The interpersonal nature of the mother–daughter relationship as it relates to women's risk behaviors has not been closely examined (Kerpelman & Smith, 1999). Although family functioning literature provides a wealth of evidence that general family functioning may increase women's vulnerability to risk behaviors such as eating disorders (Hart & Kenny, 1997; Heesacker & Neimeyer, 1990; Kenny & Hart, 1992; Kern & Hastings, 1995) and suicidality (Cohen, Spirito, & Brown, 1996; Qin, Agerbo, & Mortenson, 2003), the communication link in these models is missing. How specifically might patterns of mother–daughter communication increase women's vulnerability to risk behaviors?

The women in the Elkwood enmeshed maternal relationships reported participating in several behaviors that placed their health at risk. Suicide attempts, drug abuse, and eating disorders were among the most frequently reported risk behaviors among these women. As indicated in Table 4.2, among the women in the enmeshed maternal relationships Sylvia, Diane, Sam, Katrina, Kelly, Meredith, Morgan, and Scout all self-reported participating in problem behaviors. However, given the difficulty in truly assessing behaviors subjectively perceived as "disordered eating" and the "abuse" of drugs, I choose to focus on participants' suicidality in explaining the proposed model of convergence and risk, because at least one or more verifiable suicide attempt was made by one member of each enmeshed family. (Sylvia, Diane, Sam, Kelly, Meredith, and Morgan all reported one or more suicide attempts, resulting in a period of hospitalization, and subsequently verified during my stay in Elkwood by one or more family members.)

Self-reported risk behaviors occurred *only* among the women in the enmeshed relationships who experienced necessary convergence. Although those in connected relationships may have omitted this information from me during my stay, based on the volume of observational and interview data collected I feel confident in offering an interpretation of how NCM might be associated with increasing women's risk. First, however, I want to present some background information on suicide that provides insight into the following theoretical speculation.

Suicidality.[25]   Suicide claims approximately 30,000 lives per year, compared with fewer than 19,000 homicides (Center for Disease Control, 2002). Suicide has become a significant public health issue as the 11th leading cause of death in the United States. Females comprise most of the suicide attempts in the United States, with a 3:1 ratio of female attempts for every male attempt (National Institute of Mental Health, 2003; Satcher, 1999).

Sylvia Canetto has conducted numerous studies to try and understand the unique issues of women and suicidality, and she has proposed an integrative model of interpersonal dynamics to understand self-harming behaviors, suggesting that high levels of dependency and difficulties with differentiation between suicidal patients and their relational partners are contributing factors (Canetto, 1994, 1997; Canetto & Lester, 1995; Canetto & Sakinofsky, 1998). Moreover, Richards (1999) studied reports of psychotherapists working with suicidal patients and discovered that intrafamily dynamics were more important than social structure as influences on suicidality. Across all therapists' reports in this study, over half (52.9%) of the patients perceived their parents as being rejecting, or their intrafamilial communication as being "dysfunctional."

Research by Firestone and Firestone (1998, 1996) and Firestone (1990, 1986) on family factors and suicide outcomes lends additional support to the importance of interpersonal communication in the family and suicide risk. Firestone and Firestone's (1998) research findings strongly suggest that relationships with significant primary figures, especially parents, that are intrusive and/or rejecting in the face of failure are likely to be internalized and, as such, can increase the risk of suicide in later life. Firestone and Firestone's work points out that covert parental control strategies for gaining child conformity may result in self-attacks and suicidal ideation (Firestone & Firestone, 1998). Moreover, participants in Firestone's (1986) clinical studies traced the source of negative or hostile thoughts toward themselves to their family-of-origin communication patterns and perceived parental rejection.

Parental acceptance-rejection theory (Rohner, 1986) provides some insight into this dynamic of parental rejection. Parental acceptance-rejection theory (PAR) is a theory of socialization that attempts to explain the correlates and consequences of parental acceptance and rejection. This theory proposes that all people experience degrees of warmth and affection from their close personal relationships, with "acceptance" at one end of the warmth dimension and "rejection" at the other. Parental rejection is defined conceptually as "the absence or significant withdrawal of warmth, affection, or love by parents toward children and takes on 3 forms: (1) hostility and aggression, (2) indifference and neglect, and (3) undifferentiated rejection" (p. 21). I contend that undifferentiated rejection is the key to understanding NCM among this sample of women in Elkwood. Undifferentiated rejection is the feeling of being rejected without necessarily having any indicators of

---

[25]*Suicidality* refers to suicide attempts and/or intense or frequent suicidal ideation.

abuse or neglect, and refers to *the subjective experiences* of feeling unloved without clearly observable indicators of rejection being present (Campo & Rohner, 1992; Rohner, 1986). The issue is not, then, to determine if the women in this study were truly [26] rejected by their mothers and grandmothers; indeed, most indicators would point in an opposite direction in these highly cohesive families.[27] The defining element is the subjective experiences of these women in enmeshed relationships, the ongoing perception of not being loved and feeling rejected when not conforming to maternal expectations of convergence. As Rohner (1986) pointed out, parental love is a belief held by the child, not a set of actions by the parent. Therefore, theories need to take into account the offspring's *experiences* of parental behavior. *All* of the Elkwood women who attempted suicide reported undifferentiated rejection and perceptions that they would lose maternal acceptance if they failed to conform to her expectations. This produced a kind of intergenerational intimidation.

Interestingly, the research literature almost universally pathologizes family processes that are considered risk factors (Fergusson & Lynskey, 1995; Miller & Day, 2002). A risk factor is any variable or condition associated with a higher likelihood of negative outcomes (e.g., suicide attempt; Durlack, 1995). According to the literature cited previously, high levels of dependency and difficulties with differentiation between suicidal women and their partners, as well as perceived parental rejection, may serve as risk factors for suicide. These factors are often labeled "dysfunctional" family behaviors (see, e.g., Martin & Martin, 2000). The term *dysfunctional* suggests a behavior that would cause psychological or physical harm to the individual (Nadien & Denmark, 1999). However, the labeling of these family processes as dysfunctional misses the point. Although these behaviors might cause harm at the level of the individual, there are very compelling—very functional—reasons for these behaviors at the relational level. I do not contend that NCM is dysfunctional. Indeed, I believe that in enmeshed, highly dependent relationships with differentiation difficulties and perceived conditional acceptance, convergence may be relationally *functional* and protect the relationship from threats to the status quo. NCM, then, may be dysfunctional at a personal level but functional at the relational level.

The suppositions listed earlier account for conditions antecedent to NCM and individual characteristics of necessary convergence, but do not address convergence as a possible risk factor. Two additional dimensions must be addressed to provide the necessary links between the phenomenon of NCM and increased risk: *degree* and the *chronicity* of the convergence. This extension of the previous model is illustrated in Fig. 6.3. The following description of these dimensions leads to two final suppositions within the theoretical framework of NCM.

---

[26]As measured in an objective fashion (e.g., assessment tool).

[27]By all accounts, others in Elkwood perceived the women in enmeshed relationships as "fortunate women" in "very close and happy families."

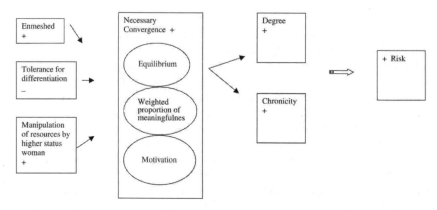

FIG. 6.3.   Model of necessary convergence and risk.

Degree.   The relative intensity or amount of convergence appears to be central to increasing risk, with a higher degree of convergence associated with higher risk. To illustrate this, I would like to once more revisit the "hair" scene and provide examples of high to low convergence.

Under conditions of high convergence, the lower-status woman would change her hairstyle extensively as a result of her mother's comment, converging with her mother's interpretation that the style was indeed horrible and altering her original interpretation to "fit" more closely with her mother's.

Under conditions of moderately high convergence, the lower-status woman would significantly change her hairstyle as a result of her mother's comment, but just to please her or reduce conflict. The lower-status woman would not alter her own interpretation to fit with her mother's interpretation; she would merely accommodate the alternative interpretation.

Under conditions of moderately low convergence, the lower-status woman might make minor alterations in the hairstyle to integrate both perceptions of what was attractive into one style.

Under conditions of low convergence, the lower-status woman might listen to her mother's comment but keep the style anyway because she likes it.

There are times when we all perceive that it is just easier, necessary, or politic to adjust our interpretations to others' view of the world. However, when there is extensive accommodation and convergence, obliterating personal interpretative frames constitutive of self, this might increase women's risk for developing negative health outcomes.

Chronicity.   When convergence is chronic or when there is a long-term pattern of convergence behavior across time and contexts, this may provide an increased potential for risk. When lower-status women experience repeated failures in negotiating meanings in transactions with a partner across time (e.g., across the life course) and contexts (e.g., attitudes, values, behaviors), this may instill a generalized expectancy of learned helplessness and "giving in." In fact, some of the women in Elkwood pointed out that as adolescents they experienced the common struggle to establish their unique frame of interpretation and establish boundaries between "me" and "we" in the maternal relationship. However, as they moved into adulthood and these boundaries became more blurred and permeable, they vowed to "not fight it anymore" and appropriated imposed attitudes, values, and expectations for behavior as their own. Chronicity might create a condition of learned helplessness (Seligman, 1975) and decrease perceptions of internal locus of control. Extant research provides overwhelming support that both attempted suicide and eating disorders are self-destructive behaviors aimed at (re)claiming personal control (see, e.g., Cohen et al., 1996; de Man, Leduc, & Labreche-Gauthier, 1993; Williams et al., 1993).

Both degree and chronicity are addressed in the final supposition in the theoretical framework of NCM. These dimensions of the model link necessary convergence with risk as an outcome.

Supposition #5.   Chronic episodes of high degrees of convergence across time and contexts will increase lower-status women's risk for negative outcomes.

SUMMARY OF THE THEORETICAL MODEL

You don't think your life will get any better. You can't conceive of it. You can't image it. You can't even dream it. It's so painful to live that it seems less painful to die. I don't know who I am anyway. I'm who and what everyone else wants me to be. I felt great satisfaction. I felt great calmness. It was real decisive. I was finally taking my fate into my own hands. I had some control. (Kelly, Family #2)

"I'm who and what everyone else wants me to be .... [When I tried to kill myself] I was finally taking my fate into my own hand. I had some control." Kelly's articulation of her experience with suicide offers a glimpse into her reasons for attempting suicide, but the experiences of the women in Elkwood contextualized within the larger relational framework can never be fully captured in these pages. The proposed model of NCM is an attempt to capture at least some of that experience. NCM suggests that coordination of meaning in maternal relationships involves power and control. In the specific case of enmeshed maternal relationships, in which there is a low tolerance for differentiation of its members and in which higher-status members exert dominance through the manipulation of emotional resources, a disequilibrium in the power to negotiate meanings may occur in which the lower-status woman perceives the threat of rejection if she does not converge her interpretive frame with her higher-status partner's. This then privileges the higher-status woman's interpretive frame in order to avoid rejection and maintain the relational status quo. Additionally, this theory speculates that chronic episodes of high degrees of convergence across time and contexts will likely contribute to an increase in the lower-status woman's risk for negative health outcomes, such as suicidality. Chronic episodes of powerlessness to negotiate unique or novel meanings in relational interactions may combine with overaccommodating the relational partner via a high degree of convergence and "giving up" all personal power to control meaning in her life.

The excerpts included in Fig. 6.4 are provided to illustrate the theoretical model of necessary convergence and risk, giving voice once again to the women of Elkwood.

TRANSMISSION

In a fascinating study by Zayas, Kaplan, Turner, Romano, and Gonzalez-Ramos (2000) that investigated suicide among Hispanic women, the researchers discovered that the interaction among three generations of grandmothers, mothers, and daughters suggested a possible intergenerational dynamic for understanding a daughter's suicide attempts. However, these authors pointed out that it is unclear what this (intergenerational) process might be, and they called for further investigation. The current Elkwood study, I believe, sheds some insight onto this intergenerational process.

This book has represented maternal relationships as enacted in dyadic transactions, but also as relational units embedded in a larger family culture with shared norms and practices—viewing the grandmother–mother–daughter relationship as the connection of two mother–daughter bonds. Moreover, a basic assumption of this research has been that families are privately transacted meaning-making systems that coordinate the actions and identities of the members, based on a constructed worldview. What I discovered was that, among the Elkwood women, there were persistent maternal cultural norms and practices—similar schemata and scripts handed down from one generation to the next. Maternal scripts, such as NCM in enmeshed relationships, guided the behaviors and values of the women, provided standards for their actions, and regulated the day-to-day interactions of relational members.

The phenomenon of necessary convergence is a form of scripted communication with relational schemata guiding its enactment *across* generational boundaries. One might ask, why would a woman who has always felt compelled to overaccommodate her mother perpetuate this pattern with her own daughter?

To understand this, one needs to recognize that middle age is a time fraught with many psychosocial changes for women. Those changes are accompanied by an altered state of power. Developmentally, by a woman's middle age she experiences an inclination toward *generativity* (concern and a sense of responsibility for guiding the next generation) and *complexity* (to selectively manipulate and control activities in multiple complex spheres; Babladelis, 1999). Recall that higher-status women who were perceived to require convergence did so "out of love" and believed they were "responsible for [my daughter's] successes

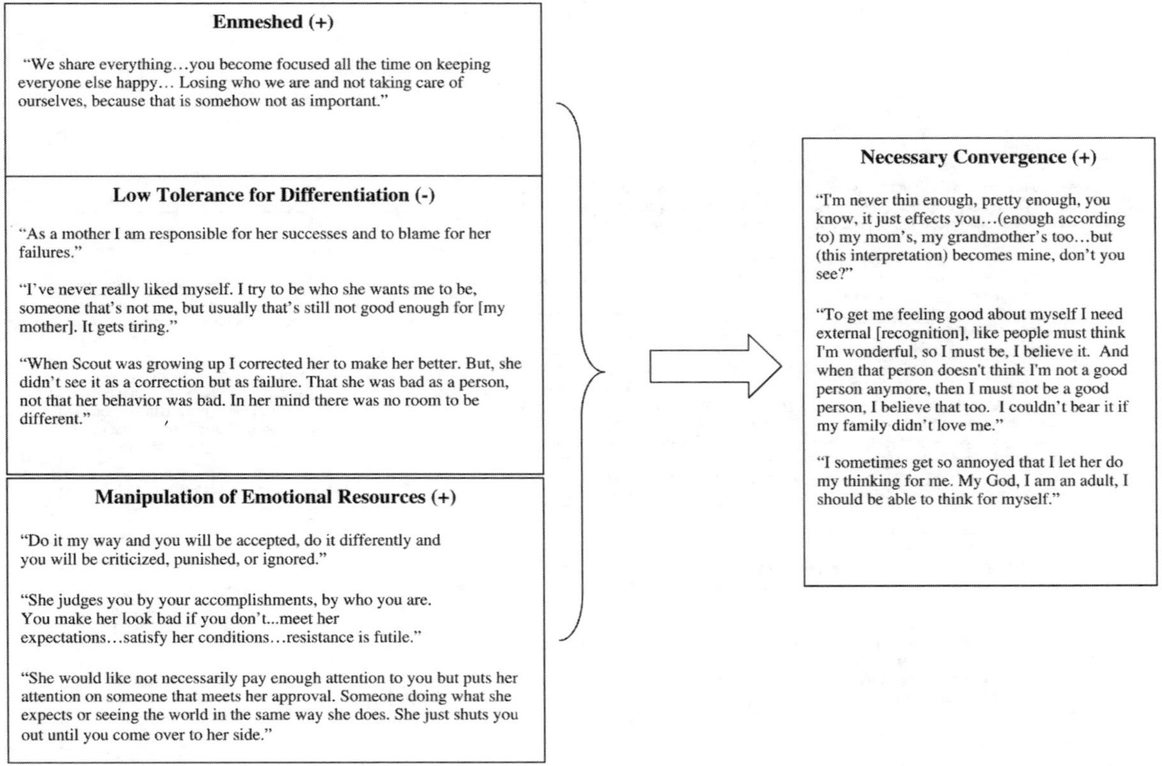

Enmeshed (+)

"We share everything…you become focused all the time on keeping everyone else happy…. Losing who we are and not taking care of ourselves, because that is somehow not as important."

Low Tolerance for Differentiation (-)

"As a mother I am responsible for her successes and to blame for her failures."

"I've never really liked myself. I try to be who she wants me to be, someone that's not me, but usually that's still not good enough for [my mother]. It gets tiring."

"When Scout was growing up I corrected her to make her better. But, she didn't see it as a correction but as failure. That she was bad as a person, not that her behavior was bad. In her mind there was no room to be different."

Manipulation of Emotional Resources (+)

"Do it my way and you will be accepted, do it differently and you will be criticized, punished, or ignored."

"She judges you by your accomplishments, by who you are. You make her look bad if you don't…meet her expectations…satisfy her conditions…resistance is futile."

"She would like not necessarily pay enough attention to you but puts her attention on someone that meets her approval. Someone doing what she expects or seeing the world in the same way she does. She just shuts you out until you come over to her side."

Necessary Convergence (+)

"I'm never thin enough, pretty enough, you know, it just effects you…(enough according to) my mom's, my grandmother's too…but (this interpretation) becomes mine, don't you see?"

"To get me feeling good about myself I need external [recognition], like people must think I'm wonderful, so I must be. I believe it. And when that person doesn't think I'm not a good person anymore, then I must not be a good person, I believe that too. I couldn't bear it if my family didn't love me."

"I sometimes get so annoyed that I let her do my thinking for me. My God, I am an adult, I should be able to think for myself."

FIG. 6.4a. Giving voice.

Degree of Convergence (+)

"(her interpretation) becomes mine, don't you see?"

"I buy into (my mother's comments) even now and I hate how she makes me question myself."

"…if I don't rock the boat, then I am embraced. If I do shake it up then I'm invisible [to her]."

Chronicity (+)

"I've never liked myself, I never liked who I was. I always tried to be somebody that wasn't me, just to please her. That's like why (I think) I've done a lot of things in my life."

"For as long as I can remember she has be telling me what I should be doing, thinking, saying, or feeling. My mother/myself—right?"

Risk

[Suicide note]: "It is too confusing. I want to be rid of me. I see no value in my life. Even writing this I see no value. What a whiner. Low life. Quit writing, what good will it do? Why the fuck dooooo I depend so much on the attention of everyone else to maintain my self-worth? If I get attention -great I feel great. If I get rejected I am ruined. I am one of the invisible many. I get no comfort- just reminders that I am invisible. Worthless. Who am I? Fuck off. Quit whining and lose your mind respectably. Signing off."

For me, my suicide attempts were about me being a failure. My feelings were that I wasn't who others said I should be and that was the whole reason I was supposed to be here! I didn't have a career (like my mother said I should), my whole life was my family and I've disappointed them… I went from letting my mother define who I was to my husband.

[Before my suicide attempt] my husband was telling me I wasn't a good enough wife and I believed him! That became my reality. He said, "Why can't you get it together, you'd just be better off dead. Why don't you just take those pills? And he goes, "I'll go buy some wine you can wash them down with it." And he goes, "Just dump them out, and I'll get a refill and you just take them both bottles." I'm like, what a good idea. You know, it's kind of like why didn't I think of this? I thought, you know he's right.

So, he gave me the valium and went out and bought wine. I took the first bottle and drank the wine and he goes, "I'm gonna get the refill." And so then he left. Now, nobody tells you not to mix booze and drugs, cause, well…you'll puke your guts out! So the whole time he's gone, I'm throwing up. And he doesn't actually know this happened. But, when he comes back I take some of the other bottle. I couldn't take that much cause I was like bluagh… See, he didn't realize I threw up before. So he's thinking all this medication is in me and we go to bed. And in the morning I wake up.

So he took me to the doctor saying I tried to kill myself and that's how they put me in the hospital the first time, blah, blah, blah...then I realized I couldn't die and then it's like I'm *really* a failure. I can't even die like he wants me to.

FIG. 6.4b.

and to blame for her failures." These women may have been perpetuating the necessary convergence script, hoping to shape their (grand)daughters, manipulate and control them for "their own good," for the positive appraisal reflected back toward their own selves, and in the name of relational maintenance. Moreover, a mother may feel that although she exerts no control over her own mother (because she can only accommodate the higher-status woman), she certainly can exert control over her own daughter across multiple contexts and "guide" that daughter out of a sense of "loving concern."

The persistence of necessary convergence across generations is also in keeping with the life-span theory of continuity (Atchley, 1989). *Continuity* suggests that as long as the older and younger women can maintain the same style of interacting, preserving the dynamic of one member being dominant and the other accommodating, then the relationship can be sustained across the life span. When this routine is upset (e.g., the lower-status woman moves toward autonomy of meaning), the higher-status woman may feel threatened by the discontinuity and strive to reassert her dominance. When convergence continues to be perceived as necessary across the life span, the higher-status woman has successfully asserted her dominance in this arena. This may explain why convergence was observed across all three generations in Elkwood, with older women doggedly resisting younger women's attempts at unique meanings and movement toward differentiation. Resisting discontinuity of interaction patterns may be one of the few spheres in which elderly women still maintain personal control in their lives and relationships.

A wealth of evidence indicates that multigenerational systems influence and are influenced by individuals who are in them, whereas interaction patterns are shared and manifested through intergenerational transmission based on a legacy of previous generations (Buerkel-Rothfuss, Fink, Buerkel, 1995; Hoopes, 1987). As for multiple generations of women, Aragno (1998) asserted that "for mothers and daughters ... residues of expectations, disappointments, assigned roles, habits, and unquestioned beliefs, colored by historical events, descend from one generation to the next, seemingly by osmosis ... transform and are transformed as they are transmitted" (p. 88). As Schonpflug (2001) pointed out, culture is carried not through a genetic code but instead via a communication code emphasizing communal over individual and positional rather than personal forms of social control. Much more information must be gathered to fully understand how communication processes function in this process of transmission. Yet, I believe necessary convergence of meaning provides one direction for building theories of intergenerational transmission processes. I contend that family-based maternal relational schemata guide the enactment of maternal scripts, with similar plots enacted across generations. I do not suggest that cultural transmission of interaction patterns leads to a constant replication of family culture in successive generations; rather, I suspect it falls somewhere between an exact transmission (with hardly any difference between parents and offspring) and a complete failure of transmission (with hardly any similarity between the generations).[28]

SUMMARY

Renowned sociologist David Maines (2003) pointed out that meaning has been seriously undertheorized and that scholars must look at the narrative plots told by interactants to identify meaning in social interaction. This chapter proposed a mid-range, grounded theory called *necessary convergence of meaning* that begins to provide a theoretical framework of relational transactions and meaning within enmeshed maternal relationships. This framework speculates that the coordination of meaning involves power and control. When a dominant partner's meanings are consistently afforded more weight—more significance—in transactions, and a lower-status woman feels threatened by the prospect of challenging that meaning or offering her own unique meaningful interpretation, this relational schema dictates a script whereby convergence with the higher-status partner's construction of meaning is necessary to secure relational acceptance and avoid rejection. Not only is necessary convergence relationally adaptive in one generation of relationships, but the phenomenon is also scripted across generational boundaries.

The most interesting aspect of this framework is its potential application to women at risk for self-harming behaviors, such as suicide. The proposed model posits that chronic convergence across time and multiple contexts might increase lower-status women's risk for self-harming behaviors. Although this was certainly the case among the maternal relationships in Elkwood, the relationships among these theoretical constructs are speculative. I strongly encourage other researchers to test this theoretical model for applicability to other Caucasian, middle-class, enmeshed maternal relationships.

All of the adult daughters and granddaughters in enmeshed maternal relationships who participated in this study continue to this day to struggle with the perception of necessary convergence that for generations has defined maternal relationships in their families. As of this writing, I have kept in touch with these women, presenting the ideas contained in these chapters to them, and receiving updates on births, deaths, marriages and divorces. In each story I hear a tale of a woman struggling, and at times succeeding, to reclaim her narrative, her story … her life.

---

[28]See Schonpflug (2001) for an extended discussion on these concepts pertaining to cultural transmission.

7

Grandmothers, Mothers, and Adult Daughters: A Force to be Reckoned With

The trouble is that I understand both my daughter and my granddaughter. But, I can't do a damn thing about it. I've been there. I know what they're going through. Amazing thing about mothers and daughters, isn't it? I guess if we summoned up a lot of our dead female ancestors, we'd hear a lot of the same stories, wouldn't we? Everybody afraid, everybody thinking that they've topped the market in being misunderstood; everybody just wanting to be loved. What if my granddaughter did understand how much her mother loves her? And I think she will eventually. Will it make her a better mother to her daughter? Perhaps. But, it'll make her understand a few things, I'll bet. They'll learn. I wouldn't be this wise old woman on top of the mountain today if I hadn't been through all that I did. You have to lose something so that you can find it again, right? When a woman gives birth to another, to someone who is like her, they are linked together for life in a very special way. Even though the resentment may seem all there is sometimes .... Ya need to face that resentment, so then the lies can be seen as truth, and the fear can turn to love . To be friends, at last. I learned a lot of hard lesson in my time. Good for me. [I still have a few to go!] And they'll learn theirs. Good for them. They'll reach a point, as I did, where you think, whoa, wait a minute! How'd I get in this old lady suit? And then you think back over all the things that happened in your life and think—"Good God! The soap opera's got nothin' on me—this is good material!" And you realize, oh, is that what that meant? And, wow, I really learned something there. And you start to relax. You pat yourself on the back and you say, "You did okay. You came through it all a little bit better and wiser—and you learned a lot about life." The bond between mothers and daughters? Well, you can't see it, and sometimes it feels like it doesn't exist at all, but it's there. No amount of pulling and yanking on it can break it. And

when you toss in that little bit of understanding, well, it becomes a force to be reck-
oned with, now doesn't it?

—Excerpt from *Grandmothers View* (Sorenson, 2000, p. 52)

In chapter 1 I stated that "agency is in the authorship." This book has been an account of women co-authoring their lives across their life span—grandmothers, mothers, and adult daughters struggling to write their own stories within the context of the relational stories. Some of the women in Elkwood were able to successfully weave their personal storylines into the fabric of the relational narrative, whereas other storylines became entangled in the fabric of relational connection.

Although some readers might interpret this relational entanglement as suffocating, others will see in it security, safety, and warmth. Even in the most conflict-ridden relationships, cohesion did not obfuscate love. Sam told me on numerous occasions, "I know [my mother] loves me. She says it." Diane corroborated this, saying, "A tremendous amount of love went out to her as a child; it still does." Yet, the juxtaposition of a smattering of their statements issued over an 8-month period reveals an entangled love, a struggle to simultaneously manage separation and connection, stability and change, ideal and real, open and closed, powerful and powerless, and person and position.

Sam: But [*pause*] I hear it rather than see it.
"I love you so much! You're my best friend!"
Oh, I'm sorry, I probably did it wrong but I
put all my eggs in a basket for you.

> Diane: She was everything I always wanted. I al-
> ways wanted children and when she was born, it
> was like I was totally fulfilled. I had a little girl. I
> can remember thinking I want a boy for [my hus-
> band], but I really wanted a girl.

Sam: "I had so many dreams and hopes for
you." She makes it sound like I disappointed
her so much. I mean dreams and hopes.

> Diane: I wanted her to be everything I never had a
> chance to be.

Sam: Even if I'm not who she wants me to
be. I'm still me, her little girl. It's those moments—when I am her little girl, when I feel
the most love for her. She really is loving and

kind and she tries to be a good mother, just
like I try to be a good daughter.

> Diane: In truth, we are all just human, subject to
> weakness and good intentions.

We *are* humans, subject to weakness, but also capable of extraordinary connection and respect for one another. The Elkwood maternal relationships were
split between those that were enigmatic and those that were untangled and perhaps less complicated. One month after I completed my residence in Elkwood,
Rowena was hospitalized with a stroke that subsequently took her life. Her
words as shared during my stay are placed with her daughter's and granddaughter's words [29] to reveal the potentiality of maternal relationships to be fulfilling,
intimate, and valued:

Rowena: I have been blessed. I have had a
wonderful life. A full life. Part of that [life], a
great part of it, has been as a mother and now
as a grandmother. It's not the whole enchi-
lada, but I wouldn't be the same person without having played that part.

> Gina: [My mother] has played a huge role in my life.
> I respect her and love her. She has always been there
> for me, and I've been there for her. Though, she is a
> pretty strong woman. She has been a wonderful role
> model for her grandchildren too. She is who she is
> and she respects them for who they are too.

Rowena: Gina's always telling me, "What
would I do without you, mother?"

> Georgie: I don't know what it will be like when my
> grandmother is gone. My mother will really miss
> her. We all will. She is a great lady.

According to Geertz (1973), humans create complex realities within their
tribes—their unique cultures. He argued convincingly that to understand
these realities scholars need to document cultures in detail, capturing behav-

---

[29]All comments were made during separate interviewing sessions.

ior, perceptions, and life as it is lived and experienced. It has been a goal of this research to document the relational lives of a handful of women in distinctive maternal cultures. This documentation and subsequent analysis discovered an array of dialectical contradictions that mothers and daughters, as well as grandmothers and granddaughters, contend with across their relational life span. Moreover, this analysis revealed two distinct patterns of dominant forces and discursive practices within the maternal relationships in Elkwood. In maternal relationships with high levels of enmeshment, there was a conspicuous appropriation of daughters and sometimes granddaughters into the realm of self. In these enmeshed cultures, younger women were considered sacred because they were closely associated with self. Personal identity became entangled within relational identities, and differentiation was framed as threatening to relational stability. Yet, for those women in connected maternal cultures, individuals were empowered to construct their own identities *within* the context of the relational culture, maintaining their personal stories while admitting to their embeddedness within maternal relational culture. For women in moderately cohesive maternal relationships, personal identity was linked to relational acknowledgment.

Maternal relationships exist with communication at their center. I have argued that to fully understand grandmother–mother–adult daughter relationships, scholars must explore the communication practices that exist in maternal cultures within generations and across generational boundaries. In doing so myself, I discovered certain relational schemata—mental structures of organized family knowledge about maternal relationships—that appeared to influence the encoding and decoding of information within these relationships.

In relationships of moderate levels of cohesion, maternal relationship scripts were enacted that cast the actors into mutually respected roles, acknowledging family status yet "rewriting" the script to adapt to developmental changes in the relationships across the life course. However, within relationships of intense cohesion, maternal relationship scripts tended to be routine and inflexible, privileging the power and position of higher-status women to determine both meaning during relational transactions and the rules for the enactment of relational scripts. Necessary convergence of meaning emerged as a script played out in enmeshed maternal relationships. Repetitive assert-response sequences across the life span that required lower-status women to time-and-again comply and accommodate the higher-status women resulted in a cultural norm of psychological dominance and submission. The theoretical model of necessary convergence of meaning may serve to extend Eichenbaum and Orbach's earlier (1982, 1984, 1989) work, which claimed that mothers (unconsciously) sabotaged their daughters' process of differentiation, by explaining how, under certain circumstances, lower-status women may abdicate authorship of their own meaning—their own stories—to the higher-status women in their lives. Loss of personal control and persistent feelings of external forces being in control of one's life (external locus of control) have repeatedly been linked to internalizing disorders such as disordered eating and suicidality (de Man & Leduc, 1995; Williams et al., 1990). It is possible that the NCM model may have important implications for understanding the communication processes involved in the development of an external locus of control, offering an explanation for how mothers may sabotage their daughters' differentiation. Other studies have pointed toward the intergenerational continuity of harsh or abusive parenting (see, e.g., Belsky, 1993), but none have truly examined intergenerational transmission of messages that more subtly eradicate or at least undermine personal agency in the creation of novel meaning. Relational culture is produced and re-produced through the communicative practices of its members, and intersubjectivity leads to shared understandings. Therefore, the NCM framework proposed in this book might provide a useful lens through which to view communicative practices and intersubjectivity in enmeshed maternal cultures.

NCM is currently a grounded theory based on suppositions and reasoned speculation; however, I truly hope that other scholars can intuit the coherence of this theoretical model and submit it to further exploration. Until then, I en-courage you, as the reader of this tome, to subject this model to your own evaluative criteria for theories in their infancy. According to Wright (1998), the following are some criteria for evaluating communication theories. First, there is *explanatory power*—do the suppositions of the NCM theoretical model enable us to explain as much of the communication phenomenon as possible? Next, is the theoretical model *parsimonious*—does it contain as few suppositions as pos-sible, is it as simple as it can be? With a grounded theory, many argue that the criteria of *testability* should not be applied, because a grounded theory is specific to a particular sample under specific conditions. However, I encourage others to test the suppositions offered in this book. Perhaps the suppositions will be falsi-fied, but perhaps not. Moreover, I suspect that this model may be extended be-yond maternal relationships to other enmeshed, dominant-submissive relationships. Is NCM *internally consistent*, that is, do the suppositions contra-dict each other? Does NCM have *heuristic potential*; does it suggest hypotheses to be tested through additional research? Finally, does NCM promote *new un-derstanding* and have *societal value*?

I admit that I am hopeful that the findings of this study—not just NCM— will provide scholars, therapists, and women with fresh insights into the nature of maternal relationships. Moreover, I feel confident that individual readers may grow from reading the experiences represented in these pages. I know that I have grown during this research process, and I thank the women of Elkwood for that opportunity.

Epilogue

I laid in bed with my son and sang,
"I will love you forever, I will like you for always,
as long as I'm living my baby you'll be."

He chimed in on the last verse singing,
"… as long as I'm living my mommy you'll be."

Squeezing my hand
he replied, "You'll never die mommy, you'll always be living."

"I plan to be around for a long time. Even when I'm not, you'll probably be a
    grandpa by then."
Without missing a beat—
"Now close your eyes, you have school in the morning."

Pulling his fuzzy blanket around him, he rolled over and closed his eyes.
I heard his breath come slowly and steadily beside me.
The rise and fall of his shoulder, a peaceful metronome …
as I drifted
off to sleep.

By some miraculous feat
without waking
I managed my way back to my
own
bed.

Only to wake in the morning to
BREAKING news of terror attacks
in New York, Washington, and
heroism over Pennsylvania.

I called my mother.
She lived nowhere near any of the attacks.
But, I needed to hear her voice, let her know she was not alone.
Assure myself that I was not alone.
Not alone as long as she was here—available.

In the end, over 3,000 war dead.
My mother cried for their loss
and for the loss of so many others.

She called me up to tell me another friend has passed away.
Her friend, a friend of the family, and my friend too.
The fourth friend in two years,
my father the forerunner in a quintet of death.
"They all seem to be dropping away and I am left here in silence," she sighed.

Tonight we sat together and talked over dinner about her losses.
Time away, time together alone—just her and me.
I am scared for her, scared with her too.
Frightened at the thought of losing my mother.
Her "dropping away."

I reach across the table.
Squeezing her hand I reassure
her (or me?),
"You'll be around for a good long time, mom."

I come face to face with what I fear.
Frightened for the loss of my self.

I grip her hand and sing inwardly,
"I will love you forever, I will like you for always,
as long as I'm living ...."

"Don't worry. I know I will," she breaks into my thoughts,
"you'll be a grandma before I've gone!"

She is me, I am she.
Together there are two of me.

References

Acitelli, L. K., Rogers, S., & Knee, C. R. (1999). The role of identity in the link between relationship thinking and relationship satisfaction. *Journal of Social and Personal Relationships, 16*, 591–618.

Adams, G. R., & Marshall, S. K. (1996). A developmental social psychology of identity: Understanding the person-in-context. *Journal of Adolescence, 19*, 429–442.

Adelson, M. J. (1998). Mothers and daughters: Secrets and lies. *Journal of Clinical Psychoanalysis, 7*, 389–399.

Allen, K. R. (2000). A conscious and inclusive family studies. *Journal of Marriage and the Family, 62*, 4–17.

Altheide, D. L. (1995). *An ecology of communication.* Hawthorne, NY: deGruyter.

Altheide, D. L., & Johnson, J. M. (1994). Criteria for assessing interpretive validity in qualitative research. In N. K. Denzin & Y. S. Lincoln (Eds.), *Handbook of qualitative research* (pp. 485–499). Thousand Oaks, CA: Sage.

Altman, I., Vinsel, A., & Brown, B. (1981). Dialectic conceptions in social psychology: An application to social penetration and privacy regulation. In L. Berkowitz (Ed.), *Advances in experimental psychology: Volume 14* (pp. 107–160). New York: Academic Press.

Ambert, A. (1999). The effect of male delinquency on mothers and fathers: A heuristic study. *Sociological Inquiry, 69*, 621–640.

The American Heritage Dictionary of the English Language, Fourth Edition (2000). Houghton Mifflin Company.

Anderson, D. Y., & Hayes, C. L. (1996). *Gender, identity, and self-esteem: A new look at adult development.* New York: Springer.

Angrosino, M. V., & Mays de Perez, K. A. (2000). Rethinking observation: From method to context. In N. K. Denzin & Y. Lincoln (Eds.), *Handbook of qualitative research* (2nd ed., pp. 673–702). Thousand Oaks, CA: Sage.

Aragno, A. (1998). "Die so that I may live!": A psychoanalytic essay on the adolescent girl's struggle to delimit her identity. In G. H. Fenchel (Ed.), *The mother–daughter relationship: Echoes through time* (pp. 85–133). Northvale, NJ: Aronson.

Archer, S. L. (Ed.). (1994). *Interventions for adolescent identity development.* Thousand Oaks, CA: Sage.

Aron, A., & Aron, E. N. (1986). *Love as the expansion of self: Understanding attraction and satisfaction.* New York: Hemisphere.

Atchley, R. C. (1989). The continuity theory of aging. *The Gerontologist, 29,* 183–190.

Babladelis, G. (1999). Autonomy in the middle years. In M. B. Nadien & F. L. Denmark (Eds.), *Females and autonomy* (pp. 101–129). Boston: Allyn & Bacon.

Bakhtin, M. M. (1981). *The dialogic imagination: Four essays by M. M. Bakhtin* (M. Holquist, Ed.; C. Emerson & M. Holquist, Trans.). Austin: University of Texas Press.

Baldwin, M. W. (1992). Relational schemas and the processing of social information. *Psychological Bulletin, 112,* 461–484.

Barry, C. A. (1998). Choosing qualitative data analysis software: Atlas/ti and Nudist compared. *Sociological Research Online, Volume 3.* Retrieved August 14, 2003, from http://www.socresonline.org.uk/socresonline/3/3/4.html

Bartle-Haring, S., & Sabatelli, R. (1998). An intergenerational examination of patterns of individual and family adjustment. *Journal of Marriage and the Family, 60,* 903–911.

Baumeister, R. F. (1998). Inducing guilt. In J. Bybee (Ed.), *Guilt and children* (pp. 127–138). San Diego: Academic Press.

Baumeister, R. F., Stillwell, A. M., & Heatherton, T. F. (1994). Guilt: An interpersonal approach. *Psychological Bulletin, 115,* 243–267.

Baxter, L. A. (1988). A dialectical perspective on communication strategies in relationship development. In S. Duck (Ed.), *Handbook of personal relationships* (pp. 257–273). New York: Wiley.

Baxter, L. A. (1990). Dialectical contradictions in relationship development. *Journal of Social and Personal Relationships, 7,* 69–88.

Baxter, L. A., & Montgomery, B. M. (1996). *Relating: Dialogues and dialectics.* New York: Guilford.

Baxter, L. A., & Montgomery, B. M. (1998). A guide to dialectical approaches to studying personal relationships. In B. M. Montgomery & L. A. Baxter (Eds.), *Dialectical approaches to studying personal relationships* (pp. 1–16). Mahwah, NJ: Lawrence Erlbaum Associates.

Becker, H. S. (1996). The epistemology of qualitative research. In R. Jessor, A. Colby, & R. A. Shweder (Eds.), *Ethnography and human development* (pp. 53–71). Chicago: University f Chicago Press.

Belsky, J. (1993). Etiology of child maltreatment: A developmental-ecological analysis. *Psychological Bulletin, 114,* 413–435.

Benedikt, R., Wertheim, E. H., & Love, A. (1998). Eating attitudes and weight-loss attempts in female adolescents and their mothers. *Journal of Youth & Adolescence, 27,* 43–57.

Bennett, L. A., & Wolin, S. (1990). Family culture and alcoholism transmission. In R. L. Collins, K. E. Leonard, & J. S. Searles (Eds.), *Alcohol and the family: Research and clinical perspectives* (pp. 194–219). New York: Guilford.

Bergman, A., & Fahey, M. (1997). Love, admiration, and identification: On intricacies of mother–daughter relationships. *Issues in Psychoanalytic Psychology, 19,* 167–184.

Bernstein, B. B. (1975). *Class, codes, and control: Theoretical studies toward a sociology of language.* New York: Schocken.

Biglan, A. (1995). *Changing cultural practices: A contextual framework for intervention research.* Reno, NV: Context.

Bishop, W. (1999). *Ethnographic writing research*. Portsmouth, NH: Boynton/Cook.

Bjerrum-Nielson, H., & Rudberg, M. (1994). *Psychological gender and modernity*. New York: Oxford University Press.

Blaine, S. (1990). Mona. In M. Miller (Ed.), *Two of Me*. Unpublished play produced by the Assemblage Group in Phoenix, AZ.

Blumer, H. (1969). *Symbolic interactionism: Perspective and method*. Englewood Cliffs, NJ: Prentice-Hall.

Bogdan, R. C., & Biklen, S. (1998). *Qualitative research for education* (3rd ed.). Boston: Allyn & Bacon.

Bonner, E. (1993). *Mothers and daughters*. New York: Vintage.

Borker, R. (1980). Anthropology: Social and cultural perspectives. In S. McConnel-Ginet, R. Borker, & N. Furman (Eds.), *Women and language in literature and society* (pp. 26–44). New York: Praeger.

Bosak, S. V. (2000). *How to build the grandma connection. The legacy project*. Whitchurch-Stouffville, Canada: Communication Project.

Boszormenyi-Nagy, I., & Spark, G. M. (1973). *Invisible loyalties: Reciprocity in intergenerational family therapy*. New York: Brunner-Routledge.

Bowen, M. (1978). *Family therapy in clinical practice*. New York: Aronson.

Bowker, L. H., & Klein, M. W. (1983). The etiology of female juvenile delinquency and gang, membership: A test of psychological and social structural explanations. *Adolescence, 18*, 739–751.

Boyd, C. J. (1989). Mothers and daughters: A discussion of theory and research. *Journal of Marriage and the Family, 51*, 291–301.

Breheny, M., & Stephens, C. (2003). Healthy living and keeping busy: A discourse analysis of mid-aged women's attributions for menopausal experience. *Journal of Language and Social Psychology, 22*, 169–250.

Brewen, C. R., Andrews, B., & Furnham, A. (1996). Self-critical attitudes and parental criticism in young women. *British Journal of Medical Psychology, 69*, 69–78.

Brown, B. B., Werner, C. M., & Altman, I. (1998). Choice points for dialecticians: A dialectical-transactional perspective on close relationships. In B. M. Montgomery & L. A. Baxter (Eds.), *Dialectical approaches to studying personal relationships* (pp. 137–154). Mahwah, NJ: Lawrence Erlbaum Associates.

Buerkel-Rothfuss, N. L., Fink, D. S., & Buerkel, R. A. (1995). Communication in the father–child dyad: The intergenerational transmission process. In T. J. Socha & G. H. Stamp (Eds.), *Parents, Children, & Communication: Frontiers of Theory and Research*. Mahwah, NJ: Lawrence Erlbaum Associates.

Burgoon, J. K. (1978). A communication model for personal space violations: Explication and an initial test. *Human Communication Research, 4*, 129–142.

Burgoon, J. K. (1993). Interpersonal expectations, expectancy violations, and emotional communication. *Journal of Language and Social Psychology, 12*, 13–21.

Burgoon, J. K., & Hale, J. L. (1988). Nonverbal violations of expectations: Model elaboration and application to immediacy behaviors. *Communication Monographs, 55*, 58–80.

Burgoon, J. K., & Hale, J. L. (1992). Validation and measurement of the fundamental themes of relational communication. In S. Petronio, J. K. Alberts, M. L. Hecht, & J. Buley (Eds.), *Contemporary perspectives on interpersonal communication*. Madison, WI: Brown & Benchmark.

Burgoon, J. K., Johnson, M. L., & Koch, P. T. (1998). The nature and measurement of interpersonal dominance. *Communication Monographs, 65*, 309–335.

Burleson, B. R. (1989). The constructivist approach to person-centered communication: Analysis of a research exemplar. In B. Dervin, L. Grossberg, B. O'Keefe, & E. Wartella (Eds.), *Rethinking communication* (pp. 29–36). Newbury Park, CA: Sage.

Burleson, B. R., Delia, J. G., & Applegate, J. L. (1995). The socialization of person-centered communication: Parental contributions to the social-cognitive and communication skills of their children. In M. A. Fitzpatrick & A. L. Vangelisti (Eds.), *Explaining family interactions* (pp. 34–76). Thousand Oaks, CA: Sage.

Burleson, B. R., Metts, S., & Kirch, M. W. (2000). Communication in close relationships. In C. Hendrick & S. S. Hendrick (Eds.), *Close relationships: A sourcebook* (pp. 245–258). Thousand Oaks, CA: Sage.

Burton, L. M. (1992). Black grandparents rearing children of drug-addicted parents: Stressors, outcomes, and social service needs. *The Gerontologist, 32*, 744–751.

Bussell, D. A. (1994). Ethical issues in observational family research. *Family Process, 33*, 361–376.

Campbell, A. (1981). *Girl delinquents*. New York: St. Martin's Press.

Campo, A. T., & Rohner, R. P. (1992). Relationships between perceived parental acceptance–rejection, psychological adjustment, and substance abuse among young adults. *Child Abuse and Neglect, 16*, 429–446.

Canetto, S. S. (1994). Review of women and attempted suicide. *Suicide and the Life-Threatening Behavior, 24*, 414–415.

Canetto, S. S. (1997). Gender and suicidal behavior: Theories and evidence. In R. W. Maris, M. M. Silverman, & S. S. Canetto (Eds.), *Review of suicidology* (pp. 138–167). New York: Guilford.

Canetto, S. S., & Lester, D. (Eds.). (1995). *Women and suicidal behavior*. New York: Springer.

Canetto, S. S., & Sakinofsky, I. (1998). The gender paradox in suicide. *Suicide and Life-Threatening Behavior, 28*, 1–23.

Caplan, P. J. (2000). *Don't blame mother* (rev. ed.). New York: Routledge.

Carbaugh, D. (1989). The critical voice in ethnography of communication research. *Research on Language and Social Interaction, 23*, 261–282.

Center for Disease Control (CDC). (2000). *National center for injury control and prevention: Scientific data, injury, and surveillance statistics*. Retrieved June, 12, 2003, from http://www.cdc.gov/ncipc/osp/mortdata.htm

Center for Disease Control (2002). Suicide in the United States. Retrieved December, 2003. http://www.cdc.gov/ncipc/factsheets/suifacts.htm

Charmaz, K. (2000). Grounded theory: Objectivist and constructivist methods. In N. K. Denzin & Y. Lincoln (Eds.), *Handbook of qualitative research* (2nd ed., pp. 509–535). Thousand Oaks, CA: Sage.

Chen, G., & Starosta, W. (1999). *Foundations of intercultural communication*. Boston: Allyn & Bacon.

Cherry, K. (1996). Ain't no grave deep enough. *Journal of Contemporary Ethnography, 25*, 22–57.

Chodorow, N. (1974). *Women, culture, and society*. Stanford, CA: Stanford University Press.

Chodorow, N. (1978). *The reproduction of mothering: Psychoanalysis and the sociology of gender*. Berkeley: University of California Press.

Chodorow, N., & Contratto, S. (1992). The fantasy of the perfect mother. In B. Thorne & M. Yalom (Eds.), *Rethinking the family: Some feminist questions* (pp. 25–36). Boston: Northeastern University Press.

Christensen, A., & Nies, D. C. (1980). The spouse observation checklist: Empirical analysis and critique. *American Journal of Family Therapy, 8,* 69–79.

Cicirelli, V. G. (1992). *Family caregiving: Autonomous and paternalistic decision-making.* Newbury Park, CA: Sage.

Cloud, H., & Townsend, J. (2002). *Boundaries.* Grand Rapids, MI: Zondervan.

Cochran, M. (1990). Personal networks in the ecology of human development. In M. Cochran, M. Lamer, D. Riley, L. Gunnarsson, & C. Henderson (Eds.), *Extending families* (pp. 3–35). New York: Cambridge University Press.

Cohen, Y., Spirito, A., & Brown, L. K. (1996). Suicide and suicidal behavior. In R. J. DiClemente, W. B. Hansen, & L. E. Ponton (Eds.), *Handbook of adolescent health risk behavior* (pp. 193–224). New York: Plenum.

Cohler, B. J., & Grunebaum, H. U. (1981). *Mothers, grandmothers, and daughters: Personality and childcare in three-generation families.* New York: Wiley.

Coll, C. G., Surrey, J. L., & Weingarten, K. (1998). *Mothering against the odds: Diverse voices of contemporary mothers.* New York: Guilford.

Conger, R., & Ge, X. (1999). Conflict and cohesion in parent–adolescent relations: Changes in emotional expression from early to mid-adolescence. In M. J. Cox & J. Brooks-Gunn (Eds.), *Conflict and cohesion in families: Causes and consequences* (pp. 185–206). Mahwah, NJ: Lawrence Erlbaum Associates.

Conquergood, D. (1994). Homeboys and hoods: Gang communication and cultural space. In L. R. Frey (Ed.), *Group communication in context: Studies of natural groups* (pp. 23–55). Hillsdale, NJ: Lawrence Erlbaum Associates.

Conville, R. L. (1998). Telling stories: Dialectics of relational transition. In B. M. Montgomery & L. A. Baxter (Eds.), *Dialectical approaches to studying personal relationships* (pp. 17–40). Mahwah, NJ: Lawrence Erlbaum Associates.

Cooley, T. M. (2000). Parent–child relations across adulthood. In R. M. Milardo & S. Duck (Eds.), *Families as relationships* (pp. 39–58). New York: Wiley.

Cowen, L., & Wexler, J. (1997). *Daughters and mothers.* Philadelphia: Courage Books.

Cragan, J. F., & Shields, D. C. (1998). *Understanding communication theory: The communicative forces for human action.* Boston: Allyn & Bacon.

Crotty, M. (1998). *The foundations of social research.* London: Sage.

Dahl, E. K. (1995). Daughters and mothers: Aspects of the representational world during adolescence. *Psychoanalytic Study of the Child, 50,* 187–204.

Davey, A., & Eggebeen, D. J. (1998). Patterns of intergenerational exchange and mental health. *The Journal of Gerontology, 53B,* 86–96.

Davis, F. (1974). Stories and sociology. *Urban Life and Culture, 3,* 310–316.

Deatrick, J. A., Faux, S. A., & Moore, C. M. (1993). The contribution of qualitative research to the study of families experiences with childhood illness in families. In S. L. Feetham, S. B. Meister, J. M. Bell, & C. L. Gilliss (Eds.), *The nursing of families: Theory/research/education/practice* (pp. 60–82). Newbury Park, CA: Sage.

Debold, E., Wilson, M., & Malave, I. (1993). *Mother–daughter revolution: From betrayal to power.* Reading, MA: Addison-Wesley.

de Beauvoir, S. (1965). *The second sex.* New York: Bantam.

de Beauvoir, S. (1974). *Memoirs of a dutiful daughter.* Middlesex, UK: Penquin.

de Kanter, R. (1993). Becoming a situated daughter. In J. van Mens-Verhulst, J. Schreurs, & L. Woertman (Eds.), *Daughtering and mothering: Female subjectivity reanalysed* (pp. 26–34). New York: Routledge.

234   REFERENCES

Delia, J., O'Keefe, B., & O'Keefe, D. (1982). The constructivist approach to communication. In F. Dance (Ed.), *Human communication theory* (pp. 147–191). New York: Harper & Row.

de Man, A. F., & Leduc, C. P. (1995). Suicidal ideation in high school students: Depression and other correlates. *Journal of Clinical Psychology, 51,* 173–180.

de Man, A. F., Leduc, C. P., & Labreche-Gauthier, L. (1993). Correlates of suicidal ideation in French-Canadian adolescents: Personal variables, stress, and social support. *Adolescence, 28,* 819–830.

de Waal, M. (1993). Teenage daughters on their mothers. In J. van Mens-Verhulst, J. Schreurs, & L. Woertman (Eds.), *Daughtering and mothering: Female subjectivity reanalysed* (pp. 35–43). New York: Routledge.

Denzin, N. K. (1978). *The research act: A theoretical introduction to sociological methods.* New York: McGraw-Hill.

Denzin, N. K., & Lincoln, Y. (Eds.). (1994). *Handbook of qualitative research.* Thousand Oaks, CA: Sage.

Denzin, N. K., & Lincoln, Y. (Eds.). (2000). *Handbook of qualitative research* (2nd ed.). Thousand Oaks, CA: Sage.

Derlega, V. J., Metts, S., Petronio, S., & Margulis, S. T. (1993). *Self-disclosure.* Newbury Park, CA: Sage.

Dillard, J. P., Solomon, D. H., & Palmer, M. T. (1999). Structuring the concept of relational communication. *Communication Monographs, 66,* 49–62.

Dindia, K. (1998). Going into and coming out of the closet: The dialectics of stigma disclosure. In B. M. Montgomery & L. A. Baxter (Eds.), *Dialectical approaches to studying personal relationships* (pp. 83–108). Mahwah, NJ: Lawrence Erlbaum Associates.

Douglass, B. G., & Moustakas, C. (1985). Heuristic inquiry: The internal search to know. *Journal of Humanistic Psychology, 25,* 39–55.

Dowling, C. (1988). *Perfect women.* New York: Simon & Schuster.

Duck, S. W. (1992). *Human relationships* (2nd ed.). London: Sage.

Duck, S. W., & Wright, P. (1993). Reexamining gender differences in same-sex friendships: A close look at two kinds of data. *Sex Roles, 28,* 709–727.

Durlack, J. A. (1995). *School-based prevention programs for children and adolescents.* Thousand Oaks, CA: Sage.

Edelman, H. (2000). *Mother of my mother: The intricate bond between generations.* New York: Delta Trade.

Eichenbaum, L., & Orbach, S. (1982). *Outside in, inside out: women's psychology: A feminist psychoanalytic approach.* New York: Penguin.

Eichenbaum, L., & Orbach, S. (1984). *Understanding women: A feminist psychoanalytic approach.* New York: Basic Books.

Eichenbaum, L., & Orbach, S. (1989). *Between women.* New York: Penguin.

Eichenbaum, L., & Orbach, S. (1992). *Understanding women.* London: Penguin.

Ellis, C., & Bochner, A. (Eds.). (1995). *Composing ethnography: Alternate forms of qualitative writing.* Walnut Creek, CA: AltaMira.

Ellis, C., & Bochner, A. (2000). Autoethnography, personal narrative, reflexivity: Researcher as subject. In N. K. Denzin & Y. Lincoln (Eds.), *Handbook of qualitative research* (2nd ed., pp. 733–768). Thousand Oaks, CA: Sage.

Ely, M. (1991). *Doing quantitative research: Circles within circles.* Philadelphia, PA: Falmer Press.

Entman, R. M. (1993). Framing: Toward clarification of a fractured paradigm. *Journal of Communication, 43*(4), 51–58.

Everingham, C. (1994). *Motherhood and modernity: An investigation into the rational dimension of mothering.* Bristol, PA: Open University Press.

Ferguson, S. M., & Dickson, F. C. (1995). Children's expectations of their single parents' dating behaviors: A preliminary investigation of emergent themes relevant to single parent dating. *Journal of Applied Communication Research, 23,* 308–324.

Ferguson, S. M., & Lynskey, M. T. (1995). Childhood circumstances, adolescent adjustments, and suicide attempts in a New Zealand birth cohort. *Journal of the American Academy of Child and Adolescent Psychiatry, 34,* 612–622.

Fielding, N. G., & Lee, R. M. (1998). *Computer analysis and qualitative research.* Thousand Oaks, CA: Sage.

Fingerman, K. L. (1989). Sex and the working mother: Adolescent sexuality, sex role typing and family background. *Adolescence, 24,* 1–18.

Fingerman, K. L. (1995). Aging mothers' and adult daughters' perceptions of conflict behaviors. *Psychology and Aging, 10,* 639–649.

Fingerman, K. L. (1996). Sources of tension in the aging mother and adult daughter relationship. *Psychology & Aging, 11,* 591–606.

Fingerman, K. L. (1998a). The good, the bad, and the worrisome: Emotional complexities in grandparents' experiences with individual grandchildren. *Family Relations: Interdisciplinary Journal of Applied Family Studies, 47*(4), 403–414.

Fingerman, K. L. (1998b). Tight lips?: Aging mothers' and adult daughters' responses to interpersonal tensions in their relationships. *Personal Relationships, 5,* 121–138.

Fingerman, K. L. (2000). "We had a nice little chat": Age and generational differences in mothers' and daughters' descriptions of enjoyable visits. *Journal of Gerontology, 55B,* 95–106.

Fingerman, K. L. (2001). *Aging mothers and their adult daughters: A study in mixed emotions.* New York: Springer.

Firestone, R. W. (1986). The "inner voice" and suicide. *Psychotherapy, 23,* 439–447.

Firestone, R. W. (1990). *Compassionate child-rearing: An in-depth approach to optimal parenting.* New York: Plenum Press.

Firestone, R. W., & Firestone, L. A. (1996). *Firestone assessment of self-destructive thoughts.* San Anonio, TX: Psychological Corporation.

Firestone, R. W., & Firestone, L. A. (1998). Voices in suicide: The relationship between self-destructive thought processes, maladaptive behavior, and self-destructive manifestations. *Death Studies, 22,* 411–443.

Fishbane, M. D. (2001). Relational narratives of self. *Family Process, 40,* 273–292.

Fitch, K. (2000). *Speaking relationally: Culture, communication, and interpersonal connection.* New York: Guilford.

Fletcher, G. J., & Thomas, G. (1996). Close relationship lay theories: Their structure and function. In G. O. Fletcher & J. Fitness (Eds.), *Knowledge structures in close relationships* (pp. 3–24). Mahwah, NJ: Lawrence Erlbaum Associates.

French, M. (1987). *Her mother's daughter: A novel.* London, UK: Heinemann.

Freud, S. (1905/1989). *Three essays on the theory of sexuality.* (J. Strachey, Trans.), Part of the standard edition of the complete psychological works of Sigmund Freud series. New York: Norton.

Freud, S. (1917/1966). *The complete introductory lectures on psychoanalysis.* New York: Norton.

Freud, S. (1923). The ego and the id. *Standard edition of the complete psychological works of Sigmund Freud* (Vol. 19, pp. 12–68).

Freud, S. (1932). Femininity. In J. Strachey (trans.), *New introductory lectures in psychoanalysis* (Vol. 22). London, UK: Hogarth.

Friday, N. (1977). *My mother/my self.* New York: Dell.

Friedan, B. (1964). *The feminine mystique.* New York: Dell.

Friedman, S. (Ed.). (1993). *The new language of change.* New York: Guilford.

Galvin, K. M., & Brommel, B. J. (1999). *Family communication: Cohesion and change* (5th ed.). New York: Longman.

Geertz, C. (1973). *The interpretation of cultures.* New York: Basic Books.

Gergen, K. (1991). *The saturated self.* New York: Basic Books.

Gerstel, N., & Zussman, R. (1999). A conversation about parenting. In B. Glassner & R. Hertz (Eds.), *Qualitative sociology as everyday life* (pp. 61–77). Thousand Oaks, CA: Sage.

Gilani, N. P. (1999). Conflict management of mothers and daughters belonging to individualistic and collectivistic cultural backgrounds: A comparative study. *Journal of Adolescence, 22,* 853–866.

Gilgun, J. F. (1999). Methodological pluralism and qualitative family research. In M. B. Sussman, S. K. Steinmetz, & G. W. Peterson (Eds.), *Handbook of marriage and the family* (2nd ed., pp. 219–261). New York: Plenum.

Gilgun, J. F., Daly, K., & Handel, G. (Eds.). (1992). *Qualitative methods in family research.* Newbury Park, CA: Sage.

Gilligan, C. (1982). *In a different voice.* Cambridge, MA: Harvard University Press.

Gilligan, C., Rogers, A. G., & Dolman, D. L. (Eds.). (1991). *Women, girls, & psychotherapy: Reframing resistance.* New York: Harrington Park Press.

Gilligan, S., & Price, R. (Eds.). (1993). *Therapeutic conversations.* New York: Norton.

Gioia, D. A., & Pitre, E. (1990). Mutiparadigm perspectives on theory building. *Academy of Management Review, 15,* 584–602.

Glaser, B., & Strauss, A. (1967). *Discovering grounded theory.* Chicago, IL: Aldine.

Goldblatt, H. (2003). Strategies of coping among adolescents experiencing interparental violence. *Journal of Interpersonal Violence, 18,* 532–553.

Golish, T. D. (2000). Changes in closeness between adult children and their parents: A turning point analysis. *Communication Reports, 13,* 79–97.

Golombisky, K. (2001). Mothers, daughters, and female identity therapy in *How to Make an American Quilt. Western Journal of Communication, 65,* 65–88.

Gottfredson, M., & Hirschi, T. (Eds.). (1994). *The generality of deviance.* New Brunswick, NJ: Transaction Books.

Gottman, J. M. (2000). *The seven principles for making marriage work.* Pittsburgh, PA: Three Rivers Press.

Graber, J. A., & Brooks-Gunn, J. (1999). "Sometimes I think that you don't like me": How mothers and daughters negotiate the transition into adolescence. In M. J. Cox & J. Brooks-Gunn (Eds.), *Conflict and cohesion in families: Causes and consequences.* (pp. 207–242). Mahwah, NJ: Lawrence Erlbaum Associates.

Gray, M. R., & Steinberg, L. (1999). Unpacking authoritative parenting: Reassessing a multidimensional construct. *Journal of Marriage and the Family, 61,* 574–587.

Greene, J. O., & Burleson, B. R. (Eds.). (2003). *Handbook of communication and social interaction skills*. Mahwah, NJ: Lawrence Erlbaum Associates.

Guerrero, L. K., & Afifi, W. A. (1995). What parents don't know: Topic avoidance in parent–child relationships. In T. J. Socha & G. Stamp (Eds.), *Parents, children, and communication: Frontiers of theory and research* (pp. 219–245). Mahwah, NJ: Lawrence Erlbaum Associates.

Guerrero, L. K., Anderson, P. A., & Afifi, W. A. (2001). *Close encounters: Communicating in relationships*. Mountain View, CA: Mayfield.

Guisinger, S., & Blatt, S. J. (1994). Individuality and relatedness: Evolution of a fundamental dialectic. *The American Psychologist, 49*, 104–112.

Gumperz, J. J. (1982). *Discourse strategies*. New York: Cambridge University Press.

Hammer, S. (1976). *Daughters and mothers: Mothers and daughters*. New York: New American Library.

Handel, G., & Whitchurch, G. G. (Eds.). (1994). *The psychological interior of the family* (4th ed.). New York: deGruyter.

Hart, K., & Kenny, M. E. (1997). Adherence to the super woman ideal and eating disorder symptoms among college women. *Sex Roles, 36*, 461–478.

Harvey, D. M., & Bray, J. H. (1991). Evaluation of an intergenerational theory of personal development: Family process determinants of psychological and health distress. *Journal of Family Psychology, 4*, 298–325.

Hecht, M. L., Collier, M. J., & Ribeau, S. (1993). *African-American communication: Ethnic identity and cultural interpretation*. Newbury Park, CA: Sage.

Heesacker, R. S., & Neimeyer, G. J. (1990). Assessing object relations and social cognitive correlates of eating disorder. *Journal of Counseling Psychology, 37*, 419–426.

Herzog, W., Kronmueller, K., Hartmann, M., Bergmann, G., & Kroeger, F. (2000). Family perception of interpersonal behavior as a predictor in eating disorders: A prospective six-year follow-up study. *Family Process, 39*, 359–374.

Hill, A. J., & Franklin, J. A. (1998). Mothers, daughters and dieting: Investigating the transmission of weight control. *British Journal of Clinical Psychology, 37*, 3–13.

Holahan, C., Moos, R., & Bonin, L. (1999). Social context and depression: An integrative stress and coping framework. In T. Joiner & J. Coyne (Eds.), *The interactional nature of depression* (pp. 39–63). Washington, DC: American Psychological Association.

Hollihan, T., & Riley, P. (1987). The rhetorical power of a compelling story: A critique of a toughlove parental support group. *Communication Quarterly, 35*, 13–25.

Holstein, J. A., & Gubrium, J. F. (1994). Phenomenology, ethnomethodology, and interpretive practice. In N. Denzin & Y. Lincoln (Eds.), *Handbook of qualitative research* (pp. 262–272). Newbury Park, CA: Sage.

Hoopes, M. (1987). Multigenerational systems: Basic assumptions. *American Journal of Family Therapy, 15*, 195–205.

Huberman, M. A., & Miles, M. B. (1994). Data management and analysis methods. In N. K. Denzin & Y. S. Lincoln (Eds.), *Handbook of qualitative research* (pp. 428–444). Thousand Oaks, CA: Sage.

Hurston, Z. N. (1942). *Dust tracks on a road*. Philadelphia, PA: Lippencott.

Jacob, T., Tennenbaum, D. L., & Krahn, G. (1987). Factors influencing the reliability and validity of observation data. In T. Jacob (Ed.), *Family interaction and psychopathology: Theories, methods, and findings* (pp. 297–328). New York: Plenum.

Jackson, R. L. (1999). *The negotiation of cultural identity*. Westport, CT: Praeger.

Jordan, J. (1993). The relational self: A model of women's development. In J. van Mens-Verhulst, J. Schreurs, & L. Woertman (Eds.), *Daughtering and mothering: Female subjectivity reanalysed* (pp. 135–144). New York: Routledge.

Jordan, J., Surrey, J. L., & Kaplan, A. G. (1985). *Women and empathy: Implications for psychological development and psychotherapy.* Wellesley, MA: Stone Center for Developmental Services and Studies.

Jung, C. G., & Kerenyi, C. (1969). *Essays on a science of mythology: The myths of the divine child and the mysteries of Eleusis.* Princeton, NJ: Princeton University Press.

Kabat, R. (1998). The conjoint session as a tool for the resolution of separation-individuation in the adult mother–daughter relationship. *Clinical Social Work Journal, 26,* 73–88.

Kahana, E. Biegel, D. E., & Wykle, M. L. (1994). Introduction. In E. Kahana, D. E. Biegel, & M. L. Wykle (Eds.). *Family caregiving across the lifespan* (pp. xiii–xxvi). Thousand Oaks, CA: Sage.

Karpel, M. A. (1980). Family secrets: Conceptual issues in the relational context. *Family Process, 19,* 295–306.

Katriel, T., & Farrell, T. (1991). Scrapbooks as cultural texts: An American art of memory. *Text and Performance Quarterly, 11,* 1–17.

Kaufman, G., & Uhlenberg, P. (1998). Effects of life course transitions on the quality of relationships between adult children and their parents. *Journal of Marriage and the Family, 60,* 924–938.

Kenemore, E., & Spira, M. (1996). Mothers and their adolescent daughters: Transitions and transformations. *Child and Adolescent Social Work Journal, 13,* 225–229.

Kenny, M. E., & Hart, K. (1992). Relationship between parental attachment and eating disorders in an inpatient and a college sample. *Journal of Counseling Psychology, 39,* 521–526.

Kern, J. M., & Hastings, T. (1995). Differential family environments of bulimics and victims of childhood sexual abuse: Achievement orientation. *Compulsive Eating and Depression, 51,* 499–506.

Kerpelman, J. L., & Smith, S. L. (1999). Adjudicated adolescent girls and their mothers: Examining identity perceptions and processes. *Youth and Society, 30,* 313–347.

Kinach, B. M. (1996). Grounded theory as scientific method: Haig-inspired reflections on educational research methodology. Retrieved August 10, 2003, from http://www.ed.uiuc.edu/PES/95_docs/kinach.html

Klein, D. M., & White, J. M. (1996). *Family theories: An introduction.* Thousand Oaks, CA: Sage.

Knapp, M. L., & Vangelisti, A. L. (1996). *Interpersonal communication and human relationships* (3rd ed.). Boston: Allyn & Bacon.

Koerner, A. F., & Fitzpatrick, M. A. (2002). Toward a theory of family communication. *Communication Theory, 12,* 70–91.

Koerner, S. S., Jacobs, S. L., & Raymond, M. (2000). When mothers turn to their adolescent daughters: Predicting daughters' vulnerability to negative adjustment outcomes. *Family Relations, 49,* 301–309.

Kornhaber, A. (1996). *Contemporary grandparenting.* Thousand Oaks, CA: Sage.

Kroger, J. (2000). *Identity development: Adolescence through adulthood.* Thousand Oaks, CA: Sage.

Laing, R. D. Psychiatrist quotations. Retrieved December 12, 2003, from http://www.gurteen.com/gurteen/gurteen.nsf

Laliberte, M., Boland, F. J., & Leichner, P. (1999). Family climates: Family factors specific to disturbed eating and bulimia nervosa. *Journal of Clinical Psychology, 55*, 1021–1040.

Langellier, K. M., & Hall, D. L. (1990). Interviewing women: A phenomenological approach to feminist communication research. In K. Carter & C. Spitzack (Eds.), *Doing research on women's communication*. New York: Ablex.

Langellier, K. M., & Peterson, E. E. (1992). Spinstorying: A communication analysis of women storytelling. In J. Haskell Spear, E. C. Fine, & D. Conquergood (Eds.), *Performance, culture, and identity* (pp. 133–158). Westport, CT: Praeger.

La Sorsa, V. A., & Fodor, I. G. (1990). Adolescent daughter/midlife mother dyad: A new look at separation and self-definition. *Psychology of Women Quarterly, 14*, 593–606.

Lather, P. (1997). *Troubling the angels: Women living with HIV/AIDS*. Boulder, CO: Westview.

LeCompte, M. D., Millroy, W. L., & Preissle, J. (Eds.), (1992). *The handbook of qualitative research in education*. Orlando, FL: Academic Press.

LeCompte, M. D., & Schensul, J. J. (1999). *Analyzing and interpreting ethnographic data: Ethnographer's toolkit #5*. Walnut Creek, CA: Altamira.

Lefkowitz, E. S., Kahlbaugh, P., & Sigman, M. (1998). A longitudinal study of mother–adolescent AIDS conversations. *AIDS Education and Prevention, 10*, 351–365.

Levinson, R. (1992). Grief and rage at the wedding: Demeter, Persephone, and the mother of the bride. *Women and Therapy, 12*, 59–72.

Levitt, D. H. (2001). Anorexia nervosa: Treatment in the family context. *Family Journal, 9*, 159–163.

Lightburn, A. (1998). Participant observation in special needs adoptive families. In J. F. Gilgun, K. Daly, & G. Handel (Eds.), *Qualitative methods in family research* (pp. 217–235). Newbury Park, CA: Sage.

Lin, G., & Rogerson, P. A. (1995). Elderly parents and the geographic availability of their children. *Research on aging, 17*, 303–331.

Lincoln, Y. S., & Guba, E. (1985). *Naturalistic inquiry*. Beverly Hills, CA: Sage.

Lincoln, Y. S., & Guba, E. (1999). Paradigmatic controversies, contradictions, and emerging confluences. In N. K. Denzin & Y. Lincoln (Eds.), *Handbook of qualitative research* (2nd ed., pp. 157–188). Thousand Oaks, CA: Sage.

Locke, K. (1996). Rewriting *The Discovery of Grounded Theory* after 25 years. *Journal of Management Inquiry, 5*, 239–245.

Lowell, A. (1916). *Patterns, men, women, and ghosts*. Boston: Houghton Mifflin.

Lykke, N. (1993). Questing daughters: Little Red Riding Hood, Antigone and the Oedipus complex. In J. van Mens-Verhulst, K. Schreurs, & L. Woertman (Eds.), *Daughtering and mothering: Female subjectivity reanalysed* (pp. 15–25). New York: Routledge.

Lyman, S. (1994). *Color, culture, and civilization: Race and minority issues in American society*. Urbana: University of Illinois Press.

Mahler, M. (1963). Thoughts about development and individuation. *Psychoanalytic Study of the Child, 18*, 307–323.

Mahler, M. (1972). On the first three phases of the separation-individuation process. *International Journal of Psychoanalysis, 53*, 333–338.

Maines, D. R. (1993). Narrative's moment and sociology's phenomena: Toward a narrative sociology. *The Sociological Quarterly, 34*, 17–38.

Mancini, J. (Ed.). (1989). *Aging parents and adult children*. New York: Lexington Books.

Mann, C. (1998). The impact of working class mothers on the educational success of their adolescent daughters in times of social change. *British Journal of Sociology Education, 19*, 211–226.

Martin, D., & Martin, M. (2000). Understanding dysfunctional and functional family behaviors for the at-risk adolescent. *Adolescence, 35,* 785–798.

Mays, N., & Pope, C. (2000). Assessing quality in qualitative research. *British Medical Journal, 320,* 50–52.

McCranie, C. W., & Bass, J. D. (1984). Childhood family antecedents of dependency and self criticism: Implications for depression. *Journal of Abnormal Psychology, 93,* 3–8.

McFarland, B., & Watson-Rouslin, V. (1997). *My mother was right: How today's women reconcile with their mothers.* San Francisco: Jossey-Bass.

McIntosh, V. V., Bulik, C. M., McKenzie, J. M., Luty, S. E., & Jordan, J. (2000). Interpersonal psychotherapy for anorexia nervosa. *International Journal of Eating Disorders, 27,* 125–139.

McMahon, M. (1995). *Engendering motherhood: Identity and self-transformation in women's lives.* New York: Guilford.

Mead, G. H. (1934). *Mind, self, and society.* Chicago: University of Chicago Press.

Meese, E. (1998). The mom of my dreams. *Feminist Studies, 24,* 553–570.

Merriam, S. B. (1998). *Qualitative research methods in case study applications in education.* San Francisco: Jossey-Bass.

Merrick, E. (1999). An exploration of quality in qualitative research: Are reliability and validity relevant? In M. Kopala & L. A. Suzuki (Eds.), *Using qualitative methods in psychology* (pp. 25–36). Thousand Oaks, CA: Sage.

Metts, S. (1994). Relational transgressions. In W. R. Cupach & B. H. Spitzberg (Eds.), *The dark side of interpersonal communication* (pp. 217–240). Hillsdale, NJ: Lawrence Erlbaum Associates.

Milardo, R. M., & Duck, S. (Eds.). (2000). *Families as relationships.* New York: Wiley.

Miles, M., & Huberman, M. (1994). *Qualitative data analysis: An expanded sourcebook* (2nd ed.). Thousand Oaks, CA: Sage.

Miller, J. B. (1976). *Toward a new psychology of women.* Boston: Beacon.

Miller, M. (1986). *A pilot examination of women, achievement, and familial expectations.* Unpublished manuscript, Department of Communication, Arizona State University, Tempe.

Miller, M. (1995). An intergenerational case study of suicidal tradition and mother–daughter communication. *The Journal of Applied Communication Research, 23,* 247–270.

Miller, M. (1997, June). *The hidden conditions: Perceived conditional acceptance in mother–daughter relationships.* Competitive paper presented to the International Network on Personal Relationships conference in Athens, OH.

Miller, M. (1998a, November). *Family stories in performance: A proposal for scripting superordinate research narratives.* Paper presented to the National Communication Association Conference in New York.

Miller, M. (1998b). (Re)presenting voice in dramatically scripted research. In A. Banks & S. P. Banks (Eds.), *Fiction and social research* (pp. 67–78). Walnut Creek, CA: Altamira.

Miller, M., & Day, L. E. (2002). Family communication, maternal and paternal expectations, and college students' suicidality. *Journal of Family Communication, 2,* 167–184.

Miller, M., & Lee, J. (2001). Communicating disappointment: The viewpoint of sons and daughters. *The Journal of Family Communication, 1*(2), 111–131.

Miller, S. (1994). *The good mother.* Delta.

Miller-Rassulo, M. (1992). The mother–daughter relationship: Narrative as a path to understanding. *Women's Studies in Communication, 15,* 1–21.

Montalbano-Phelps, L. L. (2003). Discourse of survival: Building families free of unhealthy relationships. *Journal of Family Communication, 3,* 149–177.

Montgomery, B. M., & Baxter, L. A. (1998). *Dialectical approaches to studying personal relationships.* Mahwah, NJ: Lawrence Erlbaum Associates.

Morse, J. M. (1991). Strategies for sampling. In J. M. Morse (Ed.), *Qualitative nursing research* (pp. 10–20). Newbury Park, CA: Sage.

Morse, J. M. (Ed). (1997). *Completing the qualitative project.* Thousand Oaks, CA: Sage.

Mortensen, C. D. (1972). *Communication: The study of human interaction.* New York: McGraw-Hill.

Moustakas, C. E. (1974). *Portraits of loneliness and love.* Englewood Cliffs, NJ: Prentice-Hall.

Moustakas, C. E. (1990). *Heuristic research: Design, methodology, and applications.* Newbury Park, CA: Sage.

Nadien, M. B., & Denmark, F. L. (Eds.). (1999). *Females and autonomy.* Boston: Allyn & Bacon.

National Institute on Mental Health (2003) In harms way: Suicide in America. NIH Publication No. 03-4594. Retrieved December, 2003, from http://www.nimh.nih.gov/publicat/harmsway.cfm

Neimeyer, R. A., & Neimeyer, G. (1985). Disturbed relationships. In E. Button (Ed.), *Personal constructs and mental health* (pp. 35–61). London: Croom Helm.

Noller, P., & Fitzpatrick, M. A. (1993). *Communication in family relationships.* Englewood Cliffs, NJ: Prentice-Hall.

Nussbaum, J. F. (Ed.). (1989). *Life-span communication: Normative processes.* Hillsdale, NJ: Lawrence Erlbaum Associates.

Nussbaum, J. F., & Bettini, L. (1994). Shared stories of the grandparent–grandchild relationship. *International Journal of Aging and Human Development, 39,* 67–80.

Nussbaum, J. F., Pecchioni, L. L., Robinson, J. D., & Thompson, T. L. (2000). *Communication and aging* (2nd ed.). Mahwah, NJ: Lawrence Erlbaum Associates.

Nydegger, C. N. (1991). The development of paternal and filial maturity. In K. Pillemer (Ed.), *Parent–child relations throughout life.* Hillsdale, NJ: Lawrence Erlbaum Associates.

Olson, D. H. (1990). *Clinical rating scale for Circumplex Model.* St. Paul: University of Minnesota, Family Social Science.

Olson, D. H. (1993). Circumplex model of marital and family systems: Assessing family functioning. In F. Walsh (Ed.), *Normal family processes* (2nd ed., pp. 104–137). New York: Guilford.

Olson, D. H., Sprenkle, D. H., & Russell, C. S. (1979). Circumplex model of marital and family systems I. Cohesion and adaptability dimensions, family types, and clinical applications. *Family Process, 18,* 3–28.

Olson, T. (1961). *Tell me a riddle.* New York: Dell.

Patterson, G. R. (1982). *A social learning approach: Coercive family process.* Eugene, OR: Castalia.

Patton, M. Q. (1990). *Qualitative evaluation and research methods* (2nd ed.). Newbury Park, CA: Sage.

Pearce, W. B. (1989). *Communication and the human condition.* Carbondale: Southern Illinois University Press.

Peck, D. L., & Dolch, N. A. (Eds.). (2001). *Extraordinary behavior: A case study approach to understanding social problems.* Westport, CT: Greenwood.

Pelto, P. J., & Pelto, G. H. (1978). *Anthropological research: The structure of inquiry* (2nd ed.). New York: Cambridge University Press.

Peterson, G. W., & Hann, D. (1999). Socializing children and parents in families. In M. B. Sussman, S. K. Steinmetz, & G. W. Peterson (Eds.), *Handbook of marriage and the family* (pp. 327–370). New York: Plenum.

Peterson, G. W., Madden-Derdich, D., & Leonard, S. A. (2000). Parent–child relations across the life course: Autonomy within the context of connectedness. In S. J. Price, P. C. Mckenry, & M. J. Murphy (Eds.), *Families across time: A life course perspective* (pp. 187–203). Los Angeles, CA: Roxbury.

Peterson, G. W., & Rollins, B. C. (1987). Parent–child socialization. In M. B. Sussman & S. K. Steinmetz (Eds.), *Handbook of marriage and the family* (pp. 471–507). New York: Plenum.

Petronio, S. (Ed.). (2000). *Balancing the secrets of private disclosures.* Mahwah, NJ: Lawrence Erlbaum Associates.

Petronio, S. (2002). *Boundaries of privacy: Dialects of disclosure.* New York: State University of New York Press.

Philipsen, G. (1992). *Speaking culturally: Explorations in social communication.* Albany: State University of New York Press.

Phillips, S. (1991). *Beyond the myths: Mother–daughter relationships in psychology, history, literature and everyday life.* New York: Penguin.

Pipher, M. (1994). *Reviving Ophelia: Saving the lives of adolescent girls.* New York: Ballantine.

Powers, S. I., & Welsh, D. P. (1999). Mother–daughter interactions and adolescent girls' depression. In M. J. Cox & J. Brooks-Gunn (Eds.), *Conflict and cohesion in families: Causes and consequences.* (pp. 243–281). Mahwah, NJ: Lawrence Erlbaum Associates.

Priest, P. (1996). "Guilt by association": Talk show participants' televisually enhanced status and self-esteem. In D. Grodin & T. R. Lindlof (Eds.), *Constructing the self in a mediated world: Inquiries in social construction* (pp. 68–83). Thousand Oaks, CA: Sage.

Qin, P., Agerbo, E., & Mortenson, P. B. (2003). Suicide risk in relation to socioeconomic, demographic, psychiatric, and familial factors: A national register-based study of all suicides in Denmark, 1981–1997. *The American Journal of Psychiatry, 160,* 765–772.

Rand, A. (1993). *The fountainhead* (50th ann. ed.). New York: Penguin.

Randall, D. (1995). "Doing" mother–daughter: Conversational analysis and relational contexts. In T. J. Socha & G. H. Stamp (Eds.), *Parents, children, and communication* (pp. 113–126). Mahwah, NJ: Lawrence Erlbaum Associates.

Rastogi, M., & Wampler, K. S. (1999). Adult daughters' perceptions of the mother–daughter relationship: A cross-cultural comparison. *Family Relations, 48,* 327–336.

Rawlins, W. K. (1992). *Friendship matters: Communication, dialectics, and the life course.* New York: deGruyter.

Rawlins, W. K. (1994). Being there and growing apart: Sustaining friendships during adulthood. In D. J. Canary & L. Stafford (Eds.), *Communication and relational maintenance* (pp. 275–294). San Diego: Academic Press.

Rich, A. (1986). *Of woman born: Motherhood as experience and institution.* New York: Norton.

Rich, B. R., & Williams, L. (1998). The right of re-vision: Michelle Citron's *Daughter Rite*. In B. R. Rich (Ed.), *Chick flicks: Theories and memories of the feminist film movement* (pp. 212–401). Durham, NC: Duke University Press.

Richards, B. (1999). Suicide and internalized relationships: A study from the perspective of psychotherapists working with suicidal patients. *British Journal of Guidance & Counseling, 27,* 85–98.

Richards, T. J., & Richards, L. (1994). Using computers in quantitative research. In N. K. Denzin & Y. S. Lincoln (Eds.), *Handbook of qualitative research.* Thousand Oaks, CA: Sage.

Robson, M. (1999). Stress and its perception in childhood. *Counseling Psychology Quarterly, 12,* 217–231.

Rogers, C. R. (1951). *Client-centered counseling.* Boston: Houghton Mifflin.

Rogers, C. R. (1980). *A way of being.* Boston: Houghton Mifflin.

Rogers-Millar, L. E., & Millar, F. E. (1979). Domineeringness and dominance: A transactional view. *Human Communication Research, 5,* 238–246.

Rohner, R. P. (1986). *The warmth dimension: Foundations of parental acceptance-rejection theory.* Beverly Hills, CA: Sage.

Romer, D. (Ed.). (2003). *Reducing adolescent risk.* Thousand Oaks, CA: Sage.

Ronai, C. R. (1995). Multiple reflections of child abuse: An argument for a layered account. *Journal of Contemporary Ethnography, 23,* 395–426.

Rose, L., Mallinson, R. K., & Walton-Moss, B. (2002). A grounded theory of families responding to mental illness. *Western Journal of Nursing Research, 4,* 516–537.

Rosenberg, M. (1990). Control of environment and control of self. In J. Rodin, L. Schooler, & K. W. Schaire (Eds.), *Self-directedness: Cause and effects throughout the life course* (pp. 147–154). Hillsdale, NJ: Lawrence Erlbaum Associates.

Rossman, G. B., & Rallis, S. F. (1998). *Learning in the field: An introduction to qualitative research.* Thousand Oaks, CA: Sage.

Ruddick, S. (1989). *Maternal thinking: Toward a politics of peace.* Boston: Beacon.

Ryan, J. (1974). Early language development: Towards a communicational analysis. In M. P. Richards (Ed.), *The integration of a child into a social world.* London: Cambridge University Press.

Satcher, D. (1999). *HHS initiatives addressing suicide/risk factors: Commitment to a national suicide prevention strategy* [Announcement]. Retrieved March 13, 2003, from http://www.surgeongeneral.gov/library/calltoaction/fact4.htm

Schafer, R. (1999). Disappointment and disappointedness. *International Journal of Psychoanalysis, 80,* 1093–1103.

Schely-Newman, E. (1999). Mothers know best: Constructing meaning in a narrative event. *The Quarterly Journal of Speech, 85,* 285–302.

Schnarch, D. (1997). *Passionate marriage.* New York: Henry Holt.

Schonpflug, U. (2001). Intergenerational transmission of values: The role of transmission belts. *Journal of Cross Cultural Psychology, 32,* 174–185.

Schwandt, T. A. (1993). Theory for the moral sciences: Crisis of identity and purpose. In D. J. Flinders & G. E. Mills (Eds.), *Theory and concepts in qualitative research* (pp. 95–117). New York: Teachers College Press.

Sciarra, D. (1999). The role of the qualitative researcher. In M. Kopala & L. A. Suzuki (Eds.), *Using qualitative methods in psychology* (pp. 37–48). Thousand Oaks, CA: Sage.

Sciarra, D. T., & Ponterotto, J. G. (1998). Adolescent motherhood among low-income urban Hispanics: Familial considerations of mother–daughter dyads. *Qualitative Health Research, 8,* 751–763.

Seligman, M. E. P. (1975). *Helplessness: On depression, development, and death.* San Francisco: W. H. Freeman.

Sheehy, G. (2002, May 12). It's about pure love. *Parade Magazine,* pp. 6–7.

Shields, C. (1987). *Swann.* New York: Viking.

Sieburg, E. S. (1985). *Family communication: An integrated systems approach.* Boston: Allyn & Bacon.

Sillars, A. L. (1995). Communication and family culture. In M. A. Fitzpatrick & A. L. Vangelisti (Eds.), *Explaining family interactions* (pp. 375–399). Thousand Oaks, CA: Sage.

Silverstein, M., & Long, J. D. (1998). Trajectories of grandparents' perceived solidarity with adult grandchildren: A growth curve analysis over 23 years. *Journal of Marriage and the Family, 60,* 912–923.

Simpson, B. (1998). *Changing families: An ethnographic approach to divorce and separation.* New York: Berg.

Smith, L., Hill, W., & Mullis, R. (1998). Relational perceptions in mother–daughter attachments. *Marriage and Family Review, 27,* 37–49.

Socha, T. J., & Stamp, G. (1995). *Parents, children, & communication: Frontiers of theory and research.* Mahwah, NJ: Lawrence Erlbaum Associates.

Soerensen, S. (1998). Predictors of anticipating caregiving in multigeneration families: An exploratory study. *Journal of Applied Gerontology, 17,* 499–520.

Solomon, D. H., Dillard, J. P., & Anderson, J. W. (2002). Episode type, attachment orientation, and frame salience: Evidence for a theory of relational framing. *Human Communication Research, 28*(1), 136–152.

Solotaroff, P. (1999). *Group: Six people in search of a life.* New York: Riverhead Books.

Sorenson, L. (2000). Grandmother's view. In M. Miller, *Two of me,* (p. 52). Unpublished play produced by Assemblage Theater Group, Phoenix, AZ.

Spradley, J. (1979). *The ethnographic interview.* New York: Holt, Rinehart & Winston.

Stipko Media. Famous Will & Grace quotes. Retrieved December 21, 2003, from http://www.strabuzz.tv/ericmccormack/features/will_&Grace.quotes_3.shtml

Stolley, M. R., & Fitzgibbon, M. L. (1997). Effects of an obesity prevention program on the eating behavior of African American mothers and daughters. *Health Education & Behavior, 24,* 152–164.

Strauss A., & Corbin, J. (1998). *Basics of qualitative research: Techniques and procedures for developing grounded theory* (2nd ed.). Thousand Oaks, CA: Sage.

Surrey, J. (1993). The mother–daughter relationship: Themes in psychotherapy. In J. van Mens-Verhulst, J. Schreurs, & L. Woertman (Eds.), *Daughtering and mothering: Female subjectivity reanalysed* (pp. 114–124). New York: Routledge.

Taylor, S. J., & Bogdan, R. (1984). Designing qualitative research. In S. J. Taylor & R. Bogdan, *Introduction to qualitative research methods.* New York: Wiley.

Tesch, R. (1990). *Qualitative research: Analysis types and software tools.* London: Falmer.

Thibaut, J., & Kelley, H. H. (1986). *The social psychology of groups.* New Brunswick, NJ: Transaction Books. (Original work published 1959)

Thomas, V., & Olson, D. H. (1993). Problem families and the Circumplex Model: Observational assessment using the Clinical Rating Scale. *Journal of Marital & Family Therapy, 19,* 159–175.

Thompson, R., & Zuroff, D. C. (1999). Dependency, self-criticism, and mothers' responses to adolescent sons' autonomy and competence. *Journal of Youth and Adolescence, 28*, 365–385.

Tinsley, B. R., & Parke, R. D. (1984). Grandparents as support and socialization agents. In M. Lewis (Ed.), *Beyond the dyad.* New York: Plenum.

Tracy, K. (2002). *Everyday talk: Building and reflecting identities.* New York: Guilford.

Turner, S. (1995). Family variables related to adolescent substance misuse: Risk and resiliency factors. In T. P. Gullota, G. R. Adams, & R. Montemayor (Eds.), *Substance misuse in adolescence.* Thousand Oaks, CA: Sage.

van Dijk, M., Wilco, W., van der Pligt, J., & Zeelenberg, M. (1999). Effort invested in vain: The impact of effort on the intensity of disappointment and regret. *Motivation and Emotion, 23*, 203–220.

Vangelisti, A. L. (1994). Family secrets: Forms, functions and correlates. *Journal of Social and Personal Relationships, 11*, 113–135.

Vangelisti, A. L., Daly, J. A., & Rudnick, J. R. (1991). Making people feel guilty in conversations: Techniques and correlates. *Human Communication Research, 18*, 3–39.

Van Mannen, J. (1979). The fact of fiction in organizational ethnography. *Administrative Science Quarterly, 24*, 539–550.

van Mens-Verhulst, J., Schreurs, J., & Woertman, L. (Eds.). (1993). *Daughtering and mothering: Female subjectivity reanalysed.* New York: Routledge.

Walker, A. J., & Thompson, L. (1983). Intimacy and intergenerational aid and contact among mothers and daughters. *Journal of Marriage and the Family, 45*, 841–849.

Walsh, F. (1998). *Strengthening family resilience.* New York: Guilford.

Walters, S. D. (1992). *Lives together/worlds apart: Mothers and daughters in popular culture.* Berkeley: University of California Press.

Warloe, C. (Ed.). (1998). *From daughters to mothers "I've always meant to tell you": An anthology of letters.* New York: Pocket Books.

Watzlawick, P., Beavin, J., & Jackson, D. (1967). *Pragmatics of human communication.* New York: Norton.

Weitzman, E. A. (2000). Software and qualitative research. In N. Denzin & Y. S. Lincoln (Eds.), *Handbook of qualitative research* (pp. 803–820). Thousand Oaks, CA: Sage.

Wells, R. (1997). *Divine secrets of the ya-ya sisterhood.* New York: HarperCollins.

Whitchurch, G. G., & Dickson, F. C. (1999). Family communication. In M. Sussman, S. Steinmetz, & G. W. Peterson (Eds.), *Handbook of marriage and the family* (2nd ed.). New York: Plenum.

Williams, A., & Nussbaum, J. F. (1999). *Intergenerational communication: Multidisciplinary perspectives.* Mahwah, NJ: Lawrence Erlbaum Associates.

Williams, C., & Bybee, J. (1994). What do children feel guilty about? Developmental and gender differences. *Developmental Psychology, 30*, 617–623.

Williams, G. J., Chamove, A. S., & Millar, H. R. (1990). Eating disorders, perceived control, assertiveness and hostility. *British Journal of Clinical Psychology, 29*, 327–335.

Wilmot, W. (1995). *Relational communication..* New York: McGraw-Hill.

Wodak, R., & Schultz, M. (1986). *The language of guilt: Mother–daughter relationships from a cross-cultural perspective.* Philadelphia: John Benjamins.

Woertman, L. (1993). Mothering in context. In J. van Mens-Verhulst, J. Schreurs, & L. Woertman (Eds.), *Daughtering and mothering: Female subjectivity reanalysed* (pp. 57–69). New York: Routledge.

Wolcott, H. F. (1990). On seeking—and rejecting—validity in qualitative research. In E. W. Eisner & A. Peshkin (Eds.), *Qualitative inquiry in education* (pp. 121–153). New York: Teachers College Press.

Wood, J. T. (2000). *Relational communication: Continuity and change in personal relationships* (2nd ed.). Belmont, CA: Wadsworth.

Wright, R. (1998). *Criteria for communication theory.* Retrieved August 2003, from http://www.ic.arizona.edu/~comm300/mary/general/criteria.html

Yerby, J., Buerkel-Rothfuss, N., & Bochner, A. (1995). *Understanding family communication.* Scottsdale, AZ: Gorsuch Scarisbrick.

Zax, B., & Poulter, S. (1997). A multigenerational inquiry into the relationship between mothers and daughters. In B. S. Mark & J. A. Incorvaia, (Eds.), *The handbook of infant, child, and adolescent psychotherapy, Vol. 2: New directions in integrative treatment* (pp. 461–484). Northvale, NJ: Aronson.

Zayas, L. H., Kaplan, C., Turner, S., Romano, K., & Gonzalez-Ramos, G. (2000). Understanding suicide attempts by adolescent Hispanic females. *Social Work, 45,* 53–63.

Author Index

Subject Index